AMERICAN AND BRITISH
LITERATURE
SINCE 1890

AMERICAN AND BRITISH LITERATURE

SINCE 1890

REVISED AND ENLARGED EDITION

BY

CARL VAN DOREN

AND

MARK VAN DOREN

STUDENT'S EDITION

D. APPLETON-CENTURY COMPANY

INCORPORATED

NEW YORK   LONDON

PREFACE TO THE REVISED EDITION

The Introduction which follows this Preface has been printed as it was written fourteen years ago. It stated the principles which guided the authors then, and those principles have not materially changed. Within the same framework, and following the same method, the present edition endeavors to bring the subject up to date. The subject of course has changed. Twenty authors have died; many of the others, either because they have written new books or because their old ones have assumed new importance, required more space and a different emphasis; some of them have dwindled in importance so that the sections devoted to them had to be dropped or abridged; and forty-one authors make their appearance here for the first time. Most of the newcomers have emerged into prominence since 1925, but in a few cases recognition has been given to work which lacked it in that year, and in one case, that of Gerard Manley Hopkins, a poet who died in 1898 has been given credit for an influence he began to exert two decades after his death. In fourteen years, as the present volume will make clear, much can happen to contemporary literature; so much, indeed, that the temptation may be felt to begin a history of that literature all over again, assuming a new start and rejecting the opinions once held. This book resists that temptation whenever it can, on the theory that judgments too hastily revised have to be revised again, and in the knowledge that much of the work it discussed as important in 1925 is still important. Scarcely a page, however, has stood without some revision; many pages have not stood at all,

v

and a still greater number have been added. The book is therefore longer than it was, both in the text and in the Suggestions for Study. The lists of recommended readings have been liberally enlarged, and the bibliographies have been brought, within the limits imposed by the plan, strictly up to date.

C. V. D.
M. V. D.

INTRODUCTION

Although intended for the use of schools, this manual of the literature produced in America, England, and Ireland during the past thirty-five years will also, it is hoped, prove useful to those general readers who are neither proficient in the subject nor unconcerned with it. Both sorts of audiences will find that the book has been adapted to their needs according to definite principles. Those principles do not include any effort to simplify the account unduly, to disguise the ideas which have been put forth by the more daring writers of the time, or to steer a safe middle course when there are points at issue. On the contrary, stress has been laid upon the modern elements, whether ideas or forms, in recent literature. But the book does not claim, as it does not attempt, to go into many vexed controversies or to concern itself with many minor figures. Such items of literary history, while fascinating to the expert, are confusing to the beginner. He has, from desultory reading, from hearsay, from lectures, from reviews, learned that there are numerous contemporary writers of note about whom he would like to have a more systematic knowledge. What he requires is not a series of specialized monographs, but a plain and untechnical exposition which will furnish a ground-plan upon which to build in case he cares to go further. That plain and untechnical exposition of its theme this volume is the first to offer to the public. So far as possible, it has discarded all non-essentials, reducing the authors studied to the minimum, commenting upon only the more important of their works, carrying no elaborate burden of dates and titles, confining itself to matters of some permanent significance.

If it devotes less space than might have been expected to certain eminent survivors of an earlier age, such as Howells, Henry James, Mark Twain, Hardy, Meredith, Swinburne, who did good work during the years covered by this record, that is in large part because they have already been dealt with in various works easily accessible to laymen. In part, however, it is because this book does not share the prevailing notion that the history of literature in English ended with the death of the great writers of the age just closed. As a matter of fact, the literature of Ireland since 1890 is unquestionably the most distinguished which the country has yet produced in the English language, the literature of America during that period is as distinguished as any it has ever produced in any period of equal length, and the post-Victorian literature of England suffers not too much by comparison with that of earlier ages of which the reputation is now higher. And even if this recent literature were of less moment than it is, it would lawfully make demands upon the student or the general reader. For literature is a continuous stream accompanying the life of the nation which writes it. At any given moment, the spectator may feel that the stream of literature has widened out over flats and shoals, lacking the concentration and direction which he now sees the literature of the past to have had. But spectators in the past thought the same thing about the literature which they then surveyed, and spectators in the future will no doubt envy the present age its strong current and sharp banks. In the circumstances, a book may be permitted to try to chart that current and indicate those banks. That is what this book tries to do.

Still, it does not aim too entirely to anticipate the judgment of the future. It has been written in the conviction that some writers may mean much to their own age whether or not they are likely to mean much to another. One of the notable functions of literature is to hold up a mirror in which manners and opinions may be studied by their contemporaries. Books written long ago or in remote lands have always a touch of strangeness which renders it difficult for the average reader to make the necessary comparisons between the reality which he knows and the reflection which he sees. Americans have been at a particular disadvantage in this respect. Inheriting on their continent the literature of a distant island, they have viewed it habitually through the slight haze which distance gives. There is all the more reason, then, why they should offset this by paying attention to their own literature. Moreover, American literature, as it grows in distinctiveness, grows increasingly more and more differentiated from the literature of the parent stock. It must therefore be estimated according to its own laws, not according to those of England. The account here offered considers the recent and contemporary literature of the United States as an independent venture on the part of an independent nation, not as a single chapter in the larger history of that imaginative activity of which London has been the center. At the same time, due attention has been paid in this account to the literature of the British Isles, which not only parallels that of America, but is at so many points interwoven with it.

That the literature of the three branches of the English-speaking race has been significant during the past three or four decades, this volume testifies; but that the volume is aimed to meet the need of American students first of all will appear from both its arrangement and its scale of treatment. The section dealing with native literature stands, obviously, at the head of the book, because for native students it is the logical beginning. Furthermore,

the British authors chosen for discussion are chiefly those
who have won a hearing in America or who deserve it by
reason of merits which are readily perceptible outside of
Britain. Trivial authors, it is true, who may have had a
vogue on this side of the Atlantic are in no case preferred
to weighty ones whose American reputation lags; nevertheless, certain international elements have been regularly
taken into account. It will be noted, too, that writers like
Hardy, Shaw, Kipling, Galsworthy, Bennett, Wells, are
treated in greater detail than has been devoted to any of
the Americans. The reasons for this disparity are two:
first, that those men have most of them had longer careers than their American rivals and have written more
books; and, second, that they require in any case a larger
amount of explanation to make them thoroughly compre-
hensible than Americans of even an equal rank require.
The second reason applies to the Irish writers, who are on
the whole even less known, though well worth knowing,
than either the English or the Americans. In the proportion given to any particular American writer, account has
been taken of both his influence and his intrinsic worth,
and where there was occasion for doubt, the preference
has been given to writers who have by careers of some
length and by outputs of some bulk afforded a basis for
critical opinion which can rarely be afforded when the
evidence is slighter.

Though every effort has been made to bring the book
down to date, it has been thought inadvisable to confuse
the layman or the average reader by mentioning number-
less interesting figures who are just now the topics of
literary gossip. Time and their own subsequent work
must determine whether they belong in such a study as
this. The thing to be kept in mind by any reader who
looks herein for guidance to the literature of the period is
that that literature is still vigorous, is still continuing a

march of which no record can be quite adequate, because even while criticism pauses to take stock, the materials increase and shift. One purpose of the book is to insist upon the continuity of the stream which it tries to describe, not to arrest.

C. V. D.
M. V. D.

CONTENTS

PART ONE

AMERICAN LITERATURE

CHAPTER I

POETRY

BY the year 1890 the most famous American poets had joined, in varying degrees, the ranks of the classics. To say nothing of Poe, who died young, Bryant, Lanier, Longfellow, and Emerson were already dead; and Lowell, Whitman, Whittier, and Holmes were at the end of their careers. There were, indeed, numerous writers of verse who had some reputation, but the public was right in feeling that these were minor poets, earnest or dainty survivors from more energetic days. No one of them had been shaped by the great national struggles of the past century and no one of them gave voice to the newer national ideals which were demanding expression. For the most part, they were content to sing pretty songs about remote emotions or to argue in meter about established ideas. They might, of course, have been significant without being strikingly national if they had been strikingly personal; but in this respect also they fell below the level of great poetry. Too many of them seemed to feel that it was their duty to limit their utterances to subjects which were polite or proper and to language which was smooth and decorous. No doubt this showed that they were good citizens and good men, as indeed they were. It showed no less truly, however, that they either lacked powerful poetical impulses or else misjudged the nature of poetry, which to be memorable must be direct, courageous, and ardent, and not merely graceful or acceptable to the majority. It has been claimed that the scarcity of poets in the nineties was due

3

about equally to the exaggerated prestige of the older school and to the exaggerated gentility of the newer school. Whatever the explanation, it is the fact that the last decade of the century had, among many poets, few that are now read or that deserve to be.

Riley
1853–1916

The most popular of these few was James Whitcomb Riley, who without being very distinctive was very representative. Rarely original and never elevated, he expressed ordinary emotions in ordinary language, with neat phrases and simple melodies, as in so typical a stanza as this from "The Old Swimmin' Hole":

> Oh! the old swimmin'-hole! In the long, lazy days
> When the hum-drum of school made so many run-a-ways,
> How pleasant was the jurney down the old dusty lane,
> Whare the tracks of our bare feet was all printed so plane
> You could tell by the dent of the heel and the sole
> They was lots o' fun on hand at the old swimmin'-hole.
> But the lost joys is past! Let your tears in sorrow roll
> Like the rain that use to dapple up the old swimmin'-hole.

His poems are full of accurate detail regarding typical American lives as they were led in his day in his part of the country and indeed in most parts of the country. Most of the men and women for whom he wrote, absorbed in hard work or dull routine, liked nothing better than to remember the pleasures of their youth before care had crept upon them and stolen away their glad irresponsibility. Most of them, too, regarded their children, or children at large, as the most touching and attractive items in a commonplace world. In Riley's verses these attitudes were agreeably reflected. He sang of the old swimming-hole, the old trundle-bed, the old haymow, the old glee-club, of old-fashioned roses, of old sweethearts, of old Aunt Mary, bringing up recollections which moved his hearers to happy laughter or happy tears as perhaps no other topic could have done. He sang no less movingly of the joys and whims and pathos of childhood, touching perhaps too often upon the grief of parents for dead children.

No doubt his concentration upon the past and upon the young was a kind of mannerism, but it did not tire people who shared his sentiments. To offset this, he had a considerable aptitude for shrewd characterization and for canny folk-wisdom. Without always justifying his optimism, he managed always to look for the bright side of human fortunes, and this pleased an audience who believed that pessimism was an unworthy trait. In view of all these things, it is no wonder that Riley, despite certain weaknesses of character, was widely admired and loved.

Santayana 1863– As different from Riley as possible was another poet who published notable verse in the nineties. George Santayana was born in Spain, saw during his youth, though he passed it in the United States, little that was typical of ordinary American life, and was a professor of philosophy at Harvard until he decided just before the World War to live thenceforth in Europe. Though a master of English prose, he admits that the roots of the language "do not reach quite to my center. I never drank in in childhood the homely cadences and ditties which in pure spontaneous poetry set the essential key." He had, being city-bred, no intimate feeling for nature such as is the basis of most poetry in England or America, and yet he did not feel called to tell stories in verse or to create characters. He was thus limited to reflective poetry of an austere sort never likely to attract many readers. Poetry, however, to be excellent does not have to be popular, and Santayana's "Sonnets" (1894) would be distinguished in the literature of any nation. They show his later philosophy [1] in the making. Without precisely telling a story, they give a subtle record of the

[1] For his prose, see pages 142–146.

emotions which went through him while he was achieving maturity. That he seems to have achieved by gradually disentangling his mind from the chains which bound it. Brought up in an orthodox theology, he found that it ceased to convince him, though custom, a desire to be loyal, and distrust of the validity of his doubts long held him from any open break. Eventually he could say, in one of his most famous sonnets:

> Farewell, my burden! No more will I bear
> The foolish load of my fond faith's despair,
> But trip the idle race with careless feet.
> The crown of olive let another wear;
> It is my crown to mock the runner's heat
> With gentle wonder and with laughter sweet.

So also he disentangled himself from another bond, that of his love for a woman who may be real or only symbolical but whom in either case he did not win. After bitter suffering he could finally address her:

> He who hath made thee perfect, makes me blest.
> O fiery minister, on mighty wings
> Bear me, great love, to mine eternal rest.
> Heaven it is to be at peace with things;
> Come chaos now, and in a whirlwind's rings
> Engulf the planets. I have seen the best.

Thus Santayana freed himself from a religion and a love in which he could not be happy, by ceasing to repine over what he could not have, keeping the purest elements of his experience in his memory, and living as civilized a life as he could in his own mind with the help of knowledge and beauty. His sonnets are a fit expression of his struggle and victory. They are lucid, sincere, eloquent, each of them almost flawlessly written and constructed, and yet so linked all of them together as to present an affecting drama of the spirit.

Although Emily Dickinson had died before
1890 she was virtually unknown till that year,
which saw the publication of her first volume
and with it the beginning of an influence which has increased ever since. Long a recluse in her father's house in
Massachusetts, she had been caught up by none of the
poetical fashions of her time but had instead practised her
art with the integrity and intensity of a hermit who had
no other occupation. She was bold with the form of her
poems, willing for them to be unsymmetrical, unconventionally rhymed, lawless in their rhythms, if only they
could be vivid and arresting. In particular she dispensed
with the customary poetic padding. She stripped her verse
to the bone, as if nothing but the essential idea or the
essential image were important. Of the earlier American
poets she perhaps most resembles Emerson, but she really
resembles no one besides herself. She is a Yankee to the
extent that she is naturally laconic; she is a woman to the
extent that she draws many of her illustrations from household matters; she is above all a poet speaking with a poet's
uncompromising directness of vision. Thus, for instance,
she expresses a lover's impatience and prodigality:

> If you were coming in the fall,
> I'd brush the summer by
> With half a smile and half a spurn,
> As housewives do a fly.
>
> If I could see you in a year,
> I'd wind the months in balls,
> And put them each in separate drawers,
> Until their time befalls.
>
> If only centuries delayed,
> I'd count them on my hand,
> Subtracting till my fingers dropped
> Into Van Dieman's land.

If certain, when this life was out,
That yours and mine should be,
I'd toss it yonder like a rind,
And taste eternity.

But now, all ignorant of the length
Of time's uncertain wing,
It goads me, like the goblin bee,
That will not state its sting.

Love is not her only topic. She speaks in her piercing way about the thrill of life, the mystery of death, the most varied objects of nature. Such a common sight as that of a bee at his daily work suggests to her that the pride of caste is a human invention without any real counterpart among the less artificial animals:

The pedigree of honey
Does not concern the bee;
A clover, any time, to him
Is aristocracy.

When she wants to say, with Keats, that "beauty is truth, truth beauty," she invents a characteristic story to make her point:

I died for beauty, but was scarce
Adjusted in the tomb,
When one who died for truth was lain
In an adjoining room.

He questioned softly why I failed?
"For beauty," I replied.
"And I for truth,—the two are one;
We brethren are," he said.

And so, as kinsmen met a night,
We talked between the rooms,
Until the moss had reached our lips,
And covered up our names.

She can be playful, she can compress her meaning into little parables, she can wring the heart with dramatic situations set forth in a dozen lines. But it is not, of course, her variety which has kept her from suffering the loss of reputation which many of her contemporaries have suffered, and which makes her now seem one of the American classics. She survives because she is what may be termed an irreducible poet, without false colors likely to fade or false contours likely to wither. What survives in her is essential poetry or wit, and it happens that there was never in her much beside these things in a concentrated form. Since 1930, the centenary of her birth, a series of biographies has been written in the attempt to fix the character of an experience in love which legend has always insisted upon emphasizing, and which many of the poems would seem to reflect. The best of these biographies makes it clear that there was such an experience and that it was unhappy, but that it alone does not account for the distinction of Emily Dickinson's poetry. Born a poet, she lived her life in devotion to the art; she left nearly a thousand poems behind her, the work of thirty years, and many of these had been revised with the most scrupulous care. She was at least as much in love with poetry as with any man.

Hovey
1864–1900
The very end of the century brought forth two poets, Mid-Westerners educated in New England, who, though they both died young and left their work incomplete, struck certain poetical notes which are still interesting for other qualities besides their promise of better things to come. Richard Hovey took in his verses to the open road, singing, as in "Songs from Vagabondia," the joys of vagabond adventure with a kind of Gipsy gusto. He celebrated also the lusty, hearty comradeship of young men, particularly in the poems which he

wrote for his college and most popularly in the song, loved
in all colleges, which ends:

> And life slips its tether
> When the boys get together,
> With a stein on the table in the fellowship of spring.

Hovey also undertook an ambitious, uncompleted cycle of
poetic dramas on the old theme of Arthur and Guinevere
and Lancelot, trying to present it, without Tennyson's sentimentalism, as a universal story of tragic love. Finally,
he wrote during the Spanish War a number of strenuous
poems glorifying the conflict with an enthusiasm which
was too seldom either humane or intelligent. In his longer
works he never entirely freed himself from his tendency
to imitate such predecessors as Swinburne, and even in
his praise of the free life there are signs that his bragga-
docio was partly borrowed from such contemporaries as
Kipling. Thus Hovey must be regarded as something less
than a true creative poet. He is remembered, however, because he represents the new spirit in American literature,
which was breaking with its recent tradition of complacency and triviality.

**Moody
1869–1910** William Vaughn Moody, though more of a
scholar than Hovey, was less of a singer. He
edited Milton and loved Greek tragedy; in his
most ambitious undertaking, like Hovey's uncompleted,
he tried to show how mankind, estranged from God by
its effort to become independent, must in the end be reconciled—through woman, who had first endangered the divine plan of union. But partly because Moody never wrote
more than fragments of the third poetic drama which was
to make his whole scheme clear, and partly because his
central idea was by its very nature large and cloudy, he
remains better known for his shorter poems, a few of
which are of genuine interest and excellence. In "Glouces-

ter Moors" the poet comes suddenly to think of the earth as a slave-ship plunging through the sea, toward a port which no one knows, with a crew which does not trouble itself about the wretches stifling and rotting in the hold. Must the earth thus sail on forever, with so little justice among its inhabitants? But in the most powerful of all his poems, rising above that jingoism which is a blot upon Hovey's fame, Moody took issue with his own country in "An Ode in Time of Hesitation," written when the country was deciding whether to annex the Philippines. To the most scrupulous Americans of the time it seemed unpardonable that, after a war which had no avowed aim but to free Cuba from a foreign yoke, the victor should then impose another foreign yoke upon distant islands which had had nothing to do with the original controversy.

> Was it for this our fathers kept the law?
> This crown shall crown their struggle and their ruth?
> Are we the eagle nation Milton saw
> Mewing its mighty youth,
> Soon to possess the mountain winds of truth,
> And be a swift familiar of the sun
> Where ay before God's face his trumpets run?
> Or have we but the talons and the maw.
> And for the abject likeness of our heart
> Shall some less lordly bird be set apart?—
> Some gross-billed wader where the swamps are fat?
> Some gorger in the sun? Some prowler with the bat?

Though the Philippines were eventually annexed, and Moody's poem thus speaks for a defeated minority, it still stands as one of the loftiest political poems in American history; and it will doubtless be cherished long after most of Moody's work has paid its natural penalty for being, when not at its best, a little imitative, a little heavy with erudition, a little obscure.[1]

[1] For Moody's plays, see pages 113–114.

1912 If the last decade of the nineteenth century was relatively unproductive of striking poetry, so was the first decade of the twentieth. Santayana had left poetry for philosophy, Moody turned to prose plays, and Hovey was dead. Though a robust and diversified group of new poets was growing up in that decade, they had not yet reached maturity, or they still lacked any considerable recognition. Nevertheless, many books of verse were published, and it began gradually to be felt that the cause of poetry was not a hopeless one. That cause was furthered in 1912 by the founding at Chicago of the monthly "Poetry: A Magazine of Verse," and the next year by the appearance in Boston of the first annual volume of the "Anthology of Magazine Verse," both of which continued to render service of a kind much needed. They gave a hearing to poets who might otherwise have been neglected, they stimulated critical discussion of poetry, they helped to fix public attention upon the art. Of course, however, they could not have done this had it not been for the sudden rise of new poets with new power. Why, after a dreary interregnum, this renewed poetical activity should have begun, is a matter which cannot be entirely explained; but the cause must be connected with the fact that the new poets were more impassioned, more outspoken, and more realistic than had been the custom with most American poets for a generation. Poetry, recently too often a kind of elegant accomplishment, now came to look upon itself as a serious concern. It challenged accepted opinions; it tried new forms and methods; it told stories and created characters; it drew near to the facts of native life, trying to lift them to significance and not merely, as had too long been its tendency, trying to escape from them to the world of fancy. In doing all this it returned to that wider world which is the home of poetry: the world of the imagination.

Robinson
1869–1935

One of the first things which this renaissance achieved was the discovery by a rapidly widening circle of readers that they had been overlooking an American poet of high rank already among them. Edwin Arlington Robinson, born in Maine and trained at Harvard, had since the nineties struggled in New York against the obstacles of poverty and obscurity. Nothing, however, had diverted him from his course. Little influenced by the current fashions in poetry, he had set out to be a poet in his own way. When other poets were tamely following Tennyson, copying his sweetness and softness, Robinson had been studying Thomas Hardy for his strong hold on common life, and George Crabbe, the bluntest of the English poets. But this study of sound models was only the beginning of Robinson's task. He had gone on to develop in himself an individual style, to find subjects which suited his gifts, to choose forms into which he could pour his material with the slightest loss of effect. Most of all, he had been interested in the interpretation of human character, particularly as it could be studied at crucial moments, and he had written a series of dramatic sonnets, biographies in miniature, which are unmatched in the language. By the beginning of the second decade of the century he had reached a maturity not to be mistaken.

The postponement of his fame may be in part ascribed to his habit, during the strenuous, optimistic era in which he laid down his plans, of writing much of the time about the vanity, not to say the futility, of human life. Leaving to other poets the delight of studying successful men and women, Robinson had bent his shrewd, kind, ironical eyes upon the misfits in society. He told hauntingly of Richard Cory, who was handsome and rich and admired, but who yet, because of some secret discontent, killed himself in the midst of his prosperity. He told humorously of Miniver Cheevy, who wept that he was ever born because he could not endure the present and longed for the romantic past:

> Miniver loved the Medici,
>   Albeit he had never seen one;
> He would have sinned incessantly
>   Could he have been one.
>
> Miniver cursed the commonplace
>   And eyed a khaki suit with loathing;
> He missed the mediæval grace
>   Of iron clothing.

There was nothing, apparently, for Miniver Cheevy to do but to keep on thinking and drinking. Robinson told about the graceless vagabond Captain Craig, discoursing forever like a trivial Socrates in Tilbury Town, the Maine village which Robinson made memorable by his frequent references to it as the home of many of his characters. He had indeed described so many pathetic or amusing failures that he has been called the poet of futility.

Even when he deserted his failures to study the successful, he had still a sense of the vanity of human efforts. No passage in all his poetry is more characteristic than the speech of Shakspere comparing men to flies, in the dramatic monologue called "Ben Jonson Entertains a Man from Stratford":

> Your fly will serve as well as anybody.
> And what's his hour? He flies, and flies, and flies,
> And in his fly's mind has a brave appearance;
> And then your spider gets him in his net,
> And eats him up and hangs him up to dry.
> That's Nature, the kind mother of us all.
> And then your slattern housemaid swings her broom,
> And where's your spider? And that's Nature, also.
> It's Nature, and it's Nothing. It's all Nothing.
> It's all a world where bugs and emperors
> Go singularly back to the same dust,

Each in his time; and the old, ordered stars
That sang together, Ben, will sing the same
Old stave to-morrow.

In something of this spirit Robinson examined an ancient
legend in his "Merlin" and "Lancelot." Though these two
long poems journey to Camelot for their scene and to
Arthur's court for their subject, they find them neither
heroic nor sentimental, as most poets have done, but remarkably like cities and courts everywhere. Camelot falls
because of its frailties rather than because of its vices.
Merlin, bewitched by his love for Vivien, leaves the court
and thus deprives it of a strong, wise man who might have
sustained it. Lancelot turns away from love, but he turns
to follow the grail, thinking thereby to show himself a
strong, wise man, and the grail proves to be a will-o'-the-
wisp; ruin overtakes Camelot as much from one man's
acts as from the others. Mankind, these poems seem to
hint, is made up of doomed creatures all moving to their
end according to some scheme which they cannot understand, with no absolute consolation except that possibly
they may be able to perceive their fate and so not be duped
by it into cherishing false hopes.

Though such a view of life is very old and has been
held by some of the wisest of men, it was assuredly not
common in the United States during the flushed years
which greeted the new century. Robinson, holding it,
seemed something of an alien in his times. Yet he was
thoroughly typical of the latest New England generation,
which, no longer so energetic as the earlier generations, has
produced numerous minds given to brooding profoundly
over the general state of man, as the people of advanced
civilizations everywhere tend to do. He was, in a sense,
another Hawthorne, more learned and more ironical. His
characters have so much of the Yankee in them that they
cannot cry out with the loud voices of most tragic heroes.

They are most eloquent in their silences. They do not invite the spectators of their fates to feel with them merely, but to understand them. Robinson does not help his readers. He demands that the dramas which he represents shall be listened to attentively, without explanation on his part. This of course has limited his audience. It is further limited by his poetical methods. He does not sing with bright, swift words, any more than he rants with high, purple words. What lifts his language is thought. Being himself very subtle, and perceiving in various situations all sorts of subtle consequences, he often deals with them when his readers are expecting him to tell a plain story. Many of his poems, especially such longer, later ones as "Roman Bartholow" and "The Man Who Died Twice" (1924), are unquestionably difficult to follow, by reason of his subtlety. They are, nevertheless, as a whole full of wisdom and beauty and irony.

What essentially sets Robinson apart from his contemporaries is the number of characters he created. Dozens of persons emerge from his pages with an unmistakable reality, though he has not put them into orthodox tragedies or comedies but has in many cases allowed each of them no more than a few spare lines of verse. It might be more accurate to say that he is less a dramatist than an etcher, hitting off human likenesses or situations with terse, crisp strokes. Nor is he like Crabbe, primarily blunt and honest. He has delicate insight into all sorts of human matters. His style, though chaste, is frequently marked by lovely melodies, as in his lines, in "The Man Against the Sky" (1916), on the poor relation who has outstayed her welcome and yet has nowhere to go:

> And like a giant harp that hums
> On always, and is always blending
> The coming of what never comes
> With what has past and had an ending,

> The City trembles, throbs, and pounds
> Outside, and through a thousand sounds
> The small intolerable drums
> Of Time are like slow drops descending.

Not melody, however, but precision is Robinson's chief quality as a writer. His words are selected with exactness, his various meters handled with dexterity. He does not write loosely, as he does not think loosely, but ponders every observation he makes upon life, every trait of a character, every image, till he comprehends it completely, and then seeks for the words which shall, so far as he can judge, most truthfully communicate his meaning. Through all the wide range of his subjects and characters he preserved in himself a combination of virtues which is very rare in a poet: he is always at once profound and precise.

With the publication of "Tristram" (1927) Robinson's reputation entered upon a new phase, though the character of his work was to remain unaltered during the eight years of life that were left to him. "Tristram" was the third and last of his Arthurian poems, and though it was perhaps not absolutely better than "Merlin" and "Lancelot" it proved to be many times more popular; indeed it is one of the best-known modern poems. It retells the tragic love story of Tristram and Isolt, purifying it of magic potions and mystic elements and simplifying it until it becomes a classic tale of human passion. The wisdom of King Mark at the end is Robinsonian wisdom: he cannot say other than that these things have happened, and that these are the kind of things which happen in a world where passion and reason alternately triumph. The melody of the blank verse is unusually clear for Robinson; its strength is a singing strength, and this is doubtless the reason that it gained thousands of new readers for its author.

Thereafter until his death he published a volume annually. Two of these volumes were made up of short poems—a collection of "Sonnets" old and new in 1928, and "Nicodemus" in 1932. The other six were long poems, no single one of which materially added to his stature, though all of them had their interest. The setting in each case is modern. "Cavender's House" (1929) is largely a dialogue between a man and his dead wife. Laramie Cavender returns to the dark house where her husband, himself a sort of living ghost, beseeches her to tell him whether he can be pardoned for the jealousy which moved him to kill her twelve years ago. She neither can nor will answer such a question; the dead are not burdened with knowledge of this kind, the past cannot come back and speak. The situation is seen by Robinson in its barest terms, and the poem which results is the poorest of all his poems in incidental riches; it is as if his voice had sunk to a whisper. It remained at that pitch in "The Glory of the Nightingales" (1930) and "Matthias at the Door" (1931), but it rose again in "Talifer" (1933), along with the comic note which Robinson had never been able wholly to suppress. "Talifer" is high comedy, being an account of one man's love of two excellent ladies—Althea first, then Karen, then finally Althea again. Karen is beautiful and learned enough to win Talifer away from Althea, but what sends him back is an impossible coldness—a quality concerning which we learn more from Dr. Quick, a friend of the three, than we do from any of them. Dr. Quick is wise, disillusioned, and witty, and it is his speeches which distinguish the poem, restoring it almost to the level of its author's best work. That level was perhaps reached in "Amaranth" (1934), whose hero, the painter Fargo, descends somewhat like Dante into a hell of dusky despair where he meets the remarkable spirits Amaranth and Evensong, and whence he emerges at the close, tried in the dark fires of doubt, to life and clear joy again. Fargo has been through everything; his happiness is a thoroughly tested one, and his wisdom cannot be taken from him. The symbolic nature of the poem renders it in places obscure, but on the other hand it gives it richness, and Robinson might have rested there. Yet one more narrative, "King Jasper" (1935), appeared after his death. Its allegory, a social one, had been less suited to Robinson's temperament than the personal allegory of "Amaranth," and it can scarcely be said that the fortunes of Jasper, Honoria, Hebron, and Zoë shed much light upon the predicament of the modern world. Robinson, however, had done too much in his best poems for his next-best to count against him. He was never bad; and the level of his good performance was extraordinarily high.

Free verse So rapid was the burst of poetry which followed 1912 that within five years the chief new poets had already made names for themselves and in some cases had done what now seems to have been their best work. To readers of old-fashioned taste it then looked as if there had been a violent revolution. The established forms of verse were suddenly put on the defensive, and free verse came into such a vogue that it had both enemies and defenders who did not always understand what they were talking about. As a matter of fact, the freedom consisted largely in the giving up of rhyme, which was no great innovation, and in the substitution of rhythm for meter as the technical element which distinguished the new poetry from prose. That is to say, instead of writing poetry in regular lines of verse with the same succession of accented and unaccented syllables in each, certain of the new poets undertook to make less regular rhythms their standard of measure and even to vary the rhythms used in the same poem. This mystified those members of the public who, having long been accustomed to rhyme and meter in poetry, had come to think of them as essential and who now questioned whether the new poetry was poetry at all. They were further mystified by a great change of method which the new poets permitted themselves, going to common life, employing common language, being realistic and satiric, mixing tragedy and comedy, and in many ways disturbing the smooth channel in which American poetry had flowed for a generation. The poets, however, persisted and quickly found supporters among a numerous class which had come to be bored by the traditional styles. There were a good many meaningless experiments with nothing but novelty to commend them, and a good many foolish arguments to prove that the new poetry could not please even when it was pleasing. But within a reasonable time the victory was won to the extent that there had come to be a reading public which realized that both old and new forms had merit and that they could exist side by side; and when, as was to be expected, a certain formal rigor returned, the lesson which had been learned in freedom was by no means lost, but on the contrary manifested itself in the many technical triumphs which have distinguished American poetry since 1925 or thereabouts.

Frost 1875–
The poets who won recognition were not in all cases connected with the revolutionary party. Like Robinson, Robert Frost has been satisfied to confine himself almost altogether to rhyme or to blank verse of a more or less accepted kind. Moreover, he has kept close to the soil of New England in gathering his material. But he has struck new notes and has made a definite contribution to native poetry. In particular, he has tried to give his poems as nearly as possible the quality of human speech, which to his ear is apparently more delightful than human singing. Behind all he has to say may be heard the sound of a Yankee voice, even when he is deeply moved, as in these lines of "Birches," one of his most noted poems:

So was I once myself a swinger of birches.
And so I dream of going back to be.
It's when I'm weary of considerations,
And life is too much like a pathless wood
Where your face burns and tickles with the cobwebs
Broken across it, and one eye is weeping
From a twig's having lashed across it open.
I'd like to get away from earth awhile
And then come back to it and begin over.
May no fate willfully misunderstand me
And half grant what I wish and snatch me away
Not to return. Earth's the right place for love:
I don't know where it's likely to go better.
I'd like to go by climbing a birch tree,
And climb black branches up a snow-white trunk
Toward heaven, till the tree could bear no more,
But dipped its top and set me down again.
That would be good both going and coming back.
One could do worse than be a swinger of birches.

It is intensely characteristic of Frost that he should hint at all he thinks about earth and heaven in the same plain language with which he has told about the boyish amusement of climbing birches and then bending them down to the ground. Whatever he expresses is expressed in this subdued tone, as if he were a man of such few words that any of them must mean a great deal. Frost owes, indeed, his brevity and simplicity to the habits of speech which prevail among the rural Yankees, in those inland towns and upland parishes which he represents as Robinson represents the more cultivated population of the New England cities. The New England back country, of course, has been the scene of countless stories and the subject of countless poems; but Frost, particularly in "North of Boston" (1914) and "Mountain Interval" (1916), has touched such themes in a fresh way. He does not deal with them sentimentally, as has too often been the custom, nor, as the custom has almost always been, in the manner of a visitor to these communities who regards them as museums of odd characters and strange dialects. He sees in them the stages on which, as on any human stage however large or small, there are transacted the universal tragedies and comedies of birth, love, work, hope, despair, death. Content to be a Yankee poet, he has been content to write of Yankee matters in a Yankee idiom, without explaining or apologizing. Being a genuine poet, he has written poems which are shrewd or wise or beautiful in themselves and which may be of interest to readers who know nothing of New England.

Having lived much of his life as a farmer in New Hampshire or Vermont, Frost has studied his chosen world with sharp eyes. He seems never to have merely glanced at natural objects, but always to have fully taken them in. He refers to country tasks with the knowledge of a man who has performed them with his own hands, to animals with the knowledge of a man who has trained and cared for them, to the characters of his stories with the knowledge of a man who has lived neighbor to such persons. Sight and insight, Frost says, are the whole business of the poet. He should first see things clearly, and then perceive their significance. Frost's practice is well illustrated in the poem called "The Tuft of Flowers," in which he tells how, once turning the hay in a meadow which another man had mowed before him, he began to think with pain that men are always alone, "whether they work together or apart." But in a little while he came upon a tuft of flowers in the hay which the mower had apparently spared out of respect for their beauty, and then the poet could

feel a spirit kindred to my own;
So that henceforth I worked no more alone.

But glad with him, I worked as with his aid,
And weary, sought at noon with him the shade;

And dreaming, as it were, held brotherly speech
With one whose thought I had not thought to reach.

"Men work together," I told him from the heart,
"Whether they work together or apart."

This is as characteristic of Frost's attitude as is his quiet speech. His poetry is the poetry of neighborliness. He neither praises nor condemns the race of man at large, but tries to become acquainted with those men and women whom he meets in his daily life and forms about them any opinions he may have about human life.

For all he works within such strict limits, he has unusual range. Now he can write a charming lyric struck off in some mood of joy. Now he can set forth an idea at which he arrived after long reflection. Now he can sketch a character with shrewd perception. Now he can tell a humorous story with the light touch of comedy. Now he can build up an episode of madness or witchcraft or guilt with the strong, sure grasp of tragedy. At the same time, he must be met on his own ground. He does not call out in the ringing voice of those poets who draw many hearers to them by the vehemence of their utterance. Though without the occasional obscurity of Robinson, Frost speaks so softly that it is possible for intelligent readers to miss his meanings. He does not insist upon his meanings, he does not point out his morals, but leaves them both to be discovered by anybody who will take the trouble to hunt for them. To value him fully a reader has to begin with a true affection for the facts of experience themselves and then has to move about among Frost's poems as if they were honest transcripts of experience, with very little emphasis upon any conclusions to be drawn from them. Such a reader, willing to dispense with rhetoric or explanations, will find that these poems grow upon him, signifying, like experience itself, more and more with each examination. He will feel an increasing delight in the accuracy with which Frost has described familiar objects and suggested familiar emotions, lifting them to the plane of beauty without adding unwarranted colors to them and lifting them to the plane of universal significance without seeming to take them out of their ordinary settings.

The publication of Frost's "Collected Poems" in 1930 was an occasion for taking stock of his work thus far, and the conclusion of most critics was that by now he had achieved a position which changes in literary fashion would fail to shake for a long time to come. The position is still unshaken. Frost has weathered every shift of taste since 1915, and he stands in a unique eminence among living poets who use the English language. He has published only two slender volumes since he was fifty—"West-Running Brook" (1928) and "A Further Range" (1936)—but they, in addition to showing his original quality unimpaired, have revealed new resources in him and made it plain that his limitations are less narrow than they once were supposed to be. For one thing, his lyric powers can no longer be relegated to second place. "Spring Pools," "Acceptance," "Once by the Pacific," "A Winter Eden," "Lost in Heaven," "Desert Places," "They Were Welcome to Their Belief," "Neither Out Far Nor In Deep"— these are lyrical in a manner known only to Robert Frost, but he has brought the manner to a high degree of perfection, and if he had written nothing else he would be distinguished. The lines seem to say little, and at first their music makes little sound; it is only upon further acquaintance with them, or upon reflection as to the character of the man speaking, that their meaning emerges. Then it is full and harmonious, as the vision behind it invariably is.

For another thing, Frost makes himself felt in his

later poems as more than a New England poet. He is still that, and his humor, which grows steadily in importance among the qualities of his work, is Yankee yet. But his subject matter is less local; his point of view takes in the largest concerns of his time. "Build Soil," for instance, contains two lines whose New England brevity are no more notable than their applicability to a world situation:

> I bid you to a one-man revolution—
> The only revolution that is coming.

The man who says this learned his language north of Boston, but he is addressing the human race.

Lindsay
1879–1931

A conspicuous element in the new poetry was due to the appearance in the Middle West of a group of poets who had an energy and a power never before associated with their kind in that region. Vachel Lindsay, for instance, after studying art in Chicago and New York, came to the conclusion that his wisest course lay in the direction of what he called "the new localism." That is, instead of looking through the wide world for beauty he would look for it at home, in his native town in Illinois. The emotions which he found there he would ennoble to the pitch of poetry. Moreover, he would accomplish these things with native methods, with the method, in particular, of what he called "the higher vaudeville." This was to combine the modes of speaking and singing with which Americans were most familiar, and was to choose the most common themes for treatment. Lindsay himself, in preparation for his career, wandered in the rôle of a poetical tramp through many States, carrying with him his "Rhymes to Be Traded for Bread" and thus paying his way with the least profitable of commodities. His first important poem, "General William Booth Enters into Heaven" (1913), illustrates all his gifts and aims. He shows Booth entering heaven to the tune of a Salvation

Army hymn, with drums and tambourines, followed by the human wreckage which he has rescued among the slums of the earth. The heaven which he enters is much like any of the Mid-Western towns which Lindsay knew.

> Jesus came out from the court-house door,
> Stretched his hands above the passing poor.
> Booth saw not, but led his queer ones there
> Round and round the mighty court-house square.

Yet it is heaven too, made suddenly important because real.

So with Lindsay's poems dealing with the negroes. Whereas most poets, dramatists, or story-tellers have seen these Americans as primarily comic, Lindsay tries to look behind their outward habits to their deeper selves. It is not enough for him to tell the biblical stories of Daniel, of Samson, of Solomon and the Queen of Sheba as an eloquent negro preacher might tell them; he contrives to raise the question why such a person should tell these stories in such a way. In "The Congo" (1915), most famous of the negro poems, Lindsay touches upon what he calls "the irrepressible high spirits" and "the basic savagery" of the blacks only to trace them to an origin which explains them. Back of the negro character, as he sees it, lie centuries of violence and ignorance in the deep jungles of Africa, where men and women now abandoned themselves to their wildest instincts and now cowered before their horrid gods. He has a vision of a mad revel on the banks of the Congo:

> Just then from the doorway, as fat as shotes,
> Came the cake-walk princes in their long red coats,
> Canes with a brilliant lacquer shine,
> And tall silk hats that were red as wine.
> And they pranced with their butterfly partners there,
> Coal-black maidens with pearls in their hair,
> Knee-skirts trimmed with the jessamine sweet,
> And bells on their ankles and little black feet.

The vision changes, and the poet sees a more spiritual religion coming among the negroes, to tame their wild instincts and to disperse their horrid gods:

> And the gray sky opened like a new-rent veil
> And showed the Apostles with their coats of mail.
> In bright white steel they were seated round
> And their fire eyes watched where the Congo wound.
> And the twelve Apostles, from their thrones on high,
> Thrilled all the forest with their heavenly cry:
> "Mumbo-Jumbo will die in the jungle;
> Never again will he hoo-doo you,
> Never again will be hoo-doo you."

Perhaps Lindsay is not quite scientific in this poem, since he ascribes to an ancient racial experience certain traits of the negroes which may be equally ascribable to their more recent fate in America. But at least he is true to his creed as a poet in that he finds poetry in things near at hand, and in things by most poets either overlooked entirely or else dismissed as merely vulgar.

In all his outstanding poems he produces his effects in this manner. Tramping across Kansas he is disturbed by the rush of motors along the highway, but instead of irritation at the noise and bustle which they make he feels a thrill of pleasure in this grandiose spectacle of his countrymen pouring back and forth across the continent, and he writes "The Santa Fe Trail," a poem full of rhythmical emotion. Turning to such native heroes, heretofore neglected by the poets, as Alexander Campbell, Johnny Appleseed, John L. Sullivan, Lindsay seizes upon the poetic or dramatic qualities in their lives and chants them much as primitive bards chanted primitive prophets or saints or warriors.

He stood, it may be said, somewhere between the poet and the orator. Always he had the sense of an audience actually before him. Meeting them half-way by choosing

subjects which they were likely to understand, he spoke
to them in language they could understand. Like a popular
preacher or politician, he played upon their habitual sentiments, most of all upon their optimistic belief that human
life may be made immeasurably better by reforming zeal.
He was the leader of crusades, the defender of fading
hopes, the singer of good causes. His enthusiasm so often
got the better of him that he frequently mistook it for genuine poetical elevation, and the consequence was that he
wrote a great deal which is hardly better than nonsense.
But at his best he still is powerful and energetic, and at
times he can be very moving, as in "Abraham Lincoln
Walks at Midnight," in which Lincoln is seen pacing the
dark streets of Springfield in an agony of distress over the
war in Europe. At such moments Lindsay can be said to
have dispensed with his usual sound and fury, choosing an
intensely local theme, and connecting it by his interpretation with the concerns of the world at large. Herein lies
his importance as a poet: he proved that poetry can begin
at home, and that it can find its forms of utterance there.

**Masters
1869–**

At about the same time with Lindsay there
sprang into sudden prominence another poet
who in temper is as little like him as possible.
Edgar Lee Masters, trained as a lawyer and therefore acquainted with a side of life which Lindsay, celebrator of
heroes, hardly notices, had come to doubt that American
village life is as idyllic as it has been painted by most
writers. Along with the good and shrewd people in the
villages, he had concluded, are others who are fools and
rogues. It occurred to him, taking his model from the Greek
Anthology, to set forth his conclusions in a series of poems
which would present a complete picture of a typical Illinois village as he believed it really should be presented.
His "Spoon River Anthology" (1915) purports to be
made up of the epitaphs in the Spoon River graveyard.

But whereas such epitaphs are customarily false or flatter-ing, those in this imagined cemetery are ruthlessly honest and sardonic. Each buried man or woman speaks the truth in uncompromising terms. All the secrets of the vil-lage are laid bare. Hardly a reputation is left unstained. The scandal which stalks among the tombs, whispering against the dead, naturally raises questions as to the living. The first effect of the "Anthology" is to wither the senti-mental notion that villages are invariably the homes of peace and bliss and industry and virtue.

One thing which greatly interests Masters is the ironic contrast between what is reported and what is true about his people. He shows the most respectable citizens con-fessing that they did not deserve their respectability; the most disreputable citizens revealing the fact that they were not so bad as the village thought. Again, he shows husband and wife, or friend and friend, telling things about them-selves or about one another which reveal points of view so opposite that unsuspected dramatic situations are thereby brought to light. He points out the difference between the old pioneers, with the courage

> Which labors and suffers and sings
> Under the sun,

and their descendants, with their

> sorrow and weariness,
> Anger, discontent, and drooping hopes.

He tells of Elliott Hawkins, who presumed upon his re-semblance to Lincoln and yet gave himself to public ac-tivities which Lincoln would have hated, and of Archibald Higbie, who, loathing the village and trying to purge him-self of all its influences, yet found that whenever he painted a picture in Rome it suggested Lincoln's face. But these ironical contrasts are not all at the expense of Spoon River.

Anne Rutledge, speaking from her humble grave in the loveliest poem of the whole "Anthology," contrives to throw a kind of glory across the whole village:

> Out of me unworthy and unknown
> The vibrations of deathless music;
> "With malice toward none, and charity for all."
> Out of me the forgiveness of millions toward millions,
> And the beneficent face of a nation
> Shining with justice and truth.
> I am Anne Rutledge who sleep beneath these weeds,
> Beloved in life of Abraham Lincoln,
> Wedded to him, not through union,
> But through separation.
> Bloom forever, O Republic,
> From the dust of my bosom!

While the scandal in "Spoon River Anthology" first catches the attention, it is by no means the sole element. The village has plenty of generosity and vitality underneath the smug and dusty way of life into which it has fallen, as is made clear by the unforgettable portrait of Petit, the Poet:

> Seeds in a dry pod, tick, tick, tick,
> Tick, tick, tick, like mites in a quarrel—
> Faint iambics that the full breeze wakens—
> But the pine tree makes a symphony thereof.
> Triolets, villanelles, rondels, rondeaus,
> Ballades by the score with the same old thought:
> The snows and the roses of yesterday are vanished;
> And what is love but a rose that fades?
> Life all around me here in the village:
> Tragedy, comedy, valor, and truth,
> Courage, constancy, heroism, failure—
> All in the loom, and oh what patterns!
> Woodland, meadows, streams and rivers—
> Blind to all of it all my life long.
> Triolets, villanelles, rondels, rondeaus,
> Seeds in a dry pod, tick, tick, tick,

Tick, tick, tick, what little iambics,
While Homer and Whitman roared in the pines?

It is the stale, conventional villagers whom Masters hates; he presents, however, the epitaphs of many others who win his tacit praise by their abundance of thought or feeling, little as the village may have valued them. The difference between him and most of those Americans who have set forth the charm of simple life is that whereas they tend to measure it by somewhat trivial codes of vice and virtue, he really condemns nothing so much as cruelty or meanness and approves nothing so much as courage or magnanimity.

In this respect, though like the greatest satirists of all ages, Masters seemed from the first a novel figure in American literature, which has not as a rule been remarkable for its satire but which has generally preferred to take a kindly attitude toward the race of man at large and toward Americans in particular. He is above all a satirist, as appears even in those later novels of his which seem to have left satire behind. He is most aroused when he hates injustice and dullness. His "Domesday Book" (1920), the inquest of an imaginary coroner and his jury into the remotest causes and consequences of a suicide which has come under their jurisdiction, is a panorama of American life throughout the disturbed twentieth century. There, as in "Spoon River Anthology," Masters shows that he has no use for outward conformity as such. In a country where the pressure of public opinion has gone too far in the matter of trying to make all men as much alike as possible, out of a false sense of the functions of equality, Masters rebels. He glorifies the men and women who dare to be something out of the ordinary, even though they thereby depart from the beaten path which the populace expects. Above all things he pays tribute to the free mind which ventures to detach itself from the mass of uniformity which makes up the bulk of human conduct. Being so much a rebel, Masters is not invariably an artist. He writes violently, and often crudely, unable in much of his later work to mark his poetry off from his prose by anything more subtle than the rough beat of verse. But satire has an important service to perform in a time when the ideals of life are being reëxamined, and Masters must be recognized as a satirist of great value as well as of great power. And even if he were not valuable for his services in challenging the minor conventionalities, he would be important for the reason that he has brought into American poetry one of its most robust intelligences, one of its most fiery and ironical tongues.

Sandburg 1878- Lindsay and Masters are both descended from the older American stocks; Carl Sandburg is the son of a Swedish immigrant and so grew up in the midst of the industrialism which faces the modern immigrant as wild nature faced the earlier immigrant. Though Sandburg was born in a small Illinois town, and during his youth drifted about the Middle West much as any youth might have done, he from the first found his natural themes for poetry among factories and railroads, in cities and slums, in the midst of noise and under a pall of smoke, and called his books by such names as "Chicago Poems" (1915) and "Smoke and Steel" (1920). Trying to voice the aspiration of some humble thing to have a share in great enterprises, he imagines steel, in "Prayers of Steel," as praying to be laid upon an anvil, beaten into a crowbar, hammered into a spike.

Drive me into the girders that hold a sky-scraper together.
Take red-hot rivets and fasten me into the central girders.
Let me be the great nail holding a sky-scraper through blue nights into white stars.

Such an image would never have occurred to one of the older American poets, who instead might have put the

prayer into the mouth of a plow eager to break the stubborn sod or of an ax eager to level the shaggy forest. Sandburg by his choice of steel as his symbol reveals himself
a poet of the new order of life in the United States.

Moreover, he is the poet not of any of the traditional
communities, such as Boston or Philadelphia or Richmond,
but of Chicago, the vast, sprawling, windy city where life
moves at a pace which could hardly have been indicated in
the smooth lines of any dainty versifier. What Sandburg
likes in Chicago is its newness and hopefulness, which a
different poet might call its rawness and callowness. In his
city Sandburg finds the unassimilated materials of poetry,
and indeed of civilization, not yet shaped into established
forms. Anything can happen here, and he is ready for anything that can happen. Above all he admires the superb
insolence of the untamed capital which, as he points out in
his poem called "The Windy City," has such a daring
motto:

Go to it and remember this city fished from its depths a text:
    "independent as a hog on ice."
Venice is a dream of soft waters, Vienna and Bagdad recollections
    of dark spears and wild turbans; Paris is a thought in Monet
    gray on scabbards, fabrics, façades; London is a fact in a fog
    filled with the moaning of transatlantic whistles; Berlin sits
    amid white scrubbed quadrangles and torn arithmetics and
    testaments; Moscow brandishes a flag and repeats a dance
    figure of a man who walks like a bear.
Chicago fished from its depths a text: "independent as a hog on
    ice."

Thus admiring the insolence of Chicago, Sandburg is
equally insolent. He too discards the past and its patterns;
he too reaches out and grasps whatever seems to him full
of life and molds it into his own uses; he too speaks his
own language, though it comes to him from the streets
rather than from the dictionaries. To the extent that Chi-

cago is the metropolis of the present and the future, Sandburg is the poet of those eras.

But he is not merely a voice for the tumultuous elements in American life; he is also a voice for human pity and tenderness. Brooding over the spectacle of existence, so torn and confused as he sees it, he writes of old men and women who have nothing left but memories, of frail spirits who have been put to tasks which are too difficult for them and who stumble along the paths of toil, of strong spirits broken by the struggle, of friendship and beauty and love. Because life is as good as it is, he forgives it for being no better. Like all vigorous men with a sense of the hardness of fate, he is very tender toward children. To one of his own daughters he addresses a poem, "Winter Milk," which in a few eloquent lines says what all fathers feel about their little daughters, in whom youth is now so lovely though it must pass so soon:

> There are dreams in your eyes, Helga.
> Tall reaches of wind sweep the clear blue.
> The winter is young yet, so young.
> Only a little cupful of winter has touched your lips.

Nor is Sandburg always somber in his attitude toward children. At times he is so gay and whimsical that he has taken the trouble to create, in his "Rootabaga" stories, a kind of nonsense language, largely drawn from slang, in which to tell stories which are roguish and grotesque and which yet serve to instruct children in much which it is important for them to know about the world in which they are to live when they have grown up. Perhaps nothing about him is more remarkable than the fact that he is at once so bold and challenging toward adults and so sympathetic and affectionate toward the young.

This same range of sympathies appears throughout his work. He can explode in "The Lawyers Know Too Much,"

with a guffaw of disgust at those persons who seem to him
to live only to make life more complicated:

The work of a bricklayer goes to the blue.
The knack of a mason outlasts a moon.
The hand of a plasterer holds a room together.
The land of a farmer wishes him back again.
    Singers of songs and dreamers of plays
    Build a house no wind blows over.
The lawyers—tell me why a hearse horse snickers hauling a law-
    yer's bones.

Yet he can also sing, in his fashion, sweet songs about the
most ancient emotions which poets ever have felt, such as
this song called "In Tall Grass":

Bees and a honeycomb in the dried head of a horse in a pasture
    corner—a skull in the tall grass and a buzz and a buzz of the
    yellow honey-hunters.
And I ask no better a winding sheet (over the earth and under
    the sun).
Let the bees go honey-hunting with yellow blur of wings in the
    dome of my head, in the rumbling singing arch of my skull.
Let there be wings and yellow dust and the drone of dreams of
    honey—who loses and remembers?—who keeps and forgets?
In a blue sheen of moon over the bones and under the hanging
    honeycomb the bees come home and the bees sleep.

This range of sympathies, indeed, is Sandburg's chief trait.
He is native and local enough to be able to make poems about
the Chicago stock-yards; he is universal enough to respond
to poetical sentiments from whatever quarter.

Very often, as in the case of Vachel Lindsay, Sandburg does not transmute his materials into poetry but leaves
them still rough or underdone. This is not, as some readers
insist, because he has chosen unpoetical materials to write
about; actually there is nothing which cannot be made into
poetry if the poet is competent. It is because Sandburg cannot always finish what he has begun. Full of pioneer audacity, he will not accept any help from any poetic method

except his own. Disagreeing with the great majority of Americans, he finds few audiences already prepared to share the thrill which he feels at sight of the undisciplined forces of modern society. He will not deal with common themes, and thus reap the harvest of other poets who have taught mankind how to enjoy those themes in verse. He will not select his words from among the words which the practice of other poets has made to seem poetical, but insists on selecting any word or phrase he likes and forcing it into good usage. The consequences are that many of his poems are hard for most readers to understand, and many others seem unpleasant to the best-intentioned readers by reason of their uncouth images and violent ideas. But at his best he is full of a huge tenderness, and at all but his worst he is full of fire and energy.

"Good Morning, America" (1928) and "The People, Yes" (1936) are particularly concerned with the American language. Sandburg has always manifested such a concern, but in these volumes he explores his country's idiom in search of its final secret. Language for him is more than syntax and diction. It is the whole way a people has of expressing itself, and Sandburg has studied this way in his biography of Lincoln and his collection of American songs as well as in his own poetry. But in that poetry he brings his study close to essentials. The title poem of "Good Morning, America" is a celebration, with many examples, of the national speech.

> A code arrives; language; lingo; slang;
> behold the proverbs of a people, a nation:
> Give 'em the works. Fix it, there's always
> a way. Be hard boiled. The good die young.

It is a celebration because it insists upon the beauty and importance of popular phrases. And it gives examples because there is no other way to define the quality of those phrases. "The People, Yes" devotes nearly three hundred pages to an extension of the task. It is enormously amusing, for like no other book of its time it expresses the good nature of a broad and varied country, and unlike most of what goes for poetry in the modern world it is frankly and directly humorous. Yet other moods have their innings too; and at the heart of the book is a conception of American man which does not differ too much from Sandburg's conception of man anywhere at his best—honest, ironic, quick to detect affectation or fraud, and ready to worship the brave or the sensible. Not the least virtue of "The People, Yes" is that it constitutes a repository of American sayings which will have permanent value. To the future student of twentieth-century national manners it will prove a mine of evidence. To any American, now or to come, it supplies an audible image of himself speaking at those moments when he is most himself and most American.

Imagism For the most part, the new poetry was produced rather by individuals than by schools, but there was one distinctive group of which something must be said. That group, working both in England and the United States more or less upon the model of certain French contemporaries, had a definite poetical theory and set out about 1915 to do definite things. They called themselves Imagists, because they believed that poetry should first of all present an image, that is, "should render particulars exactly and not deal in vague generalities, however magnificent and sonorous." They believed, in addition, that poetry should use the language of common speech, employing "always the *exact* word, not the nearly exact, nor the merely decorative word"; that it should "create new rhythms—as the expression of new moods—and not . . . copy old rhythms, which merely echo old moods"; that poets should have "absolute freedom in the choice of subject," whether chosen from the present or from the past;

that a poem should be "hard and clear, never blurred nor indefinite"; and that "concentration is of the very essence of poetry." These doctrines, the Imagists realized and insisted, were not new, but had latterly been neglected, with the result that poetry had become either too smooth or too cloudy. Like Wordsworth in his time, the group was making war upon poetical diction and the restriction of poetry to a few established themes; but they went further and made war also upon Wordsworth, and more explicitly upon Whitman, for their "vague generalities." "It is for this reason," they said, "That we oppose the cosmic poet, who seems to us to shirk the real difficulties of his art." It might almost be maintained that they were deliberately turning from Whitman to Emily Dickinson; and while they were not quite doing that, they were at least basing their principles upon her kind of practice. They were, in other words, doing what they could to reduce poetry to its irreducible elements, making it simple and direct and vivid, even though in so doing they might have to discard many of the riper and ampler charms to which poetry has traditionally laid claim.

Amy Lowell 1874-1925   Of the American Imagists, without any question, the best-known poet was Amy Lowell. She was, however, more than a member of a school. She had already thought a great deal about poetry, and had tried numerous forms of it in her own work, before she became interested in Imagism; and she brought to the new doctrine a vigorous critical intelligence and a pugnacious disposition which helped it to win a hearing. Cultivated and energetic, she wrote and spoke in behalf of experimentation in verse, defending poetic practices which were ridiculed or misunderstood, explaining the aims of neglected poets, turning to the poetry of many other literatures to find illustrations which would prove her points. She thus furnished a basis for argument in favor of free verse of

various sorts which it did not have before she joined the
cause, at least so far as the larger public knew. Her own
work, too, shows the range of which the new poetry is
capable. She composed in severely classical forms as well
as in more novel ones. She chose now to reproduce the
delicate formality of Japanese verse and now to manipulate the effects of cadenced prose. She explored the past for
her subjects or took them from familiar legends of New
England. She adorned her narratives with gorgeous colors
or permitted them to be as bare as dialect demands. In
particular she showed that the methods she upheld can be
applied not only to brief snatches, merely glittering fragments, but to long stories in verse as well. It would, indeed,
be difficult to overestimate her services to the new movement. She gave it prestige by her culture, which was that
of a stock long eminent in Massachusetts, and yet did not
shrink from the robust task of leading a cause which has
had to be emphatic and iconoclastic in order to make its
way in the world.

Her positive achievement as a poet was doubtless less
than her achievements as a critic and a spokesman. Though
the body of her work is impressive, she produced almost no
individual poems which sting and haunt as the triumphant
poems of the more memorable poets do. Reading a volume
by Amy Lowell is, in a sense, like walking through a museum in which many objects of art have been arranged
with admirable taste. The light falls upon them at the
proper angle; they are grouped to the best advantage; they
exhibit charming colors and textures and forms. But, as
has been said, this poet seemed to be interested hardly so
much in the stuff as in the stuffs of life. That is, she painted
the vivid surfaces of human existence and did not always
communicate the drama stirring beneath them. True to
her creed, she confined herself to the essential image, drawn
with a hard, clear outline, contemptuous of the softer

moods in which the eye relaxes its vigilance and takes in beauty without always testing it very precisely. She rarely burst into spontaneous eloquence or flowered instinctively into song. The objects in her lovely museum therefore do not always come to life, and have sometimes the appearance of something not much better than specimens. By and by they cause a kind of eyestrain, from having demanded so close an attention. Occasionally, however, Amy Lowell struck an unmistakable note, as in "Men, Women, and Ghosts" (1916), with "Patterns," which is justly the most famous of her poems. There the lady who speaks has lived so long in a stiff, formal world that the tightness of her garments and the squareness of the paths in her garden have come to symbolize her fate, which keeps her at home in a tense anxiety while her lover is away at war. Then comes the news of his death, and the lady, aware that he can now have no chance to rescue her from her prim life, cries out in rebellion against it. At that moment the actual woman, however cramping the pattern of her life may be, is revealed in a flash. Such flashes are poetry.

"H.D."
1886–

Amy Lowell was the best-known Imagist while she lived, but another poetess of the school has since come to seem its finest representative. "H.D." (Hilda Doolittle), whose poems were collected in 1925, has since that date published further work, but her procedure has never changed, just as her excellence has never flagged. She employs a short, nervous, irregularly-lengthed line in poems whose sole intention is to render with a minimum of verbiage the essence of a scene, a mood, a moment. The point of view is within the observer's mind rather than his eye; if images are her stock in trade, they are not surface images. More is implied than stated:

> I was splintered and torn:
> the hill-path mounted
> swifter than my feet.

What seems to be exaggeration is upon second thought discovered to be intensity, as when in the poem "Garden" she speaks of heat

> that presses up and blunts
> the points of pears
> and rounds the grapes.

"H.D.," who has lived in Europe since 1911, is devoted to ancient Greece as a source not only for her images but for her ideas. Increasingly, through translations of Greek poetry and through poems celebrating the power and beauty of the Greek divinities, she reveals that she is most at home in remote gardens of the spirit. Yet this does not deprive her of contemporary force. She is not archaic so much as timeless; her desire is to give emotions permanence by treating them as gems to be carved, as stones to be reshaped with grace. Her success is perhaps minor, but it has its importance in days when form is paid less than its proper homage.

Edna St. Vincent Millay 1892– Associated with no poetical school, Edna St. Vincent Millay is yet associated, at least in the popular mind, with the new poetry as is no other American. To this eminence she has undoubtedly been helped by the simplicity of her methods. She has not devoted her energies to experimenting with new technics or to arguing about them. Her only novelty lies in her freshness and her directness. Her only concern, apparently, has been to drive home the arrows of her wit and beauty, singing as they go. Her readers, grateful for her art without, in many cases, being aware of it, have therefore fixed their attention upon the ideas and emotions which she expresses.

Her career began in 1912, when, at the age of twenty, she published her remarkable poem called "Renascence." It set forth a vivid experience in vivid words. She had been visited by a powerful mood in which she felt that her soul filled all the world, and that she could hear "the ticking of Eternity." But the suffering and pity of mankind so pressed upon her that she shrank from it, and imagined herself buried in the cool earth, happy in her escape. In this comfortable death, however, she suddenly remembered the beauty which she had left behind. The memory was stronger than her desire for peace.

> Ah! Up then from the ground sprang I
> And hailed the earth with such a cry
> As is not heard save from a man
> Who has been dead, and lives again.
> About the trees my arms I wound;
> Like one gone mad I hugged the ground;
> I raised my quivering arms on high;
> I laughed and laughed into the sky.

Exultant in her rebirth, she concluded that it lies with the soul to be the master of space and time, or to be the victim of them.

> East and West will pinch the heart
> That cannot keep them pushed apart;
> And he whose soul is flat—the sky
> Will cave in on him by and by.

Though born in Maine, she came soon to be thought of in connection with Greenwich Village, that district of New York City most favored for a time by all kinds of artists as their place of residence. There, according to the popular notion, art and gaiety flourish without a care, safely removed from customary dullness. The spirit of the place has been supposed to be distilled in Miss Millay's volume "A Few Figs from Thistles" (1921), particularly in a quatrain laughingly called "First Fig":

> My candle burns at both ends;
> It will not last the night;

But ah, my foes, and oh, my friends—
It gives a lovely light!

This is actually no more than a merry version of Emerson's grave statement that "Beauty is its own excuse for being," but it aroused responsive echoes in many readers who had grown tired of hearing life forever called real and earnest, and who wanted to admire verve and audacity no less than prudence. It is these brighter qualities which Miss Millay celebrates. Her poems are concerned not with sacrifice but with freedom, not with duty but with joy, not with obedience but with rapture. They may touch the deepest themes, but they are never somber, because they are always gallant. At the same time, they are not shallow. A very alert intelligence confirms Miss Millay in her instinctive feeling that if it is better to be alive than to be dead, so is it better to be wholly alive than to be half alive. And as she does not believe in brooding, so she does not believe in keeping silent. She speaks out boldly on all the topics which interest her or the imagined speakers of her poems. Indeed, it has distressed certain of her readers to find Miss Millay permitting women in her poems to speak as candidly about love as men have always been permitted to do. Her women do not tremble at the thought of being loved or whimper at the thought of not being loved again. They are eager for love; they praise the beauty of their lovers; they can laugh at love in the midst of its desperations; they recover from it, if it fails them, and live to love again. In "The Harp-Weaver and Other Poems" (1923) Miss Millay thus expresses a sense of love's variety and variability:

I know I am but summer to your heart,
And not the full four seasons of the year;
And you must welcome from another part
Such noble moods as are not mine, my dear.
No gracious weight of golden fruits to sell
Have I, nor any wise and wintry thing;

And I have loved you all too long and well
To carry still the high sweet breast of spring.
Wherefore I say: O love, as summer goes,
I must be gone, steal forth with silent drums,
That you may hail anew the bird and rose
When I come back to you, as summer comes.
Else will you seek, at some not distant time,
Even your summer in another clime.

This sense of love in Miss Millay is in keeping with her sense of life at large. But like all who love life and beauty, she is always haunted by the knowledge that both are mortal. Because she loves them so much she knows they cannot last, and because she knows they cannot last she loves them all the more while they do. She who has written lyrics and ballads of the most dashing insolence, has written exquisitely tender dirges, such as her "Prayer to Persephone," in "Second April":

Be to her, Persephone,
All the things I might not be;
Take her head upon your knee.
She that was so proud and wild,
Flippant, arrogant and free,
She that had no need of me,
Is a little lonely child
Lost in Hell,—Persephone,
Take her head upon your knee;
Say to her, "My dear, my dear,
It is not so dreadful here."

This is all the more lovely for the reason that Miss Millay has made the mother in her poem speak a little lightly as well as tenderly. Light words are often as strong as the heaviest. Because she has known this, Miss Millay has added a very special quality to the poetry of her time.

Since "The Harp-Weaver" Miss Millay's poetry has grown more grave in its subject matter and more complex in its structure. "The Buck in the Snow and Other Poems"

(1927) carried on the familiar lyric strain in certain of its pages, but other pages were shadowed by current events. The section called "Justice in Massachusetts" was in effect a requiem for civilization inspired by Miss Millay's distress over the execution of Sacco and Vanzetti in Boston for a crime which many persons believed they had not committed. The reverberation of this case throughout the literature of its decade will be noted elsewhere in the present volume. Miss Millay's somber elegies are distinguished among the many protests called forth in America because their distinction, like that of her work generally, is among other things formal. She speaks briefly, but weightily and to the point. Her next book, "Fatal Interview" (1931), was a collection of love sonnets, but their note was deeper than that of their predecessors. The title is, significantly, a phrase from the English poet John Donne, whose complicating influence on English and American poetry was everywhere being felt when Miss Millay's sonnets—her best ones thus far—appeared. Love had ceased for her to be a playground; it had grown until it was as important as life itself, and her analysis of it in this volume becomes finally mature. "Wine From These Grapes" (1934) is still further touched by the times; the imminence of new wars clouds its pages, and its rhythms break up as a result, so that instead of the former crispness there is a frequent use of long, irregular, ominous lines. The final section is a group of sonnets called "Epitaph for the Race of Man." But Miss Millay was to vary her sonnet technique in still another way. "Conversation at Midnight" (1937) is a dialogue between seven men, met together in a New York house, on the state of the current world. In vernacular lines, sometimes broken and harsh, they discuss women, hunting, fishing, poetry, painting, Communism, capitalism, the decay of culture, and their own troubled minds. Only the acutest ear will discover that they are talking in sonnets, and only an acute intelligence will presume that Miss Millay has perhaps most sympathy with Anselmo, the priest who remarks on one occasion:

> No man can be at peace with his neighbor who is not at peace
> With himself; the troubled mind is a trouble maker.

Miss Millay has not altogether avoided the danger which dialogues invariably run: that of seeming implausible. And a certain feverish eagerness in everybody to empty the whole content of his mind increases the reader's sense of artifice, of maneuvered argument. Yet the volume is rich in wit and understanding, and many valuable things are said. Miss Millay has come a long way in it from the charm of her early poems. They are still charming, as Miss Millay herself is still an effective poet.

Elinor Wylie 1885–1928 An American poetess who rivalled Miss Millay in popularity while she lived, and who keeps her eminence unimpaired in death, is Elinor Wylie, author of four volumes of poetry published in the short space of eight years (1921–1929). Elinor Wylie was also a novelist and an extraordinarily brilliant person, but it is her poetry that will keep her name longest alive. This poetry is never without decisiveness, whether, as in "The Eagle and the Mole," it counsels the reader to

> Avoid the reeking herd,
> Shun the polluted flock,
> Live like that stoic bird,
> The eagle of the rock,

or whether, as in the sequence of posthumous love sonnets, "One Person," it discloses a personal, indeed a secret passion for whose depth there are no adequate words or gestures:

> My lord, adjudge my strength, and set me where
> I bear a little more than I can bear.

The poetry of Elinor Wylie is also steadily luminous; it glistens with the jewelry of wit, which sometimes is worn in a holiday mood, but which most of the time is the adornment of an impressive intellectual talent. Certain of her shorter pieces, notably "Let No Charitable Hope," "Confession of Faith," and "True Vine," are masterpieces of personal statement: analyses of a self aware of its own intricacy but aware also of the perspective in which the self must always be viewed if the truth is to be known and told. Elinor Wylie's brilliance occasionally conceals a tendency to be diffuse; she could say things so well that she sometimes said them in more than the necessary number of ways. But it is an infrequent fault in a poet whose performance is delightful even when it is not high. And it nowhere occurs in the culminating effort of her career, the nineteen sonnets to One Person.

After the Renaissance The renaissance of poetry which occurred in 1912 or thereabouts was beginning in the late 1920's to lose some of its original force. The reputations established during its first decade abundantly held their own; but they were established, and new ones of the same sort did not follow at the same quick pace. The public enthusiasm for poetry died down; magazines devoted exclusively to the art no longer were a fashion; and poets returned to the private existence which is their proverbial lot. This did not mean, however, that excellence had been lost. Public enthusiasm had put a premium on obvious effects, and in large part had signified an interest in the thing being said rather than in the manner of its saying. The new phase of American poetry now entered upon has never been a popular one, but it has its great importance, and its contribution is probably permanent. Poetry since the renaissance has been learned, ironic, intellectual, and disillusioned; and the manner of it has been difficult.

Sometimes this manner has been obscure, either because
the poets set out to achieve obscurity or because their
themes demanded the kind of handling which the hasty
eye may not appreciate at a glance. At any rate it is true
that a certain discipline is necessary for the understanding
of the poetry in question, and more than one of its masterpieces has taken years to come into its own.

**Eliot
1888–**
The most famous and influential example is
T.S. (Thomas Stearns) Eliot's "The Waste
Land" (1922), which came to be the most discussed poem of its decade, but only after two or three years
of persistent misunderstanding and ridicule. Eliot, born in
the United States but since 1914 a resident of England,
had published "Prufrock" in 1917 and "Poems" in 1920.
Both volumes had aroused intense interest and admiration
in limited circles. The stanza invented by Eliot for his
poems about "Sweeney" was recognized as an invention—
a rare thing in poetry—and had many imitators. And the
exquisite boredom of "The Love Song of J. Alfred Prufrock," along with its free verse which so perfectly fitted
a mood, fell in with the post-war disillusion on both sides
of the Atlantic. Eliot, then, had found his audience of
poets. But it remained for "The Waste Land" to carry his
name across the entire literary world. In good time it did
so, and it was discovered that he had written it, as indeed
he has written all of his poems, even the humorous ones,
out of a deeply held conviction. "The Waste Land" expresses that conviction by suggesting that the modern
world, being without a culture of its own, can have one
only if it pieces together the scraps of ancient culture which
survive here and there by inexplicable accident. The absence of a culture means for Eliot the absence of an integrity and a faith. His poems are delicate and mournful
songs sung in sorrow for a vanished unity; or else they are
harsh in their indictment of the ugly world that results.

In the years since "The Waste Land" he has sought and found some kind of faith for himself, expounding it both in further poems and in an important body of literary criticism.[1] Its first expression was "Ash-Wednesday" (1930), a group of lyrics one of which commences:

Lady, three white leopards sat under a juniper-tree
In the cool of the day, having fed to satiety
On my legs my heart my liver and that which had been contained
In the hollow round of my skull.

This is enough to indicate that Eliot's new-found faith was not a simple one. It was in fact a very interesting one, and not only poems but plays—notably "Murder in the Cathedral" (1935)—have appeared in the process of its elucidation. Its influence has been no less than the influence of his early despair; nor should the point be missed that despair is the very basis on which it has been built. Meanwhile he has continued to write verse of the most accomplished and delicate kind; merely as a technician he holds a dominant place in the contemporary field.

**Pound
1885–**
One of his teachers in technique, and a teacher of many other poets of importance, was Ezra Pound, whose literary reputation is greater than his public name, if the latter can be said to exist at all. He has lived in Europe since 1908, and from there has kept up a rapid fire of nervous, unconventional comment on the art which he himself practises with a highly professional skill. Many writers of the first rank have acknowledged their indebtedness to him. His criticism is voluminous, his personality widely felt. His poetry, however, is known chiefly by other poets. They value it for its wit, its learning, and its virtuoso's dexterity. Pound has one of the sharpest satirical tongues known to his time, and it would be known more

[1] For his criticism, see pages 155–156.

widely by that time if its occupation were with other than literary matters. So has he a fine lyric gift, but again he avoids the subjects which lyric poets habitually cultivate. As a translator from many languages he has led the way to new discoveries in form and theme; he was the first contemporary poet to give an acceptable English dress to Chinese and Japanese poetry, but he is equally interesting for his renderings from Anglo-Saxon and Provençal. Since 1925 he has been laboring at his chief work, a long poem called simply "Cantos" which appears from time to time in sizable instalments. Its materials are assembled from every obscure corner of the literary and human past, on a scale much larger than that of Eliot's "The Waste Land" and in a tone prevailingly comic rather than tragic or melancholy. Eccentric shifts of century and setting express its author's sense of the confusion which human history is, and they express this brilliantly. The poem, however, will continue to be a possession of the learned minority while shorter pieces like "A Girl" and "The Return" continue to please the larger minority to which Pound's vogue seems definitely confined.

Stevens
1879–

Wallace Stevens is another expert who writes for experts. For a quarter of a century he has worked reticently at the composition of exquisite masterpieces whose oblique allusions he can expect only the most sophisticated readers to comprehend. They have comprehended them, and they have paid homage to him as one who knows best of all poets in his time how to paint pictures in words and how to manipulate syllables so that they will be music. But the painting and the music are modern; the colors are fragmentary and the harmonies are half-heard. His account of the contemporary world is an account of its surfaces, beneath which he seems to say there is nothing. His perception of tints and shadows is a perception at the same time of the irony involved in the fact that these were once supposed to conceal meaning. They conceal for him nothing but emptiness, the depth of which he sings with an accomplished, almost an insulting indifference. His poems are most to be enjoyed by one who does not, at any rate in the beginning, worry about what they say. There is pleasure to be had from the mere sounds they make, and from the patterns they provide for the reading eye. They say more than that; Stevens is in fact a satirist of note, and he is utterly free of delusions. "Sea Surface Full of Clouds" is not pure painting, and "Sunday Morning" is not pure music. But they use the techniques of those two arts to convey their ultimate meaning—a meaning which will not be possessed by the reader until he has seen and heard them, simply and superficially, without imposing his own will or understanding upon the poet.

Ransom 1888–

Another kind of difficulty is presented by a Southern poet, John Crowe Ransom, who both by his example and by his criticism has been an artist of wide influence. Chiefly instrumental in founding the Tennessee group called the Fugitives, who for several years after 1922 published their poems in a magazine to which they gave their name, he has since that date come steadily up in the estimation of his peers, and there are those who claim for him the first position among contemporary poets. If he occupies this position, it is not by the vote of general readers, for he is in no sense a popular poet. Yet he is not a cultivator of surfaces like Wallace Stevens. He is serious, ironic, tragic, and passionately Southern—an expression of the last trait being his poem "Antique Harvesters," which recalls the past dignities of a section, the lost rituals, in a setting where those dignities and rituals may no longer be seen. Devoted with other "Agrarians" of his region to the cause of restoring or at any rate stating the best that there is in the traditional South, Ransom in his poetry is particularly effective as a discoverer of contrasts between the old and the new, between the established and the fashionable, between the passionate and the sentimental. He has no illusions about the possibility of restoring another age in this one, for he is not romantic. He is ironic—often bitterly so, though several of his shorter pieces, such as "Lady Lost," "Blue Girls," "Here Lies a Lady," and "Piazza Piece," reveal in him a streak of gaiety which is elsewhere repressed. Not that the subjects of these pieces are gay, for they are usually aspects of death; but the poet's touch in them is quick, light, nervous, and fine. His human endowment is felt by any sensitive reader to be rich, however he may hide the fact under a somewhat bristling exterior. And his poetic endowment is even richer.

Tate
1899–

Another member of the Fugitives group was Allen Tate, whose reputation as a poet would seem to be out of all proportion to his output. A rigorous critic of others, he has been as rigorous with himself, publishing comparatively little and subjecting that little to constant revision from one printed version to another. His "Ode to the Confederate Dead" has been rewritten more than once, and some of his sonnets in their later form are all but unrecognizable. But his distinction lies precisely in this conception of himself not as one who writes his autobiography in verse but as one who writes poems for the best judges to read. At the same time a definite character, and one of pronounced strength, is to be felt behind the severe surface of his art. He too, like John Crowe Ransom, is passionately devoted to a vision of the Southern past, and like Ransom, though in an individual fashion, he institutes a series of implied comparisons between that past and the present. His Ode is so far from being a conventional tribute to the Confederate dead as to become an ironic commentary on the convention; and "The Mediterranean," perhaps the best of his shorter poems, only gradually reveals the interest its author has in a still remoter past than that of his own region—the past of Rome, and back of that the past of the exiled Trojans who sailèd west to found Rome. Yet Tate is not exclusively concerned with history and geography. The human theme is always alive in his work, as it is in the work of any important poet. In "Death of Little Boys" it is present without reference to place or time. So is it in "Mother and Son," or in any of several concentrated poems whose lines are impressive for their precision, their intellectual grasp, and their controlled melody. His "Selected Poems" (1937) contains only fifty-four pieces, but upon them a secure reputation has been founded.

Crane
1899–1932

The maladjustment to modern life of Hart Crane, who committed suicide in 1932, does not mean any lack of modernity in his poetry. On the contrary he is often taken as the type of modern poet in America; for contemporary poetry has as one of its dominant themes the difficulty of an ordered existence, and much of it expresses a conviction that this is the worst possible world wherein a harmonious spirit might attempt to live. Crane's education, in poetry as in other matters, was uneven; but by a sure instinct he went to the sources which would help him. His poems are in most cases difficult to read, though anyone with a knowledge of great poetry will recognize its accent everywhere. He is bold, concentrated, ambitious, and musical; this is clear, even if it is true that he seldom hit upon the perfect form into which to pour his content. His first volume, "White Buildings" (1926), which carried a preface by Allen Tate, contained one of his most finished pieces in "Praise for an Urn," whose third and fourth stanzas deliver, in addition to praise of the dead man who is the occasion for the elegy, a commentary upon past and present :

> The slant moon on the slanting hill
> Once moved us toward presentiments
> Of what the dead keep, living still,
> And such assessments of the soul
>
> As, perched in the crematory lobby,
> The insistent clock commented on,
> Touching as well upon our praise
> Of glories proper to the time.

The interruption of the rhythm in the fifth line is intentional, and in itself expresses much of what Crane wanted to express. Four years later, in "The Bridge," he attempted a synthesis of America through a series of poems theoretically bound together by the symbol of Brooklyn Bridge. They are only theoretically unified, and "The Bridge" is probably a failure on the whole. But it contains passages of the greatest magnificence, and remains one of the most ambitious efforts by a contemporary American poet to deal with the entirety of his country's culture.

MacLeish 1892– The poetry of Archibald MacLeish has passed through many stages. The author of "Ars Poetica," insisting that

> A poem should not mean
> But be,

was something of an Imagist, for the Imagist doctrine was that poetry, rather than conveying its subject matter, should embody it in itself. This represented a change of mind from that which had inspired MacLeish's earliest volumes, where various things of a personal sort were said without special distinction. But as time went on MacLeish moved to new ground. "The Hamlet of A. MacLeish"

(1928) showed him involved in the mysteries of self then being explored through psychology. "New Found Land" (1930) revealed him to be a lyric poet of fine and sustained power, as in "You, Andrew Marvell," which quickly became famous for its handling of the theme of time and the turning earth. "Conquistador" (1932), approximating epic length, retold a phase of Mexico's conquest in verse conspicuous for its technical originality and dexterity. But then MacLeish shifted to still further ground, entering the field of contemporary affairs in "Frescoes for Mr. Rockefeller's City," which he used as a medium for direct address to an immediate public. After that came a series of plays two of which were for delivery over the radio, whose announcer MacLeish likened to the chorus of Greek tragedy, and whose voice he used to an equivalent end. "Panic" (1935) dealt with the bank crisis of 1933, "The Fall of the City" (1937) with dictators, and "Air Raid" (1938) with the terrors of modern war. MacLeish, in other words, has fitted his poetry at all times to current thought; and has reaped his reward in a reputation which recognizes his usefulness along with his skill. But his skill is no less important than his usefulness. He is one of the subtlest of contemporary stylists, and one of the most versatile of modern word-musicians.

Jeffers
1887–
In 1925 a new poet from California took the public by storm. Robinson Jeffers had published other volumes before "Tamar and Other Poems," but this one did for him what none of its predecessors had done; it made him famous. Its title poem was a lengthy and violent narrative written in a long, swinging line of Mr. Jeffers's own invention—a line which he has used for all his subsequent work. It is not a singsong line but a spoken one; a ground rhythm makes itself gradually felt through phrases that do not have the surface appearance of music:

I sadly remember smiling that the flower fades to make fruit, the
    fruit rots to make earth.

The poem called "Tamar" introduced the themes which
Jeffers has developed throughout his later work: murder,
incest, slaughter, fire, and desperate tenderness. His view
of man is of a creature who has perverted himself and his
society by too much inward thinking; the theme of incest
as Jeffers uses it represents, he says, "symbolized racial in-
troversion: man regarding man exclusively—founding his
values, desires, a picture of the universe, all on his own
humanity." Jeffers is more in love with other creatures—
hawks, eagles—who can "love outwardly," and with unconscious entities—mountains, the sea, the distantly burn-
ing stars—whose beautiful existence does not depend on
thought at all. Such existence is not aware of itself, or, if
it is, it longs for a return to primeval night.

    Truly the spouting fountains of light, Antares, Arcturus,
    Tire of their flow, they sing one song but they think silence.
    The striding winter-giant Orion shines, and dreams darkness.

So he speaks in one of his shorter poems, "Night," which
should be read along with "Apology for Bad Dreams,"
another short poem where the same statement is made in
terms of human life. The public best knows Jeffers, however, for the long narratives—"Tamar," "Roan Stallion,"
"The Tower Beyond Tragedy," "The Women at Point
Sur," "Cawdor," "Dear Judas," "Thurso's Landing," and
others—in which he has told sensational stories with a
steady, almost sullen power. "The Tower Beyond Tragedy"
is especially interesting because it retells from Jeffers's
point of view, though not in a modern setting, the ancient
Greek tale of Agamemnon, Clytemnestra, Orestes, and
Electra.[1] But any of his narratives finds him true to his
theme; in each of them an attempt is made to "break

    [1] For another version of this tale, by Eugene O'Neill, see pages
126-127.

through" the trance in which man stands beholding his own image; and since it is difficult to do this, violence accompanies the effort. Jeffers's future reputation will depend upon the intelligibility of his doctrine in a later age; and upon the ability of his long, loose line to continue impressive as a unit of verse composition.

Stephen Vincent Benét 1898–   Another narrative poet, Stephen Vincent Benét, has achieved popularity without benefit of a special doctrine. Benét's epic of the Civil War, "John Brown's Body" (1928), is fresh in its view of that familiar event, but the freshness is in the enthusiasm of the poet rather than in the novelty or the depth of his thought. A man of quick human sympathies, Benét presents the conflict in terms of its effect on a number of individuals he has chosen and created for the purpose. The scattering of emphasis which this implies finds its parallel in a multiplicity of poetic devices, so that the unity of the work comes from its author's feeling rather than from its form. The poetry of "John Brown's Body" is uneven, and sometimes it is bad. On the whole, however, it is interesting; and that alone is an achievement at a time when most poets strive to be admired rather than liked, discussed rather than read. Benét's poem shows how a return is possible at any time to the familiar matter of American history and legend, and his popularity is deserved. His ballads, of which there are several volumes, generally find him absorbed in such material. They are likewise brisk and fresh, and they are native in their rhythms; but "John Brown's Body" is still his representative poem.

CHAPTER II

PROSE FICTION

PROSE fiction in 1890 was not so near the end of an epoch as was poetry. Though William Dean Howells, for instance, had done nearly all his best work and was recognized to be the leader of the realists who were the prevailing school, he had still a score of years before him in which he was to continue his suave representation of American life. Henry James, having completed his middle period, as it subsequently proved, had not yet quite made up his mind that it was vain for him to hope to win a wide audience and that he might as well decide to please himself since he could not please any considerable number of novel-readers. Mark Twain had published most of his most characteristic books, but had hardly entered that fascinating chapter of his life which was to reveal him as a man of bitter thought as well as a humorist, a commentator upon the times in unstinted language, a kind of prophet who was to be listened to with more respect after his death than before it. Among the minor writers of fiction, however, a change was impending. Ever since the Civil War there had been under way a more or less concerted effort to exploit the materials for fiction which the whole country afforded. In every section and in almost every State some novelist or story-writer had set forth the peculiarities of local custom and speech and mental attitude until there had resulted a body of literature which might have been called an imaginative census. But this fiction tended, unfortunately, to be thin. Too much of it had been written by men and

58

women who were collecting curiosities instead of looking through surface peculiarities to the general truth of life; too much of it had been written by men and women who were led by their nearness to their material to feel obliged to be amiable toward it and therefore to omit from their records much that might not seem pleasant. Now a group of younger novelists was beginning to hold that it was less important to be pleasant than to be truthful, and they set out with zest to find the truth and to bring it to the light. Without doubt they tended, being in rebellion against the older school, to believe that the official realism of the time was less truthful than it was, but they did intensify and deepen the concerns of fiction, and they founded the tradition of naturalism which has more or less persisted ever since.

Crane
1871-1900

Modern American fiction may be said to begin with Stephen Crane. From the first he believed that conventional ways of thought are only so much cotton in which mankind likes to pack itself. Too unschooled to look for reality behind the accepted manners of the race, he was too honest to pretend that he saw it there. If he could not see life eye to eye, he did not care to see it at all. Reality for him, to be reality at all, had to be obvious and intense, as he thought it is in the slums or on the battle-field. Born in New Jersey, he laid the scene of the first of his two significant novels in a New York slum, with what at the time seemed daring candor. In "Maggie" (1893) a girl of the old Bowery neighborhood, driven from home by the drunken brutality of her mother, seeks refuge with a young tough of her acquaintance, loses him to a more practised woman, and drowns herself. Crane did not expurgate or moralize his story. Such things, he knew, happen, and he required no other excuse for his narrative. At a time when most American novelists would have hesitated to touch this theme at all, or if they had touched it would have tried to justify themselves by disguising it as a sermon, he let the facts speak for themselves. He wanted to communicate the matter directly to his readers, so that they would have lived something and not merely have learned it. To him any apology or comment would have seemed heartless, an intrusion of his private opinion into Maggie's tragedy.

This first novel of Crane's was neglected by the public till after the publication of his second, "The Red Badge of Courage" (1895), which was too striking to be overlooked. It was a war story of a sort new to the United States. Crane had refused to pay any attention to the books which had been doing what they could to make the Civil War out an epic conflict, full of pomp and heroism. Instead, he had talked to old soldiers in their franker hours of reminiscence. As a result, he chose for his hero an ordinary recruit, fresh from an inland farm, and carried him through his first experience in actual fighting. As the recruit naturally has no notion of the general plan of battle, he has to obey commands that he does not understand, that he resents, that he hates. He suffers agonies of fatigue and almost a catastrophe of fear before he becomes accustomed to his situation. Perhaps he seems unusually imaginative, but he is represented without too much subtlety. He speaks a convincing boyish dialect. His sensations are limited to something like his spiritual capacity. He is a pawn of war, but he is the item which, Crane held, must not be forgotten in any consideration of war. For when all has been taken into account, war must be judged by its effect not upon the statesmen who start it or upon the generals who wage it but upon the average men who actually endure it. And this idea of Crane is reflected in the art of the "Red Badge." The young soldier is the focus of the whole action, the lens through which the battle is perceived.

Being in the fear of death, he is not a mere transparent lens. The battle takes a kind of mad shape within his consciousness as the tangled details of it stream through him. Though Crane had never seen a battle when he wrote this book, he managed to make it extraordinarily convincing. Even readers who must have felt that he was unjustifiably disregarding the heroic and throwing the grand style overboard, admitted his concentrated power.

During the few years remaining to him after the publication of his masterpiece Crane lived a vivid life, chiefly as a war correspondent in various parts of the world. Of his later fiction, his short stories are on the whole better than his novels. "The Open Boat" tells a straight story of adventure with breathless ferocity. "The Monster" exposes the stupidity of public opinion in a narrow town. "The Blue Hotel" shows fate working blindly and causelessly in the muddled lives of chance-met men. At times Crane has a good deal of comic force, but always he is spare, pungent, intense. By his intensity, above all else, he attracted attention, and for that he is still noted, even though he has had many followers. Yet he is never obscure. Unlike Emily Dickinson, a poet whom he admired and in some respects imitated, he is as much a journalist as an Imagist. Such lucidity as his, indeed, is almost poetry. It perhaps accounts for his persistent charm, the charm of a free mind resolutely revealing itself. Though he is often, in his writing, crude and incorrect, he never ceases to be intelligent. This intelligence of his brings him very close to his material, which he does not thereafter hold at arm's length. He delights in every aspect of reality, however ruthlessly he may expose it. It does not matter that he is ironical, for irony may be only the other side of tenderness, as it is with Crane. But the generation before Crane had so often been sentimental that he, as a rebel against it, could not allow his passion for life to have a loose tongue. He kept it under control and thus gave added color to representations of life to which he seemed to be giving only clearness of outline.

Norris 1870-1902 With Crane it is customary to associate Frank Norris, another novelist who died young after a brilliant and effective career. Born in Chicago, a student in Paris, he became an author in California, and thus had a wide view of the continent on which he lived. As a protest against provincialism he wanted to continentalize American literature, and planned two vast trilogies, neither of which he lived to finish. One would have been concerned with the battle of Gettysburg, a novel for each day, and would have exhibited the whole nation as struggling on that fateful ground; this he left untouched. Of his Epic of the Wheat he wrote two parts: "The Octopus" (1901), which deals with the production of wheat in California, and "The Pit" (1903), which deals with the distribution of wheat through the Chicago Board of Trade. There was to have been a third part called "The Wolf," dealing with the consumption of American wheat in Europe; this too remained undone. But though these plans were too large to be carried out in a short life, their largeness is reflected in the work Norris actually did.

"The Pit" is on the whole inferior to "The Octopus," perhaps because trafficking in wheat is essentially a less significant process than growing it. The Octopus to which the title refers is a railroad which holds the wheat-growers of California in its cruel tentacles, able to say whether or not they shall ship their grain to market, and thereby to illustrate the power which economic machinery has over the primary elements of life. Agriculture and Trade have come to grips in a grandiose drama. Norris sympathizes with the farmers so thoroughly that he heaps upon the head of the villain every accusation, making the agent of the railroad the symbol for all the novelist hates in the system which thus comes wantonly between food and hunger. In the end, though the farmers are beaten, the agent is suffocated under a stream of wheat which is again a symbol— "the wheat which comes up from the abundant earth and moves irresistibly to its appointed purpose, guided, of course, by men, and fought and played over by them, but always mightier than they and always their master as well as their sustenance." These cosmic implications, however, do not keep the story from presenting a picture of actual life in California, of plowing, planting, harvesting, sheepherding, merrymaking, rabbit-hunting, with the human matters of love, labor, birth, and death. Though the struggle itself is sordid and tragic, there are many incidental details of loveliness and goodness. The style is strong, the movement rapid, the pictures alive. If the book falls short of the first rank, it is only by reason of a certain emotional exaggeration which was one of the results of Norris's fiery zeal to find some general truth behind all appearances.

Though Norris called himself a naturalist in fiction, his zeal for reality has more than a touch of the romantic in it. Less clearly an artist than Crane, and perhaps less intelligent, he could not be content to tell a story and let it hint its meanings; he had to interpret them. He was constantly looking, too, for elemental instincts to chronicle. His heroes are nearly all violent, wilful men; his heroines are nearly all women of a rich, deep vitality. What is virtually the same pair of lovers appears in each of his novels, as if he could not imagine any other kind of love. And whether or not his characters are concerned with love, they do not have much range of intellect, so largely are they taken up with the operation of those instincts which have come to be known as red-blooded. Norris had, in short, rather more force than direction. But he had so much force that it is impossible not to be stirred when he is at his best, and not to regret that his work ended so soon. He thought and wrote about his art in a way to show that he was laying the foundation for achievements which might have been re-markable if his mind had eventually caught up with his emotions.

London 1876–1916

What was elemental in Frank Norris became abysmal in the third member of this gifted trio, Jack London. A Californian, the son of a pioneer who had not prospered, he spent his youth as a laborer and a tramp and an explorer, with no thought of writing books. But when he did take to the pen, he had an enviable amount of experience to work with. Moreover, having become a socialist and a revolutionist, he was full of resentment against the established order of society and full of hope that it would shortly be overthrown. His doctrines serve as the basis of his many controversial and autobiographical books, and hardly less as the basis of his fiction. Believing that there is a natural war between the classes, London saw human history in terms of the strug-gle for survival. Life for him was one long epic of which his stories were episodes. His favorite heroes, whether wolves or dogs or pugilists or sailors or vagabonds, have all of them much the same kind of instincts and the same kind of fate. The hero of "Martin Eden" (1909) is Lon-don under another name, learning to write; the struggle seems as enormous as if life and death were the issue. In "The Sea-Wolf" (1904) the principal figure is a ship-captain who dominates his crew with a cold brutality, which he justifies by an appeal to Nietzsche and to the dogma that the strong are entitled to command the weak; he becomes finally, however, the victim of a paralysis against which even his strength is insufficient. And in London's master-piece, "The Call of the Wild" (1903), all his ideas are given dramatic expression in the story of a dog which es-capes from human control to go back to the wild as leader of a pack of wolves.

As in most stories about animals, the narrative is sentimentalized. Buck, the dog, has a human psychology. Though no man can know whether a dog has thoughts or not, Buck is shown thinking throughout the story. His thoughts are suspiciously like his creator's. He learns the law of the wilderness with a philosophical quickness; he dreams of his ancestors and instantly recognizes in them the source of the new traits which are developing in him now that he too is running wild. But whether or not London was justified as a scientist in making Buck so nearly human, he was justified as an artist. The story, after all, was meant to be read by human beings, and it was written by one of them. Something autobiographical in "The Call of the Wild" gives it much of its power. Telling of Buck's initiation into a hard and dangerous life, London remembered his own initiation into vagabondage; telling of Buck's adjustments to the climate and customs of Alaska, London remembered his own struggles with the Klondike in the days when he had felt that all nature was conspiring to destroy him and that he could preserve himself only if he resorted to every trick and used all the strength he had. Memory stirred his imagination as well as furnished him with realistic details. The narrative is no more overburdened with superfluities than an Arctic expedition; it is swift and alert, packed with excitement and peril. And it has in addition certain qualities which were later to become less evident in London's work. It exhibits a fine sensitiveness to natural beauty, a robust, moving, genuine current of poetry which enriches both style and plot.

This decrease in beauty, which accounts in part for the inferiority of some of the many books which London wrote after he became famous, was due to the hasty, casual habits which he formed. There grew upon him, moreover, a kind of obsession for primitive emotions, for violent conflicts, for terrible sufferings. He came to write as if he thought that reality is to be found only upon the plane of naked warfare between man and man, between man and society, between class and class, between mankind and nature. In a world which is much of it civilized, he was thus limited in the range of his subjects, and he tended to repeat himself, all the more so since his public, liking what he had done, demanded that he continue indefinitely in the same channel. The consequence was that, though he wrote many more books than Crane or Norris, he did not write many more good books than they. He did, however, carry on the program laid down by the other two, and won a victory for those novelists who felt that they need not restrict themselves to dealing with the surface lives of respectable Americans. It is hardly his fault if his successors have gone beyond him to the point where red blood is made to appear as conventional a thing as blue blood ever was.

O. Henry
1862–1910

Somewhat apart from these three novelists, and yet of a temper not so different, was a remarkable writer of short stories who used the pseudonym O. Henry instead of his real name, William Sydney Porter. Like Jack London, O. Henry saw much of life before he began to write about it. Born in North Carolina, he spent his boyhood there, went as a young man to Texas, visited South America, served a term in a Federal prison for embezzlement, and had reached the age of forty when he settled down in New York for the remainder of his life. His rapid popularity came first as a result of his cleverness, in the management of surprising plots and in the reproduction of slangy vernacular speech. It was soon increased by the realization on the part of his public that he had discovered what seemed to be a new province of fiction: the world of those ordinary New Yorkers who make up the bulk of the city's population, and who had hitherto been rather neglected by literature. But O. Henry did not confine himself to the metropolis;

he wrote stories which had their settings in the South, in the Southwest, and in Latin America; and finally it was seen that he had discovered not so much a new province as a new process of finding and setting forth the romance and the comedy and the tragedy of average existence.

Technically speaking, O. Henry is a raconteur. His stories are all short, his plots simple, his manner free and easy. He constantly interjects himself into his narratives, commenting upon them to his hearers. Seeming to have been everywhere, and to have seen everything, he reports his observations. What has interested him, however, is not himself but the persons he has encountered on his travels. He appears never to have overlooked any of them, and indeed appears to have got at all their secrets. Yet it is their customary hours which he has chiefly noted. He prefers not to probe too deep. As a raconteur, he avoids the somber, private emotions which cannot be discussed in a light tone. As a raconteur, too, he chooses episodes or situations which can be made to startle by the outcome. In this he was aided by the delight he took in such little accidents of fate as that which happens in his most familiar story, "The Gifts of the Magi." A husband and wife are each anxious to give the other a Christmas present, though they are very poor. The wife sells her hair, which is her greatest charm, to buy a chain for her husband's watch; the husband sells his watch, which is his proudest possession, to buy a set of combs for his wife's hair. The irony of the double sacrifice is of course far from tragic, since the husband and wife, whatever their disappointment, can promptly forget it in their joy over the affection which prompted their acts. Almost always O. Henry has what has been called the short memory of comedy. Instead of assembling evidences to prove that fortune is malign, as persons of a tragic disposition do, he looks at each prank of fortune separately, laughs, and passes on.

So much good humor might grow tiresome were it not for the wit and variety with which it is accompanied. As it is, O. Henry at times is undeniably sentimental. And yet he has a comic vigor which distinguishes him from the tribe of sentimentalists. His humor keeps his good humor from cloying or from turning sour. In what is probably his best story, "A Municipal Report," he had a chance to be merely pathetic in his account of a woman hopelessly bullied by her worthless husband. But he was no more content to do that than he was content to exploit his materials for their own sake, without making anything of them. He rounds the action out with a robust deed, the murder of the husband by a faithful servant. Though the plot is romantic enough, it is complete, not a mere fragment of local color.

In two of his books, "Cabbages and Kings" and "The Gentle Grafter," the same personages are repeated from story to story, but as a rule the volumes have no more unity than comes from their restriction to some special community as the scene, and this only in the case of the volumes devoted, like "The Four Million" (1906), to New York, or like "Heart of the West" (1907), to a wider region. The total effect of the body of O. Henry's work is that of a gigantic miscellany. He wrote in haste. He did not avoid the cultivation of certain mannerisms, such as the almost invariable surprise in his endings. Being extraordinarily full of his materials, he poured them out in a profuse stream. Being extraordinarily successful in pleasing his public, he made no particular effort to improve his art. Other writers imitated his methods without being able to capture his peculiar charm, and the art of the short story became as a consequence looser and more casual than it had been before him. In a sense, he cheapened the form, but he extended its scope and made it the most democratic form of literature in America.

Garland
1860–

Meanwhile there was a freshening of the tendency toward realism in the Middle West, where the tendency had begun as far back as the seventies and had never quite been lost. Even before Crane, Hamlin Garland of Wisconsin had parted company with the smoother novelists of the established school. In particular, he called attention to the hard lives of prairie farmers in "Main-Travelled Roads" (1891), which was a protest against the idyllic pictures of rural life then common. The men in his book wrestle despairingly with their bitter tasks, never sure when they may be beaten by nature or by the money-lender. The women are sacrificed to overwork until they have lost all their charms along with their hopes. The pressure of life is too heavy to be borne except by the ruthless or the crafty. This frontier, Garland wanted to point out, had its victims who must not be forgotten in the romantic chorus raised to celebrate the victors. He propounded their dilemmas, with pity less than with anger, in level language. That he knew farm life, on the whole, better than most other novelists then writing about it, does not alone account for the excellence of his book. Back of it lay a long course of thought about the problem of needless poverty. And if that imparts to "Main-Travelled Roads" its intellectual consistency, a genuine human affection imparts to it the note of human dignity which characterizes it.

Having written a few other books in this vein, Garland for years gave himself to the writing of inferior romances about the Rocky Mountains. They were inferior because in these regions he was a visitor, and not a native, and he tended to fall into the errors of enthusiasm which he had challenged in his prairie novels. He later returned to his true material in "A Son of the Middle Border" (1917), which is indeed autobiographical, but hardly more so than

"Main-Travelled Roads" or "Prairie Folks." Whether autobiography or fiction, Garland's best work concerns itself with essentially the same theme. The golden hopes of the pioneers, it keeps saying, were largely illusion. Only those among them who could live on hope could feel sure that the glory of the westward march made up for its discomforts and agonies. Many of them, his stories show, were like the young recruit in "The Red Badge of Courage." They could not see any intelligible whole of which they were a part. Of such pioneers Garland offers this most convincing record. After him, as after Crane, novelists could not lose the individual in the type quite so easily as their predecessors had done.

Dreiser 1871– From Indiana came the novelist who is generally admitted to be the leader of the new school in American fiction, Theodore Dreiser. His "Sister Carrie" (1900) was both neglected and abused, and he has ever since been a center of controversy as no other native novelist has been for so long a period. Just why, it is not quite easy to say. Perhaps the explanation may be found in the thorough way in which he manages, in his novels, to cast doubt upon almost every rule of life which is accepted as certain by the majority of men. This he does by narrating, without reproach, the lives of persons who seem, for some reason, to avoid the expected penalties of their misdeeds and the expected rewards of their good conduct. For example, Carrie drifts from her native village first to Chicago and then to New York, seems to feel little repentance for her irregular course of life, and in the end becomes a noted actress with hardly any serious effort. And if she seems to have few of the standard moral sentiments, so has Dreiser so far as she is concerned. He does not judge her, he only pities her when she is distressed. Likewise with Hurstwood, who leaves his wife and family to take up with Carrie, gradually loses his standing and his self-respect, and goes to pieces; though the account of Hurstwood's downfall is one of the triumphs of fiction, Dreiser nowhere assumes that the man got what he deserved for his offenses. To assume that, for Dreiser, would be to imply that he accepted the ordinary moral code of society as fixed and just. Instead, he appears to hold that such codes are only customs and that individuals are rather unfortunate than blameworthy when they come in conflict with them. He refuses to believe that the novelist is obliged to be a moralist.

In all his novels Dreiser has vexed those readers who want to meet in fiction only the sort of persons they would like to meet in life. He has insisted upon choosing his characters as he pleases, and upon tracing their careers without reference to current susceptibilities. Cowperwood, the hero of both "The Financier" and "The Titan," rises from obscurity to fame and wealth, but he does so by shocking methods. He bullies his rivals, evades the laws, and takes his pleasures along the way with a high hand. Witla, in "The 'Genius,' " no less irresponsibly pursues the life of art. What interests Dreiser in these men is their vitality. Unlike more timid creatures, who struggle to make themselves conform to the established patterns of life and suffer if they cannot, the true Dreiser hero sets out for a definite goal, plods resistlessly toward it, and does not mind if at times he runs counter to the customs and morals of his age. His desire for something or other is all the authority he asks. That is to say, he trusts his instincts. Dreiser's blunt chronicles of the working of such instincts make many readers uncomfortable, because they feel, perhaps dimly, that if human society is to hold itself together it must demand that many individual instincts be subordinated to the general good. A writer like Dreiser, who is interested more in those instincts than in the general good, therefore seems dangerous. He in effect glorifies the natural man at the expense of the obedient member of society.

What makes Dreiser so irritating to certain of his readers is not that he is at war with society, which he can hardly be said to be, but that he is in doubt as to the reality of its laws and customs. Positive enmity can be forgiven more easily than indifference or skepticism. The same quality, however, gives him an advantage when it comes to creating characters. He is willing to tell all he knows about them, just as he is willing to take them wherever he finds them. His "Twelve Men" (1919) illustrates this. Rarely generalizing, he portrays a dozen actual persons he has known. All his native honesty is brought to the task of making his account fit the real facts precisely. All his large tolerance is exercised to present the truth without malice or excuses. These, he seems to say, are members of the human race. They might, no doubt, have been better or wiser than they were, but they were not. They had each of them a set of qualities which no other person has ever combined in quite the same pattern. Since they existed at all, they have a kind of excuse for being known; and since they existed thus, they must thus be represented. Handled so candidly and so tolerantly, they become real and affecting. They may have worn disguises in life, but they no longer do so. They may have been, as seen by their acquaintances, rather trivial persons, but they have been made somehow important. The truth about them dignifies them.

It is the truth about Clyde Griffiths, hero of "An American Tragedy" (1925), that dignifies him in Dreiser's eyes. In himself he has little or no dignity, since the desires that dictate the course of his life are cheap desires— for "dressy" clothes, for "right" friends, for "classy" connections—and since his outstanding trait is cowardice. He has not the courage to face the consequences of his love

for Roberta Alden; he cannot, that is to say, either marry
her or explain to her why he will not; and though he commits the error of imagining her murder he can neither suppress the fancy nor with positive will carry out the act. He
is the cause of her death by drowning, but only because one
of his confused and tentative gestures pushes her out of
a canoe; and he can swim to shore believing that he is not
wholly responsible for her end. A jury thinks otherwise and
Clyde is executed, and the story might seem to end there.
But for Dreiser that was where its interest began. Docu-
menting his novel from an actual murder case which had
absorbed the newspaper world for months, he tried to get
behind the simple moral issue which the prosecution had
presented. The question for Dreiser was not whether Clyde
Griffiths had been vicious; it was why he had done what
he did, or rather how he had become the young man for
whom such a deed was possible. Dreiser in other words
proceeded as a naturalistic novelist, concerning himself
with causes and effects, conditioning situations, and all
the other determinisms proper to his theory of life and
fiction. He went back to Clyde's boyhood in Kansas City
and explained the nature of his later desires by showing in
full detail the shabby, unsatisfactory life he had lived as
the son of an unsuccessful evangelist. He took his hero
through all the stages, including his period of service in a
great hotel, by which he arrived at a notion of what he
wanted to be; and he brought him at last to Lycurgus,
New York, to work in a collar factory and to fall in love
with Roberta Alden—who, however, was in the long run
inadequate to his desires because she was not "swell" like
Sondra Finchley, glittering in the distance as a more profitable catch. The entire progress of the youth is stupid and
pitiable, nor does Dreiser deny that it is. Dreiser's explanation is not by way of excuse, or to the end of a sentimental defense such as is often provided criminals by those

who dislike truth in any form. It is explanation rather than justification. But it is explanation on so great a scale, and so close up to the individual concerned, that the reader cannot but find the prosecuting attorney at the trial a shallow and even cynical moralist. Perhaps Clyde Griffiths deserved to die; but he is condemned by those who scarcely know him. We who have known him from boyhood, even if we have never approved of him or liked him, would have treated him with such dignity as any individual earns merely by his existence. It is only we as readers who possess the full materials bearing upon Clyde's tragedy. Whatever our moral judgment, our understanding is as complete as Dreiser could make it. And he has been substantially complete. The Kansas City section—the mission, Clyde's home, the hotel—remains a triumph of the naturalistic method, and indeed no episode of Clyde's career goes without the most painstaking and penetrating treatment by a novelist who always has been distinguished for the depth no less than the breadth of his sympathies.

Though unquestionably a great novelist, Dreiser has always been handicapped by his defects as an artist. He writes bunglingly and heavily. He piles detail upon detail till the main outline is lost. His imagination is not trustworthy when it tries to penetrate the secrets of subtle people. He loves beauty, but he appreciates only a few aspects of it, and does not always know how to reveal them. Nevertheless, he has rendered an indispensable service to American literature. As the leader of his school, he has received the heaviest blows of his opponents and has thus saved his followers. The work which Crane and Norris died too young to carry out, Dreiser has carried out through stubborn, persistent years. If they, and Jack London, proved again that life may be studied by the novelist in the slums, in the wilderness, at sea, on the battle-field, he has proved that it may be studied in more daring places: in the con-

duct of men and women who, without leaving society, lead
their own lives in the midst of it, and find that there is,
provided the individual has desire or courage enough, an
opportunity now and then to be first of all an individual
and only incidentally a member of the human hive.

**Tarkington
1869–**   At the other extreme from Dreiser stands
Booth Tarkington, also an Indianian, who has
won the widest popular approval. This may be
said to be due about equally to his ideas and to his art.
His ideas, at least those which appear in his novels, are
the ideas of the majority. He neither challenges nor dis-
turbs complacent readers. If one of his heroes for a time,
during an inexperienced youth, shows signs of wanting to
be a hero or a poet or a saint, he is sure in the end to
settle down and to be at most points like anybody else.
This, for Tarkington, is the happy ending, as he shows in
"The Turmoil" and "The Magnificent Ambersons." He
accepts the world on something like its own terms. Many
generations of men, he knows, have tried their best to learn
how to live to the best advantage. They have found out
that honesty and prudence and decency and temperance are
likely to lead to prosperity and happiness. To aim too high
is to run the risk of disappointment. It is better to aim
low and not be disappointed. This is the kind of story of
which Mr. Tarkington never tires. He has told it, in one
form or another, over and over even in the serious "Alice
Adams" (1921), in which the heroine, having pathetically
failed to win a rich husband, decides to go to work for her
living. As most people suspect or fear individualism, they
are pleased by novels which tell of the defeat of ambitious
individualists. It must, indeed, be admitted that the individualism of Tarkington's characters is never in any sense
genius. It is more or less the wild oats of some person
of average intelligence and emotions.

Tarkington's art is more notable than his ideas. He has

the knack of comedy. He observes the absurdities and follies of mankind and displays them with a swift, light touch. He can be, with about equal success, either romantic or satirical, though he is more frequently satirical. When he is satirizing a person or an age he picks up laughable details with an endless gusto. As if he were a little chary, however, of touching more serious themes, he has specialized in what he appears to consider the minor comedies of the young. That children and adolescents have something like the same concerns as adults he does not take into account. Since their loves and hates and rivalries and aspirations and frustrations do not visibly move the world, which is administered by their elders, he sees such things as amusing only. Doubtless he would not observe them so closely if he were not sympathetic, but the use he makes of them in his stories is far from being sympathetic in all respects. In reporting the deeds and affectations of the heroes of "Penrod" (1914) and "Seventeen" (1916), Tarkington is really not interpreting them. He is winking over their heads at men or women who are able to smile with him at the ridiculous figures the youngsters cut. The genuine merit of these books does not lie, as is sometimes held, in their insight into childish souls. It lies in the vigor and humor with which the manikins are manipulated. Penrod finds all the types of mischief which a boy of his age can find; Baxter practises every affectation which a boy of his age can practise. Tarkington extracts all the comedy which can be extracted from his materials without going beneath the surface, where, indeed, not all is comic.

**Ade
1866–**

George Ade is still another native of Indiana who, while his fiction is of a special kind, must be dealt with in any treatment of recent fiction. During his early days a newspaper man in Chicago, he wrote amusing novels, and he later turned with temporary success to comic operas; but he struck his most distinctive note when he published "Fables in Slang" (1899), and he has continued in that vein ever since. Before him there had been, of course, many Americans who had tried to utter homely wisdom in homely language, but Ade invented, or at least applied, a new device. Taking some moral maxim, he tells a story to illustrate it. Whereas Æsop, however, chose the most general kind of morals and illustrated them in the most simple and direct language, Ade chooses gay or cynical morals and illustrates them in broad slang. The moral itself does not interest him so much as the chance to give it flesh and blood, that is, to prove it by showing it in operation in the lives of more or less actual people. If he wants to say, in effect, that the shoemaker should stick to his last, he tells the story of two brothers, one of whom stayed on the farm and prospered, and the other of whom, having in mind to make a fortune more quickly, went to a neighboring town and never rose above a minor clerkship. The moral of this fable is "Drink Deep, or Cut Out the Pierian Spring Altogether." If Ade wants to hint that charity begins at home, he tells the story of a woman who meddled with the poor in her neighborhood and discovered to her horror that they were not grateful. The moral is "In Uplifting, Get Underneath." And so on, with scores of stories and hundreds of characters, he translates the wisdom of life into action and makes it amusing by the slang in which he discourses.

The fables bear much the relation to ordinary stories that caricatures bear to portraits. The names of the persons in them are deliberately grotesque. The actions are exaggerated. The plots are content merely to make some satiric point or other. That is, Ade thinks first of his general idea, and then invents characters and actions to fit it. But for all that they are laughably lifelike, as caricatures frequently are. Exaggerated themselves, they ridicule exaggeration in their heroes and heroines. Aspiration and affectation both seem absurd in these fables. Though their range of intellectual sympathies is modest, however, they cover a wide ground of knowledge. They are "minutely conversant with the ins and outs of common households; with the wiles of maidens and their swains; with the ways of men with dogs and horses and motors and stenographers and customers and competitors, in the bleachers, on the golf links, at the poker table; with the ways of women with servants and pets and clergymen and house-cleaning and candy and cosmetics, in cotillions, on picnics, at bargain counters; with all the comic nooks of American life." And they are far from being complacent in their attitudes. They make fun of solemn and dull people who are forever reciting solemn and dull maxims, and believing them. With a certain healthy cynicism, they insist that things do not always turn out exactly as the copy-books predict. "Early to bed and early to rise," says the copy-book, "makes a man healthy, wealthy, and wise." "Early to bed and early to rise," says Ade, "and you will meet very few of our best people." One of his most notable fables, "The New Fable of Susan and the Daughter and the Grand-Daughter, and Then Something Really Grand," is a kind of comic history of American luxury, from the eighteenth century to the twentieth. It does not condemn luxury in its various stages; it accepts them as amusing, and smiles at the successive generations that have practised them. And over the contemporary scene the fables, taken as a whole, spread their garment of satire with a bland impartiality. More thoroughly than do the works of any other recent writer, they caricature the age.

While the tales in such a later book as "Ade's Fables" (1914) are longer and more complex than those in "Fables in Slang," the method in all of them is essentially the same. It is merely that of a man telling a humorous story to illustrate a shrewd truth. The fables would be striking without the slang. Yet the slang gives the needed touch which drives them home. That the language has varied a little with the changes of comic speech during the past quarter-century makes less difference than might be expected, for it is not altogether derived from reality. It is partly a creation. Ade has that sixth sense for language which is one of the marks of Americans. Like them, he enjoys words and phrases which seem to have been turned out to grass and to be kicking up their heels. Moreover, he goes a step beyond most of his compatriots; he outdoes a nation of slang-makers at their own game. Without using many new words, he uses new combinations of words. Telling about a family which had got ahead in the world he says: "The Goddess took her Mocha in the Feathers, and a Music Teacher came twice each week to bridge the awful chasm between Dorothy and Chopin. Dinner had been moved up to Milking Time." No ingrained American will fail at a glance to understand that the mother had her breakfast in bed, that the daughter had little gift for music, and that the household now dined later in the day than formerly. Such slang is a caricature of language, but the caricature, while less enduring than the classic, may be extraordinarily effective while it is preserved.

Edith
Wharton
1862–1937

That the literature of an age may exhibit very different qualities side by side is made clear when it is pointed out that George Ade has been the contemporary of Edith Wharton. If he has broadly satirized the average Hoosier, she satirized, with exquisite irony, the fashionable New Yorker. The noisy smart set, indeed, never interested her; she wrote about the inner circles which are so remote from the approach of the vulgar that they are almost secrets to them. Within these circles a severe and uncompromising decorum is the rule of life and the price of success. The people there live in such intimate solidarity that no one of them may leave the established paths of conduct without outraging the others and thereby bringing disaster on himself. Outsiders have little chance to enter, for the reason that the rules are known only to those already inside. Lily Bart in "The House of Mirth" (1905) has the advantage of belonging by birth to the golden region and of knowing all its customs, but she lacks a fortune. Given the opportunity to marry one, she hesitates because she does not love its possessor. This, in her circumstances, is a fatal weakness, and she gradually finds herself an exile with no hope of any return. Newland Archer and Ellen Olenska, in "The Age of Innocence" (1920), belong and remain within, but they do so only at an immense sacrifice of personal happiness and free action. In all this Mrs. Wharton did not specifically take sides. She only set herself the task of portraying a very compact community in certain of its conflicts with its errant members.

Even when she left New York, as in her masterpiece, "Ethan Frome" (1911), she was still concerned with the same theme. Rural New England seemed to her, a native of New York, a no less compact community than fashionable Manhattan. Moreover, to the code of manners which there exists is added in New England the compulsion of poverty, which binds its victims as even a code could not. Ethan Frome, whom life has cheated out of every opportunity for joy, finds an exquisite love blooming on his bleak hillside and for a time forgets his fate. But poverty holds him fast, refuses to let him escape from the deadly existence which he has been leading, and drives him, in a mad hour of rebellion, to try to commit suicide with the girl he loves. The outcome is something more dreadful than the condition against which he rebelled. Himself crippled in the attempt at suicide, he is obliged henceforth to bear the presence in his house not only of the wife whom he never loved but of the girl whom he did and who is now a querulous wreck of her former charming self. Doubtless a more energetic man would have found some way out, despite his poverty, but the character of Ethan has been shaped by his environment. To bear is the only art he knows. And circumstances have conspired against him to make his burden infinitely heavy and yet to place upon him such a responsibility that he can do nothing to save himself and his fellow-victims. Not since Hawthorne had a novelist laid in New England the scene of any tragedy of such power and elevation as this. The book is so constructed as to reveal gradually, piece by piece, details which hint at the nature of the long catastrophe, and then suddenly to let its full extent be known. Many writers of New England stories during the last generation might have been glad to undertake this story, but most of them would have handled it as a tragic curiosity of rural life. Mrs. Wharton, acquainted with the great world, lifted her theme to the mood and the dimensions of universal tragedy.

Tragedy, however, was not her sole concern. She had the gift of satire as well. Particularly in her short stories she threw the light of her irony into many corners where sentimentalism ordinarily flourishes. As she found herself drawn to tales of conflict between the individual and his group, so she found herself repelled by stupidity and affectation and muddy confusion of mind and purpose. She disliked dingy and characterless lives. She did not dislike arrogance if it was well bred. Sometimes thought snobbish because of her preoccupation with the affairs of rich and cultured persons, she was nevertheless remarkably unpartisan in her irony. The short novel "The Spark" furnishes an example. Delane, the story runs, has all his life had in him a spark of humanity which most of his associates cannot equal. One of them learns that the quality is to be traced to Delane's contact during the Civil War with a certain attendant in a Washington hospital, "a sort of big backwoodsman." In the end it turns out that the backwoodsman was Walt Whitman, though Whitman, with delicate reticence, is never once mentioned by name. But when Delane is shown some of Whitman's poems, he completely fails to appreciate them, because his own poetical taste has been formed upon other models. Quiet irony could hardly go further than this. And yet it is approached, if not matched, many times in Mrs. Wharton's works. Being an ironist, she does not achieve the march or rush of rapid narrative, as she does not devote herself to the sturdy or burly or homely aspects of comedy. But in most of her books she keeps to a high level of satirical intelligence, and to sophisticated minds she is a delight.

Willa Cather 1876– Though no less intelligent than Mrs. Wharton, Willa Cather is less interested in intelligent characters and more interested in the general run of mankind. Two native types, however, have especially taken hold of her imagination. One is the pioneer; one is the artist. Born in Virginia, she grew up among pioneer conditions in Nebraska, where heroic deeds were still being done. The pioneers in her books are for the most part unreflective creatures, driven by powerful inner forces which they do not comprehend. They are primitive and epic in their dispositions. And yet they do not outlast the circumstances in which they do their hardest tasks. By and by comes the end of the frontier. Its wild freedom is degraded by clumsy towns, prosperous vulgarity, a monotonous standardization. Of the children of the pioneers Miss Cather finds herself concerned chiefly with those who are again pioneers, pioneers of art. Her artists, too, are active rather than reflective. They work much by themselves, contending with definite though ruthless obstacles and looking forward, if they win, to a freedom which cannot be achieved in the routine of crowded communities. Thea Kronborg, in "The Song of the Lark," is a Colorado village girl with the voice of a genius. Nobody in her village knows how to help her, and everybody mistakenly tries to reconcile her to a tame career. But she cannot be thus limited. She has a kind of hard pioneer integrity which compels her to escape toward her destiny, almost as a powerful animal shoulders its instinctive way through scratching underbrush to food and water. In her the old qualities are joined to the new. So are they in all Miss Cather's novels. She is interested in the passion for freedom, but not for the limp passion which whines for freedom in a stuffy corner. Her characters strike out and make their own ways, whether to the end that they may subdue the soil to usefulness or to the end that they may subdue ugliness to beauty.

Living, to Miss Cather, is an art in which men and women have to be, in some degree or other, pioneers and artists both. Marian Forrester in "A Lost Lady" (1923) practises her art badly. Exquisite by nature, she lives in a cramped community on the Nebraska plains, bound to an aging and invalid husband, surrounded by neighbors who none of them knew how to value her and her capacities. In a somewhat earlier day she might have found an outlet for her energies in the labor of her hands; in a somewhat later day she might have found it easier to go elsewhere to a more diversified community; in her own day she stifles. Unable to live without love, and finding none worthy of her, she declines to lower planes, as if she were not aware, or were aware too late, that no love at all is better than unworthy loves. She does not in the end come to any melodramatic downfall, but she is lost none the less, because she has drifted away on the tide of cheapness against which she was designed to struggle. She lacks the strength to be a pioneer and the conscience to be an artist. On the other hand, Ántonia Shimerda in "My Ántonia" (1918), has both these virtues. Her life, indeed, begins unpromisingly. Her childhood is full of hardships;

she is tricked by a scoundrel lover. But adversity cannot destroy or dry up the well of her spirit. Without the ordinary instincts of self-preservation, a gentle and confiding woman in whose nature service to others is the first law, she has so deep and true a current of goodness that it extricates her from the dangers of mediocrity. Goodness, so often negative, in Ántonia is so positive a thing that it seems to bring vitality to all it touches. "She was a rich mine of life, like the founders of early races." Nor is Miss Cather content merely to say how profoundly good her heroine is. She somehow proves it by the effect which Ántonia has upon all who come near her. Her excellence lies in her essence. She has the courage to live genuinely, and is therefore a good artist as Marian Forrester is a bad one.

It will be noted that Miss Cather most frequently chooses women for her principal characters. This denies her the opportunity to deal often with the more violent kinds of adventure. But if the actions of her novels are not epic, the moods are likely to be. High emotion blows through her chief actors like a free, wholesome, if devastating wind. She herself has the energy to feel high emotion and the honesty to reproduce it. She has tasted the savor of abounding health; she has exulted in the sense of great distances, the rapture of the earth rolling through space, the consciousness of past and future meeting in the present. At the same time, she does not let herself fall into vagueness or into the glorification of mere noise and bulk. Taste and intelligence hold her emotions in hand. The result is a combination of qualities to be discovered in few of her contemporaries. If she is not so powerful as some of them, she is more graceful; if she is not so dexterous as some of them, she is more full of generous life.

Taste, intelligence, and grace are present in the later novels of Miss Cather to the extent of becoming the prime and sometimes the only qualities of her people. They stand forth in less relief than before, with the result that these novels, while exquisite in their analysis of virtue, are not enough more than exquisite to have the dimensions of great fiction. Miss Cather's method has grown lyric rather than dramatic, her vision having narrowed to the point where it cares to contemplate excellence in its pure state, not mixed with the alloys of error and event. There is a relative absence of action, and a corresponding development of atmosphere. The hero, or as is more often the case the heroine, gives off an aroma of perfection such as only a distinguished artist could create, and some of these later books are within their limits surpassingly beautiful. But the limits are clear; it is fine rather than great fiction.

The action of "The Professor's House" (1925), if action it can be called, consists in the withdrawal of its hero from the world about him—his new house, his family, even his work. Professor St. Peter's life as we see it is chiefly reverie, for its focus moves farther and farther into the past. He remembers Tom Outland, the best student he had ever had, not as the scientist he later became, or as the aviator who died in France, but as the noble youth who had come up out of the Southwest and brought with him the flavor of a remote and ancient perfection. It is this flavor which the Professor gradually recalls, until at the end his only desire is to live in a recess of his own mind where he has restored the image of the western boyhood he himself had spent. The things he now thinks he cannot communicate either to his wife or to his daughters; only Miss Cather, indeed, can put his case for him, as she does in an incomparably written conclusion. Something of the same sort can be said of her next two novels, "Death Comes for the Archbishop" (1927) and "Shadows on the Rock" (1931). The first is a saint's life rather than a full-bodied novel; Father Latour, stationed among the Southwest Indians a little less than a century ago, is admirable and of course interesting, not only in himself but against a background of contrasting and supporting episodes, yet he is not realized through action so much as through attitude. The second moves farther back in time to late-seventeenth-century Quebec, where the clear spirit of the apothecary's daughter, Cécile Auclaire, flowers in the fine, cool air of Catholic piety—an air which only from time to time is enriched by rumors of the fur trade and of the *coureurs de bois,* one of whom, Pierre Charron, reappears at the end to marry her. Nobody can make virtue more attractive than Miss Cather, though other novelists, and she herself in her major works, can make it more powerful than it is here by giving it more work to do, more obstacles to overcome. The heroine of "Lucy Gayheart" (1935) plays an almost entirely passive rôle. Gentle, beautiful, and softly gay, she slips into love for Clément Sebastian, the musician with whom she studies in Chicago, without desiring to do so or even knowing that she does; until a timid confession of the fact to Harry Gordon, her Nebraska suitor, misleads him into the malice of marrying another woman and, after Clément has died and Lucy has returned home, into the error of treating her so cruelly as to become at last the unwitting cause of her death. Lucy is one of Miss Cather's most irresistible heroines, but she moves us by pretty helplessness rather than, as Ántonia did, by magnificent strength.

Cabell
1879–

The special distinction of James Branch Cabell among all the American novelists of his time is that more than any other he has laid down for himself a large program and has thoroughly carried it out. He has even invented an imaginary medieval country called Poictesme in which his principal actions take place, has drawn a map of it, given it a folk-lore and a history, and populated it with characters who are the ancestors of all his other characters in England or America. Being himself formerly a genealogist, and living in Virginia, he has hit upon the scheme of carefully tracing the line of descent of his heroes and heroines from Manuel, Count of Poictesme, as far as to their Virginian descendants. And with this scheme he has fitted his central conception of human life. This is that life is a comedy perpetually reënacted. Every man is born, aspires, succeeds or fails (no matter which), and dies. His son and his son's son and that son's son do the same thing over again, much as if some eternal comedian were playing the same rôle in the different costumes which might be the fashion in different ages. Cabell's books are thus, as he calls them, the Biography of Manuel, who will serve as well as anyone to represent the eternal comedian. But if the Biography is a comedy, so is it a romance. As a romance, the Biography need not keep looking for new stories. Old ones are good enough, provided they are worthy. The aim of the romancer, as Cabell sees it, is to write perfectly of beautiful happenings.

He himself writes with virtual perfection about many happenings which are undoubtedly beautiful, but which do not always seem so to people of humane sentiments or of narrow views. His medieval characters, whose trade is commonly war, are often ruthless and cruel and bloody, esteeming the end rather than the means when there is a clash of interests. And all his characters are concerned rather with the beauty or ugliness of their behavior than with its goodness or badness. Over their sins Cabell is not greatly worried. He would rather see them up to some high-hearted mischief than sitting in a smug chimney-corner. He has written about a remarkable number of rogues, knowing that the race of man loves a rogue for the color of his achievements even when it condemns him for their consequences. The hero of "Jurgen" (1919) is a rogue if there ever was one. Being permitted by a devil to do precisely as he likes for a day, Jurgen travels irresponsibly through space and time, having many amorous and satirical adventures, and so exhausting the possibilities of his freedom that he settles down with a positive relief to his ordinary occupations when his time is up. Yet the conclusion is not merely edifying. Whereas most moralists would like him to conclude that his humdrum life is better than his period of wild oats, Jurgen only concludes that he has not the courage or the strength to keep on enjoying himself forever. He still believes that the poetry of existence is more attractive than its prose, and he regrets that he cannot endure more poetry than he can.

Yet no one knows better than Cabell that beauty has its own austerity. The happenings which he finds most deserving of perfect language are the actions of chivalrous, gallant men in the face of heavy odds, above all when they win some great victory over themselves. Ironically believing that no man has too much courage, Cabell nevertheless celebrates courage. Ironically believing that fidelity by and by grows cold, Cabell nevertheless celebrates fidelity. In "Domnei" (1913), the simplest and loveliest of his longer tales, he celebrates both. There Perion and Melicent are separated by obstacles which they cannot control. Though the obstacles seem infinite, the lovers never once despair. Perfectly loyal not only to each other but to the idea of love, they see in it something divine against which they would commit blasphemy if they weakened. Not that they are seriously tempted to give up the quest. In all his battles Perion never wavers; in all her lonely waiting Melicent never doubts. A love so perfect in time infects their world. Their enemies out of respect for such devotion surrender certain of their advantages, and Perion and Melicent are united, and seem to each other no less desirable for the long separation. Perhaps it was a kind of madness which had made them persist, but it was a madness which was a glory.

In a sense "Domnei" stands with Cabell's short stories more truly than with his novels, for it is lucid and unified as the novels not always are. He is, in some of them, occasionally difficult to follow. Chiefly this is because of his cryptic and allusive manner. He hints at things which he does not tell. He makes references which may be deceptive. He humorously jumbles geography and history and mythology without warning. "The Rivet in Grandfather's Neck" is full of laughing satire; "Figures of Earth" (1921) is full of allegory; "The High Place" (1923) turns out to have been most of it a dream; "The Cream of the Jest" keeps shifting its scene back and forth from a real world to an imaginary one. It is sometimes impossible to tell when Cabell is making fun of his characters and when he is making fun of his readers. His Poictesme at first glance seems very remote from any common experience. But whoever makes a little effort can find the way into Poictesme and will soon be able to find his way about in it, surely one of the most exquisite worlds in fiction, devoted to magnificent adventures, high speeches, memorable personages, in spacious, noble, harmonious landscapes. All is order and art. And whoever wonders how it is that such a world could have been planned and completed during a turbulent season can read in Cabell's "Beyond Life" and "Straws and Prayer-Books" a cogent account of the theories upon which Poictesme was founded. The theories, however, are of course less important than the bold and deft-handed genius which invented Poictesme and keeps on peopling it, with less strength as time goes on but with as much finesse as at the start.

Sinclair
1878–
Argument, not art, is the preoccupation of Upton Sinclair, who writes, moreover, with the special creed of the socialist as the basis of his

argument. At first a poet, he was drawn from his native Maryland to Chicago to study the conditions of the workers in the packing-houses, and wrote "The Jungle" (1906). The book made a stir, because it claimed, as a later investigation proved, that meat, intended for millions of people all over the world, was being prepared under filthy conditions. But this was not the only fact which outraged Sinclair; equally horrible to him seemed the fact that the workers in the yards were compelled to live in a virtual slavery to their employers. Thanks to a kind of conspiracy among their masters, these workers could not help themselves; thanks to the weight of public unconcern they could get no help from popular opinion, which indeed saw their plight as something essential to the very structure of society. Against such a state of affairs Sinclair raised his voice. Moreover, he drew from it the general conclusion that the worker is everywhere at the mercy of the possessor, that labor and capital are naturally at war. Such a doctrine not only sent him in search of further evidences; it furnished him with a method which made all his later books exciting. In them the oppressed heroes are pitted against the villainous oppressors with the fury of melodrama. Stories like these are as full of adventure as the old chronicles of frontier warfare, and in addition are full of comment upon the actual circumstances in which men live in industrial communities. Nor has Sinclair confined himself to industrial conditions alone. He has ranged among his villains all those persons who out of some selfish interest or other wish to maintain any set of circumstances not founded upon simple justice to mankind in general. One by one his heroes and heroines try to make their way in the world and find it already in the hands of rich or learned or prejudiced or avaricious masters who will not share their possessions. Furthermore, the masters enter into conspiracies to protect themselves against the demands of justice. The hero is not only snubbed, but persecuted. If Sinclair's strength lies in the vigor of his belief in the rights of plain men, his weakness lies in his habit of scenting conspiracies on every side. He drives his argument so far as to vex or amuse those of his readers who are not of his opinions. He manages to be solemn in his bitterness. Twice only has he been ironical, in his "100%" (1920), the record of a disgusting creature whose patriotism leads him to carry his actions beyond the bounds of human decency, and in "Mountain City" (1930), whose western hero, Jed Rusher, grows to be the greatest man in America with the aid of every unscrupulous and vulgar device known to the black art of business, including the device of turning against his own class. But as a rule Sinclair is hampered by a zealous formula, even when he most vigorously upholds the cause of living men against the dead hand of tradition and the hard hand of injustice.

His contribution to the literature of protest against the Sacco-Vanzetti execution was "Boston" (1928), a novel in two volumes which documented the story of the two Italians by showing them through the eyes of an old lady, Cornelia Thornwell, who runs away from her rich family and lives by the work of her own hands among the poor people of the suburbs. In her eyes Sacco and Vanzetti are saints, and the judge at their trial is a sinner against every human law. The novel is frankly prejudiced, but it is none the less powerful; Sinclair's view of the famous case is built up elaborately and systematically, and loses force only at those not too infrequent moments when he forgets he is telling a story and becomes a pleader at the bar of justice. For at such moments he is wasting the great strength he has; a narrative is effective only when it is narrative.

Lewis
1885–

The enormous popular success of "Main Street" in 1920 showed that a new spirit had arisen in America. In that book Sinclair Lewis, looking back from New York to the Minnesota in which he had been born, told an old story in an unfamiliar way. His heroine rebels, as many heroines had rebelled before her in fiction, against the dullness of her village. But whereas the usual story had represented such a rebellion as a sign of snobbery in the rebel, this story represented it as a sign of aspiration. Carol Kennicott is not, it is true, a genius; her protest, however, is for that reason the more significant. If so humble a person as she has made the discovery that dullness is a vice, not a virtue, many other persons must have made the same discovery. And the reception of the book proved that they had. Whatever the various motives which impelled millions to read the book, it could not have caused so great a sensation if it had not touched a theme which was already interesting. Throughout the country, the reception of the book proved, people had begun to resent the increasing tendency to standardize human beings as machines and machine products were standardized. They had begun to feel, no doubt dimly, that if it was wrong to expose the character to the contamination of vicious company, so it was wrong to expose the mind to the contamination of dull company. Instead of blaming Carol, they unexpectedly sided with her, or at least grew excited over her story. They suddenly showed themselves to be aware that there is a conflict between the free intelligence and the meaningless conventions which cramp its movements.

To the charge that Lewis was merely making sport of village customs a reply followed in "Babbitt" (1922), which shifted the ground to a city of some size. In a sense, he had repeated his earlier story, in this record of a man who has always desired to be at every point as much like his fellows as he can be, but who catches disturbing glimpses of happiness and beauty and excellence not to be attained by those who give themselves too thoroughly to a routine existence. "Babbitt," however, goes deeper than "Main Street," for it traces the discontents of its protagonist to their roots, as the earlier book had not done. In the midst of his noisy efforts to conform, Babbitt perceives that he has never done the work he actually wants to do, that he is not even sure the work he does is worth doing, that he has been cheated out of joy in his personal life because he has not had the courage to insist upon taking his profounder instincts into account. He has lived upon the surface, as all purely conventional men and women do, and he has thereby lost hold of reality. In the end his discontent avails him little, but he has at least decided not to hold his children back from the paths of freedom if he can help it. Lewis, arraigning dullness as before, had also pointed the way to escape it. He had made unmistakable his conviction that happiness in the long run is to be achieved only by obedience to the genuine impulses of the individual, never by conformity to the outward habits of the mass of men.

Though Lewis's ideas are clear enough, they have, without much question, been effective only indirectly. His readers have often hardly noticed them because of the delight they were taking in his comic gifts. A natural mimic, he takes off a hundred absurd characters, reproducing their looks, gestures, speech, with amazing accuracy. He seems to have overheard all the average citizens of the republic, and to have made notes of their average conduct. He knows just how they will respond to a given situation, just how they will behave when any topic comes up for discussion. He does not, indeed, leave them quite on their average level of speech, for he is a satirist, and he tends by little touches of exaggeration at every turn to lift the language of his characters up so that it may be noticed, if only for its eminence of dullness. What the men and women say in his books is what they would say if they had the knack of expressing themselves a little better than such persons actually can. As Lewis has observed human beings, so has he observed the background of their lives, their costumes, houses, schools, churches, clubs, amusements, politics, with a swift, remembering eye. He has reproduced the outward life of the Middle West as no other novelist of the century has done. Its inner life he reproduces less exactly, because as a satirist he is concerned with making certain points, not with setting forth the eternal drama of birth, love, hope, death, which is the basis of imaginative literature. Many readers who sympathize with him in his dislike of conventional ways of thought and action, still find themselves unable to keep up with him in his delight in exposing such conventions. His proofs of an indisputable thesis seem too numerous. Nevertheless, he rarely loses himself in his materials. He has that first of qualities in a novelist, narrative energy. His stories move rapidly and consecutively. With all his cleverness, he takes great pains with his plots, building them up with that scrupulous conscience which is, rather unexpectedly, no less characteristic of him than his satiric wit.

With "Arrowsmith" (1925) Lewis staked a new claim for himself and extended his range as a satirist. His subject now was not a typical town or a typical city but the medical profession in all of its aspects from low to high. And his emphasis was as much upon the ideal as upon the actual. "Arrowsmith" deals candidly and eruditely with the shortcomings, the chicaneries, and the cheapnesses of doctors who consult only their own interest. Yet the reader does not forget the vision of the healing art which Dr. Martin Arrowsmith finds growing in himself through a varied career as practising physician, health official, fashionable pathologist, research bacteriologist, and crusader against a plague in the West Indies. This vision grows in him partly because he himself has integrity and the passion of a scientist, partly because he comes into contact with the great Max Gottlieb. At any rate it is what Lewis honors, and in the end he gives his benediction to Arrowsmith's gesture of retirement from the medical scramble in order to devote himself disinterestedly to his science in the back country of Vermont. If this is satire it is richly so; it is not so much an attack upon its subject as an attempt to understand that subject fully, to leave us without illusions about it—least of all the illusion that it is unimportant. With "Arrowsmith" Lewis made it clear how serious a man he was. He was still witty, and he has never ceased to be so, nor has he ceased to be high-spirited; but it was never possible after "Arrowsmith" to dismiss him as a scoffing clown, as indeed it should never have been before.

The temptation so to dismiss him was offered two years later by "Elmer Gantry" (1927), which, because it exposed the vulgarity and immorality of one American preacher, or rather one type of American preacher, brought down the charge that Lewis had attacked the clergy. Elmer Gantry was perhaps not worth the labor Lewis spent on him, but it is clear that he was not intended to represent more than his own kind of bully and fool. And it is true that Lewis did not, as in the case of "Arrowsmith," balance his hatred of mountebanks with a vision of good men. "Elmer Gantry" is in short one of Lewis's ugliest books, though it is not his least energetic or his least valuable. "Dodsworth" (1929) moves on to still newer ground. The scene now is international, and Lewis is treating a theme which for at least a century has been traditional in American fiction —the American in Europe. Cooper, Hawthorne, Henry James, and Mark Twain had formed the tradition, in their various fashions striving to establish a perspective in which the American might be truly observed. Dodsworth, a millionaire automobile manufacturer of Zenith, and a decent if somewhat limited fellow, goes with his wife on a sort of grand tour of the Old World—losing his wife when he discovers the shallowness and disloyalty he had never had time to see in her before, and in pathetic loneliness making the cultured rounds. Lewis has never been wiser or more sympathetic in his perceptions than he is in "Dodsworth." He conceals none of his hero's limitations, yet he keeps him solid and likable; and he compares America with Europe as sanely as any of his predecessors ever had. Four years later it was generally agreed that "Ann Vickers" (1933) had not succeeded so well with a purely American subject—the woman with a career, the career in this case being social work and prison reform.

Meanwhile, in 1930, Lewis had been awarded the Nobel Prize in literature, and in Stockholm had delivered an address of acceptance which struck out at the deficiencies of contemporary American literature—deficiencies of courage, knowledge, and candor. The criticism was just, but the three novels he has published since that address are not his best, though there is no lack in them either of courage or of candor, and one of them has exerted a wide influence upon its time. "Work of Art" (1934) is too obviously ridden by an idea, or perhaps a paradox, to be altogether successful as fiction. The two Weagle brothers, Myron and Ora, start out as hotel man and poet respectively, but they exchange rôles as they grow up. Myron, who has always thought of himself as a prosaic business man, becomes a "dreamer" who at much sacrifice of his own practical interest pursues the vision of a perfect inn until it lands him in poverty and obscurity; Ora, who has always thought of himself as a dreamer, matures into a successful and cynical author. The reversal of rôles is somewhat mechanical, though on Myron's side of the pic-

ture Lewis has another opportunity to prove himself a
scholar in contemporary affairs. He knows hotels from
the basement up, and what virtue the novel has is certainly
connected with this learning. "It Can't Happen Here"
(1935) is an attempt to show what would happen in
America under a dictatorship similar to those of Europe,
and is an answer to the optimist who insists that no such
dictatorship is possible on this side of the Atlantic. Do-
remus Jessup, a Vermont newspaper editor, is hero of the
novel and chief victim of "It"—of a political situation
which permits the triumph of three successive "chiefs"
in Washington, the destruction of all civil liberties, and
a progressively fiendish extermination of self-respecting
American citizens. There is a radio spell-binder, there are
sneaks and informers galore, and finally a New Underground is established in Canada for the conveying to
safety of persecuted Americans. Lewis has attempted to
incorporate in his first "chief," Buzz Windrip, certain
American traits supposed by optimists to be our guarantee
against "It"; he is a humorist, with something of Mark
Twain and George Ade in him, and he is what usually
passes in America for a "realist." The novel in its time
aroused much excited controversy, and there were those
who objected that Lewis had only copied the horrors of
Europe to frighten his own people. Others accepted him as
a prophet. Anyone could have seen that his extraordinary
invention and energy were again at work; and perhaps that
his fancy had a little outrun itself. Nor would anyone have
predicted that the next novel, "The Prodigal Parents"
(1938), would be so ineffectual. It has to do with the solid,
sensible Americanism of Frederick William Cornplow,
automobile dealer of Sachem Falls; with his wife Hazel;
and with his children, Sara and Howard, who make fools
of themselves by going "red" and violating the bluff Cornplow tradition. The point would be interesting, and the

book would be as much as "It Can't Happen Here" a defense of Americanism at its best, were the father in the case more intelligent and the children less trivial. Neither side proves anything; though it goes without saying that many incidental details of the novel are bright and recognizable, and that the whole tale is told with relish and vigor.

Anderson
1876–

Sherwood Anderson has little of Lewis's wit, but he too is in rebellion against what he thinks the standardized lives of Americans. Born in Ohio, he had little formal schooling, and drifted into business without any definite aim or consciousness of his gifts or desires. Gradually, however, there came over him the conviction that he could no longer find any happiness in the kind of life which seemed to satisfy the majority of his fellows; he must at least try to be an artist, to create beauty, to grow and not conform. "A Story Teller's Story" (1924) is an avowed record of his career, but his earlier books most of them deal with a similar theme under one disguise or another. They keep telling how some ambitious, bewildered youth leaves his native village, makes his way elsewhere, and yet can arrive at no final conclusions as to the meaning of existence. Life seems to them, as it apparently seemed to Anderson, a nightmare, wherein men troop back and forth and round and round, never coming to rest in any settled order, never feeling quite sure what they want or how to get it. By the aid of certain traits a man may emerge from the ruck, but he is then little better off than he was before, for he does not know what to do with the freedom which he has thus purchased. Instinct drives him toward excellence, but does not guide him. Anderson neither hates nor satirizes the world from which his characters are struggling to escape. He is mystified by it, and he broods over it with an intensity which gives his work its haunting tone. "Winesburg, Ohio" (1919) is typical. A young man, on the eve of his departure from the small town in which he has always lived, becomes aware of the drama stirring under the surface on every side. Because he partly hates to go, he views his neighbors with a good deal of tenderness; but because he is going, he has a sense of detachment which leads him to see them as cramped souls, repressed and distorted by the stern customs which have refused them any outlet for the forces working within them. Whereas Lewis's characters have a dusty complacence in their dullness, Anderson's have within them all a ferment which will not let them be at peace.

The difference is that Anderson is more a poet than Lewis is, and credits his characters with something of his own fire. This appears clearly in "A Story Teller's Story," in which the author is himself the hero, but in which he is the sort of hero he has regularly written about. Perhaps there are as many elements of fiction in his autobiography as there are elements of autobiography in his fiction; in any case, his life as here recorded turns out to be more interesting than any of his novels. And though he is bent upon giving the truth about himself as an individual, he incidentally helps to explain a certain recurring type of person which the age has produced in America. That person can no longer remain contented with the material prosperity which was for so long the chief boast of Americans and which contented them at large. He feels that, the goal of comfort having been reached, the nation should now look ahead to intellectual and spiritual triumphs. Instead, he believes that it has slowed its march, has grown fat with overfeeding, and has ceased to aspire. A nation cradled in revolution has given itself to a deaf fundamentalism and a blind patriotism. Resisting change, it does its best to suppress every one who counsels the pursuit of new aims. Thus suppressed, such censors of the age no doubt tend to dream wild dreams. Anderson has all his life, by the testimony of "A Story Teller's Story," hardly known how to distinguish between fact and vision. But there can be no question that he, like others of his type, has been engaged throughout in the search for the path which leads to goodness and excellence. To be dead-alive, they feel, is not enough. They long to be full of vitality, richly sensitive to beauty and heroism. They have the ruthlessness of saints, turning their backs on the world, and condemning it for its sloth and self-indulgence.

Lardner 1885–1933 The publication in 1929 of "Round-Up: The Stories of Ring W. Lardner," drew critical attention to a satirist who until then had passed as a purely popular writer. Ring Lardner's popularity is by no means inconsistent with his excellence, which in a certain vein of satire is supreme. His baseball stories are classic in their field, rich as they are in observation of the simple ways in which the athletic mind works, and right as they are in the art with which they communicate through syntax the flavor of that mind. As a satirist, however, Lardner went after bigger game in such stories as "Alibi Ike," "Champion," "A Day with Conrad Green," "Haircut," "Some Like Them Cold," and "I Can't Breathe." These stories, and many others of their kind, are savage in their exposure of frauds, practical jokers, snobs, hypocrites, and bullies. Lardner saw alarmingly far into human depravity; remaining himself, however, on the sane ground of those who love generosity and truth above all things. That is why his stories, in addition to being masterpieces of irony and mimicry, are moral tales of the first importance.

1920 The year of "Main Street" saw an outburst of fiction not to be compared in volume and reputation with any since that which had followed the war with Spain; but whereas that earlier episode had been characterized by historical romances, most of them concerned with glorifying the national past, this later episode was characterized by realistic novels, most of them examining the national present. The temper of the public had undergone a marked change. It settled down to peace in a mood which demanded more than patriotic or sentimental flattery. Strictly speaking, no doubt only a section of the public was affected; that, however, was the most intellectual section, and the best books of the new mode were directed at it. Everywhere it was felt that an old order had passed. Established sanctions had broken down, and authentic ones had not taken their place. In the meantime, it seemed, men and women were obliged to live their lives as independently and as courageously as possible. Fiction but reflected this new attitude, and a set of characters was created who won or lost in proportion as they dared or did not dare to rely upon their own instincts to guide them. The bounds of fiction were widened by the range of ideas it was thus permitted to suggest and by the discussion which it consequently aroused.

Wolfe
1900–1938
By the end of the following decade American fiction had begun to take advantage of the range and freedom which had been won for it by Lewis and others. It could now settle down to the cultivation of its own field without having to grow controversial about methods or to ask permission for the use of certain themes. In the South particularly it came with great quickness to an interesting and even surprising maturity. Thomas Wolfe's "Look Homeward, Angel" (1929), as Lewis took occasion to point out later on, was a novel not only of promise but of achievement. It brought into American fiction a passion and energy such as are felt only in the work of great novelists, and it brought to life a fascinating gallery of human beings. It is the biography of Eugene Gant, and it is also quite clearly the autobiography of Thomas Wolfe. Towards the end it runs the risk and commits the fault of becoming pure autobiography; the

pity of the author for his hero becomes, that is to say, self-pity, and the narrative effect is lost. But before that happens "Look Homeward, Angel" does great things in its portraiture of Eugene's father and mother and in its reconstruction of American life, particularly in North Carolina, as it was lived shortly after 1900. In addition to the Homeric Gant and his avaricious wife there are dozens of other live persons in the novel; and in addition to all of them there is the sense of a full, strenuous, painful, and sometimes beautiful collective American life, comic in its detail but tragic in its mass. "Of Time and the River" (1935) carried on the story of Eugene Gant through college and beyond, across America to Europe and back home again, and still with much of Wolfe's original richness. The autobiographical fault is loud in the second book, however, and Wolfe's announcement in "The Story of a Novel" (1936) that he intended to go on without limit infected some readers with the fear that he would some day wade beyond his depth in ravings about the painful and beautiful importance of life. Death cut the project short in 1938, so that no one now can say what Wolfe would have learned or whether he would have saved himself from the dangers inherent in his rhapsodic method. It remains clear, however, that his virtues were huge and valuable, and that life as all people know it did get into his fiction with less loss than usually occurs in America.

In the same year with "Look Homeward, Angel" appeared another novel from the South to astonish a public familiar with the soft traditions of that section. William Faulkner's "The Sound and the Fury" (1929) was not his first book, but it was the first one to bring him critical attention. It was difficult reading because of its eccentric time scheme and because of its internal or unspoken dialogue; but it was clear to anyone that Faulkner, writing from Mississippi, had sent a record

Faulkner
1897–

of human depravity to join the other records of its kind which both Europe and America had been collecting for a generation. Not only is there an idiot in "The Sound and the Fury," and in the person of Jason a man mean beyond measure, but there is everywhere over the town of Jefferson, Mississippi, where Faulkner has set his plot, an odor of latter-day decay. This odor continues strong through most of the novels which have followed "The Sound and the Fury." "As I Lay Dying" (1930) underlines the ignorance of poor farmers; "Sanctuary" (1931) the viciousness of backwoods debauchery; "Light in August" the warped morality of outcasts with mixed blood; and "Pylon" the sad, stubborn will to live of itinerant mechanics whose only loyalty is to their machines. Faulkner has traded too much perhaps in misery and sensation; but he has done so as a serious artist, and as one skilful in the nuances of pain. He has permanently extended the range of possible subject matter in American fiction.

Caldwell 1902– It is as meaningless to inquire whether Erskine Caldwell's fiction is "true" of Georgia, where most of it is set, as it is to infer from Faulkner's novels that Mississippi society is rotten at the core. Both writers deal in squalor and degradation, but their background is as much literary as social; their connections are with the main stream of the naturalistic tradition as it reaches its goal—for it would appear that it could scarcely flow on beyond this point. Caldwell, whose first successful book was "Tobacco Road" (1932), a novel which when it was made into a play had a New York run of unprecedented length, has a quality which few of his colleagues in the tradition have had. This is humor—a broad, native, impulsive humor of the sort that nothing except a natural gift will explain. He is known to feel serious concern over the plight of the poor Southern farmer, the sharecropper who is bound to his land almost as tightly as the slave once was, and he has been an active journalist in the cause of this economic unfortunate. Nor is it unlikely that he thinks of his short stories and novels as documents descriptive of a certain area of American life. But his instinct as he writes is to fill his pages with fun—grim it may be, or even ghastly, yet nevertheless fun. The conversation of Jeeter Lester in "Tobacco Road" and of Ty-Ty Walden in "God's Little Acre" (1933) has in spite of everything a magnificence about it, a richness of phrase such as only a gifted ear could catch or reproduce, and a syntax which betrays the presence in either speaker of an indigenous, witty, fantastic mental force. This force is doubtless Caldwell's own, for the endowment carries over from one book to another; yet in each book it seems natural to him who has it, and it is the thing that has made these books not only appalling but delightful, not only sordid but splendid. Caldwell has published fewer novels than volumes of short stories; in both forms, however, his method is the same, and his success is constant. He has one of the finest talents of his time.

Elizabeth Madox Roberts 1886–   Elizabeth Madox Roberts is a Southern novelist with a difference. Her tales of rural Kentucky present an uneducated folk, but the emphasis is on the word folk. Her first and best novel, "The Time of Man" (1926), was pleasant and fresh because it returned to the traditional folk manner of story-telling; its people, from the heroine Ellen Chesser down to the least of passing strangers, were quaint and timeless in their talk, and the land they walked on was redolent of folkways—superstitions, old-fashioned idioms, and inarticulate faiths. Not that Miss Roberts had written an old-fashioned sentimental romance; the story of Ellen had its harsh and veritable aspects, and there was no falsification of the human creature. But the style both of the writing and of the story-telling had a murmurous, unaccented charm.

Miss Roberts's later novels have carried on in the same direction with greater or less success, and tended more and more to be exercises in style. The heroine of "The Great Meadow" (1930), a story of Kentucky in the time of Daniel Boone, reads Bishop Berkeley as a girl in Virginia and develops a habit of thinking of the world as existent only in her senses; when she is not looking at it it is not there. This is symptomatic of Miss Roberts in general; her heroines, for she mostly has heroines, are specialists in perceiving—they look at things with that exaggerated interest which short-sighted persons feel in objects that for normal visions are quite ordinary. They look, listen, and feel with such an especial care that we are left at last with an impression that they are myopic in all their senses; a cloud surrounds them through which they must thrust themselves if they are to be certain of anything at all. In consequence there is always a dreamlike, trancelike medium through which the story comes to us, a layer of cloud which softens everything and makes it remote and beautiful. Perhaps it is significant that the hero of "He Sent Forth a Raven" is a farmer who swears when his wife dies that he will never set forth on God's green earth again, and never does—remaining a prisoner in his own house where he receives reports from the outside world but cannot apprehend it directly. Miss Roberts's women touch us because we know their processes so well; but we observe that they are not practically successful in the world, they lose their men to brisker rivals, or at any rate play humble rôles before them. So with the wife in "A Buried Treasure" (1931), and so with Dena Janes in "Black is My Truelove's Hair" (1938), who loves Will Langtry but cannot gain his final loyalty, and who transfers her affections to a merrier and better-hearted fellow, Cam Elliott the miller's son, but a less vivid lover. The novels of Miss Roberts are minor, but there is nothing better in their mode today.

Heming-
way
1898–

Earlier in the decade that followed 1920 there emerged from the longitude of Paris, where he was one of many post-war expatriates, the story-teller who of all contemporary story-tellers is oftenest hailed as the most expert. Ernest Hemingway's "In Our Time" (1924) announced his talent in the short story, and "Men Without Women" (1927) made that talent clear once and for all. A collection of his short stories in 1938 spread his whole accomplishment on the record. It is a superb accomplishment, for none of his rivals has ever matched him in compression, color, and force. He writes slowly and publishes relatively little; but what he writes succeeds because an artist has been tightly in control of its every sentence. His specialty is the clipped dialogue—a famous example is to be found in "The Killers"—which implies more than it states and accumulates tensions with a mysterious quickness. The same method displays itself more elaborately in his novels, though not with a corresponding shift of form; the novels tend to be series of brilliant tales. "The Sun Also Rises" (1926) was the classic picture for its decade of expatriates caught in a round of death and liquor—death by way of bullfights and liquor by way of incessant drunkenness. "A Farewell to Arms" (1929) was less heartless, and indeed in its story of the love of its hero for an English nurse at the Italian front it went deeper than Hemingway has gone in any other book. In "To Have and to Have Not" (1937) he returns to the tough and the terrible; Harry Morgan, a rum-runner of Key West, is represented as a significant social phenomenon, a strong man in other words whom desperate conditions have driven to lawlessness and murder, but he is not very different from the brutal type most common in Hemingway's work, and the interest of the book is in the last analysis sensational. "Death in the Afternoon" (1932), a treatise on bullfighting, and "Green Hills of Africa" (1935), a treatise on big-game hunting, make it clear that Hemingway has a weakness for death as a subject; and the rather infantile style in which these books are written suggests obsession. Whatever the truth may be, Hemingway is limited in his fiction not, certainly, by any technical deficiencies, for he has none, but by the monotony with which he lets blood in his pages. It is done for its own sake, and for the sake of vindicating the cause of manliness. But the final effect is not masculine, and a strain of the febrile keeps him from being a very great writer. He is a brilliant one, however, and a generation has taken him for its tutor in the art of putting words down on paper.

Farrell 1904– In 1932 a document of genuine social importance was published as "Young Lonigan: A Boyhood in Chicago Streets." Its author, James T. Farrell, seems to have thought it best to be sponsored by a sociologist, for the novel was prefaced by an authenticating statement from an expert on Chicago gangs. "Young Lonigan," however, was at the same time a novel of the first excellence, and in due course it was followed by two sequels, "The Young Manhood of Studs Lonigan" (1934) and "Judgment Day" (1935), which with it made up a trilogy. The hero is William (Studs) Lonigan, an Irish boy who grows up inadequately in an environment of the most dreadful intellectual and moral shabbiness. Whatever gave meaning to this society once has ceased to do so, and Studs, like each of his tough young friends of the streets and poolrooms, has no guidance in the sorry adventure of life. He is likable because in spite of everything he retains a certain innocence of soul; his habit of day-dreaming, which brings him close to us as we read, shows him capable of conscience up until the day of his death from pneumonia, contracted while walking in the rain in search of a job. His family, his various schools, his friends, his sweethearts, his reveries in which he fancies himself a great

athlete, his encounters with moving pictures and newspaper headlines, his debauches, his walks in the parks of
Chicago, his pitiful misunderstandings of world events—
misunderstandings never corrected by his elders—and his
misconceptions with reference to everything of ethical or
abstract importance are in their various turns rendered by
Farrell with an accuracy that leaves nothing to be desired.
The trilogy is a document then of the first value, being a
responsible indictment of society. But it also is fiction of
the most breathless and terrible interest. Farrell is rapid,
sure of hand, and relentless as a story-teller; and he is full
of color. A later series of novels, with Danny O'Neill for its
hero, is more successful in its first member, "A World I
Never Made" (1936) than in its second, "No Star Is Lost"
(1938); but the energies of Farrell do not seem to have
flagged, and the only danger he now runs is that of growing monotonous. Already, however, he has made a vital
contribution to contemporary American fiction.

The Nobel Prize in Literature was given
Pearl Buck
1892–
in 1938 to the author of "The Good Earth"
(1931), one of the most successful of modern
novels. Its author, Pearl Buck, knew the China of which
she wrote, for she had lived a good share of her life there
as the daughter of a missionary and later as a teacher at
the University of Nanking. "The Good Earth" was followed by "Sons" (1932) and "A House Divided" (1935),
the three novels composing a trilogy, now called "House
of Earth," upon the theme of the Chinese family. Pearl
Buck has said that the fortunes of the house of Wang are
typical of all Chinese life: a man raises himself from the
earth to greatness and his heirs share that greatness, but
those who come after begin to lose it when contact with the
original earth is broken or forgotten. "The Good Earth"
shows the rise of Wang; "Sons" commences the story of
cleavage between members of another generation; and "A

House Divided" reveals in the third generation a total, not to say ominous, set of cross-purposes. Pearl Buck is interesting for other reasons, of course, than that her story is typical of China; it is interesting in itself, for it is rich in incident and fundamental in its importance. The Chinese setting would not be necessarily an advantage; it has been made so by combining the exotic with the eternal, partly through the invention of a simple, fluid, even monotonous style which accents the simplicity of the matter. The matter is simple, however, without being flat, nor are the incidents mild. The famine in "The Good Earth," and the migration to the Southern city—these are events of the most vivid force, and the same thing can be said of nearly everything in the volume, as also of Wang the Tiger's life in "Sons" and of life in the coastal city in "A House Divided." Pearl Buck has written other novels with a Chinese setting, and one with an American setting. The most important of her remaining works, however, is her translation of a great thirteenth-century Chinese novel under the title "All Men Are Brothers" (1933). It is romance on a vast scale, having one hundred and eight Robin Hoods for its heroes—noble bandits who hide on a mountain and issue forth to redress wrongs—and covering the whole of China in its course. The China of "The Good Earth" seems little different from this ancient one, except that it is less rich. "All Men Are Brothers" is one of the great novels of the world, and Pearl Buck has done nothing more valuable than her translation of it; though the novels she has written have their lasting value too.

CHAPTER III

THE DRAMA

AMERICAN literature has always been weakest in the department of drama. Until the present generation there has been little dramatic work worth the serious attention of the historian, and there have been few or no playwrights of deserved eminence. Not until 1890 did any arise of even respectable quality, and not until 1915 did talent of a high order enter the field. Between those years, indeed, flourished three playwrights, two of whom were efficient practitioners of social drama and melodrama as they were known in contemporary Europe, and one of whom promised, but only promised, to become an artist of the theater. During these twenty years, too, the prosperity of the theater in the United States became great; New York and its Broadway tradition dominated the national scene; hundreds of well-made plays held the boards for long or short periods. But seldom was any contribution made by the theater to the more significant literature of the country. Theatrical psychology rarely rose above the level of that represented in England by Pinero and Jones. No Wilde or Shaw or Galsworthy or Barrie offered himself as a relief from the prevailing shallowness and flatness.

Fitch 1865–1909 For a time Clyde Fitch, whose career coincides with the period under discussion, was hailed as a significant dramatist. But although he was immensely successful with his numerous plays, and was a master of the technic required in the work he set himself to do, he ceased to hold a high position when his plays no longer appeared, and after his death his reputation rapidly declined until it is impossible now to grant him any considerable worth as a maker of literature. In all the devices which work for theatrical effectiveness he was obviously proficient; in all the situations where maturity of emotion and strength of thought are things to be desired, he was ill-equipped. He was honest and earnest, and he had a sense of humor; but he had little or nothing to say.

Fitch produced many lighter plays which may be classed as farces; yet he continues interesting chiefly by virtue of the serious social dramas which constituted him a rival of Jones and Pinero in England. "The Climbers" exhibits two families in an American city, the Hunters and the Sterlings, at a time when financial difficulties test their characters. Richard Sterling, a young business man, the weakest of them all, is the person around whom the action of the piece develops. His integrity cannot stand the strain of poverty, and he commits suicide at the end after he has entangled the fortunes of many friends in his rash speculations. Honesty is never the theme of great drama; it is one of the easiest of the virtues, and writers of supreme spiritual endowment do not spend much time upon it. It is significant of Fitch's mind that he dealt with it again and again. "The Truth" (1907) concerns itself with Becky Warder's inveterate habit of fibbing when she is in uncomfortable circumstances. Such a habit is annoying to others, perhaps, and a definite blemish in one's character; but the tragedy, or the near tragedy, which Fitch builds around it in the present case fails to be impressive. The most fatal quality which a tragic theme can have is triviality. "The Girl with the Green Eyes" explores a more passionate and more fundamental sort of error—jealousy. Jinny Austin is able to conquer only after much agony of spirit her instinct to suspect her young husband of divided affections. Here again, however, the treatment is far from profound, and the issue never is elevated. "The City," to name another social drama, studies the consequences to the members of a provincial family of their removal to New York. The Rands, who were eminent and fairly respectable in Middleburg, disintegrate rapidly in the city toward which their ambitions have pulled them, and are saved from ruin only by the resolution of George Rand to reform his life and confess his sins as a politician and business man. The somewhat old-fashioned device of a campaign for the governorship is resorted to for theatrical excitement, and such excitement is abundant throughout. The play, however, fails to establish for Fitch the place which his champions have sought to make for him among the first of American dramatists.

Thomas
1857–

Augustus Thomas was an effective influence in the American theater at the same time that Clyde Fitch was dominating it. He began with sonorous melodrama, typified by two plays, "Alabama" and "Arizona," in which rather stale codes of honor are argued about and men are manly in the most obvious fashion—the fashion favored for good or for ill by the average theater audience. With the twentieth century Thomas advanced in sophistication and adroitness, but remained essentially commonplace in mind. "The Witching Hour" (1907) and "As a Man Thinks" are thoroughly competent dramas, rich in incident and interesting in their by-play; the themes by which they were intended to be subtilized, however, are unimportant morally and intellectually. In the first of the two much is made of telepathy; in the second, as its title indicates, much is made of spiritual healing—spiritual error is cured by taking thought. The errors which Thomas employs for the foundations of his dramas are at the best unreal errors. No great human issue is involved, and no strong light is thrown upon human motive. The way was still clear after Augustus Thomas for a playwright who should contribute imagination and understanding to a relatively barren stage.

Moody 1869–1910   There were those who believed that such expectations had been fulfilled when William Vaughn Moody, poet [1] and scholar, appeared with his play "The Great Divide" (1906). This was a study on a large scale and in intense terms of the conflict which in the course of nature arises when temperaments sprung from different civilizations come together. More concretely, it tells the story of Ruth Jordan and Stephen Ghent, the first representing the culture of New England, proud, scrupulous, and morally supersensitive; the second representing the culture of the Far West, rough and ready, and, though genuine, uncouth. The fundamental conflict of the drama is in the mind of Ruth, who, having in a moment of romance submitted to her abductor Stephen, eventually is unable to endure the thought that she is his primitive prize and escapes from his Rocky Mountain house into the East again. Upon his following her there, she is reconciled to him only when she is convinced that he has suffered for her sake and has looked into the depths of her conscience. The reputation of "The Great Divide" has declined with the passage of time. Yet it was an advance upon the drama of its day for the reason that it had a meaning and was written by a man of indubitable talent and culture. What Moody might have done in the following years is now only a matter of speculation. Before his early death he produced another play, "The Faith Healer," which was generally accepted as inferior to its predecessor. Its hero, Ulrich

[1] For his poetry, see pages 10–11.

Michaelis, is possessed of the power of healing the lame and the sick by spiritual suggestion. Upon his coming into the presence of Rhoda Williams, the niece of a woman whom he has cured of paralysis, he at first fears that love for her will destroy his divine powers; but in the end he is brought to understand that such love only increases his gifts, and he faces a happy future with her who is to be his earthly wife. The danger here is that the audience will not be convinced, and it is true that "The Faith Healer" failed of great effect because the religious energy supposed to reside in Michaelis was not fully communicated by the action or the dialogue.

Moody was the author also of an uncompleted trilogy in verse dealing with the relations between the spirit of God and the spirit of man. "The Fire-Bringer," based upon the old Greek legend of Prometheus, who attempted by the gift of fire to make man independent of God, is the first member of the trilogy. The second is "The Masque of Judgment," wherein it is made clear that God cannot afford to annihilate man because in so doing he would annihilate Himself. "The Death of Eve," a fragment, was intended to show God and man reconciled through the woman who had put them apart. The theme of the whole is the inseparableness of men from their deities and the utter dependence of deities upon the men who have created them. Moody appears here as the mystic that he prevailingly was, and in many passages as one of the most generously inspired poets of his day.

The New Theater The second decade of the present century brought with it a veritable renaissance in American drama. The separation between literature and the stage, between art and the drama, tended to cease under the influence of many forces. Most of these forces emanated from abroad. Certain American producers and critics, traveling in England, Germany, Russia, Scandinavia, and Hungary, became aware of

astonishing new possibilities in the dramatic form, and
returned to write books or to produce plays which should
embody their discoveries. It had long been the custom to
import French farces; now plays of greater consequence
from other countries began to appear, and sophistication
advanced rapidly not only among authors but among their
audiences. The art of scene-painting and stage-setting
was literally revolutionized within the space of a few
years. Whereas the old formal four-act play had been
content with conventional sets and stiff verisimilitudes,
or in the better cases with a meticulous realism among the
properties, now fancy, imagination, allegory, vision, and
the profounder principles of esthetics operated to create
new and fascinating worlds of canvas, metal, wood, and
electricity. Two artists of the stage in particular, Lee Si-
monson and Robert Edmond Jones, demonstrated what
could be done by trained minds working freely with unconventional materials. The theater had begun to be a
place where art could thrive.

What was more important for the drama as literature,
playwrights now became aware that there were fewer
limits upon their minds than they had been taught to
suppose. Bolder thinking was encouraged; a more honest
realism was demanded; and when realism itself grew tiresome, fantasy or allegory found space in which to expand.
In particular there was a liberalizing of technic. The nineteenth century had handed down a more or less rigid set
of rules. There must be three or four acts, with three or
four curtains; a theme must be developed plainly and
directly within this mold; the dialogue was to be the
natural dialogue of men and women; there must be no
soliloquies, because in actual life men do not talk aloud
to themselves; and there must be no asides, for it would
be illogical to suppose that what the audience could hear
at its distance a fellow-actor on the stage could not hear.
These rules had made for a certain superficial likeness to

life; they had not made for poetry, or philosophy, or essential likeness to the immemorial elements in human nature. One by one they tended to give way before methods borrowed more or less directly from Europe. Some of the new practices were ill-adapted to American psychology, were fads, and so died a quick death. Others survived, and still survive as elements in a new technic which continues to regenerate the whole art of writing plays. A term often rather loosely applied to this technic is "expressionism"—a term itself borrowed from European criticism. Expressionism, if it can be defined at all, means immediacy of communication; that is to say, it means that the playwright, having an idea or a mood to communicate, proceeds to express it not bluntly or didactically through the speeches of his characters but by inference and by image through selected scenes and situations which he hopes will powerfully suggest the mood or the idea to the audience. More specifically, expressionism affects the style of play-writing by its insistence on the right of the author to use as many scenes as he likes, and to leave these as incomplete as their nature demands; it encourages the symbolic touch. Thus it is not unusual in a modern American play to find ten or fifteen scenes, each suggesting a development in the action but never stating it. A return has been made not only to the best European practice of a generation but to the practice of all the great playwrights of history who have been conspicuously free to do what they liked—to the Elizabethans, for instance.

1915   All this implies the existence of audiences trained to novelty and experiment. Such audiences had been prepared by the institution known as the little theater, an institution which, likewise under the influence of Europe, multiplied itself in many forms throughout the United States. The little theater, or as it is sometimes called the institutional theater, was conceived in reaction against the commercial theater of Broadway, dominated in most cases by men insensible to art and committed to the star system of acting. The management of the little theater was generally in the hands of a few devotees of dramatic art on its more serious side; the actors were frequently amateurs to begin with—and hence impressionable to novelty; the plays were likely to be plays for which there was no large popular demand, plays perhaps written by obscure authors who were more interested in excellence than in success. The little-theater movement was abortive in many cities of the country, either because of quixotic management or because of a frailty in the plays offered. But in New York at least three ventures attained a remarkable artistic success. Three little theaters were by chance opened in the same year, 1915. The Neighborhood Playhouse, the Washington Square Players, and the Provincetown Players are historically of great importance. They succeeded in maintaining themselves; they encouraged the writing and performing of intelligent plays; they experimented to admirable effect. The Washington Square Players gave birth to the Theater Guild. The Provincetown Players, commencing their work at Provincetown, Massachusetts, in a theater made out of an old building on a wharf, established themselves in a small room on Macdougal Street in New York and there did an invaluable service in introducing original playwrights of purely local origin—and in two cases of unprecedented imaginative power.

Susan Glaspell 1882–   The career of Susan Glaspell as a dramatist is closely bound up with the career of the Provincetown Players. Her first piece was performed in the Wharf Theater at Provincetown, and when she published her first collection of plays, it was observed that all of the eight had appeared under the

auspices of the company to which she had given her
devotion both as author and as player. Her reputation
was established by this volume. Most of the items included in it were one-act plays, after the fashion which
the little theaters of the country, reacting against the
dogmas of the older stage, had already set. They were
conspicuously the work of an intelligent and passionate
mind; when they were not gay with the feather touch of
satire they were intense and concentrated in the quality
of their examination into human—particularly feminine
—motive. They were obviously the work of a woman,
and most readers agreed that they were the product of a
genius, if a narrow one.

"Trifles" (1917) is perhaps the best known of these
shorter plays by Miss Glaspell. Briefly and sardonically
it shows the accumulation of circumstantial evidence
proving that a woman has killed her brutal husband, the
crowning bit of evidence being a dead bird (her especial
pet as all people knew), wrapped in silk and put away
in her sewing-box. The husband, it seemed plain to the
neighbor women who came with the sheriff to investigate,
had wrung the bird's neck; and the wife had at last
struck back. "Bernice," a longer play, contains an ingenious analysis of a woman who has died before the
beginning of the action, her character being reflected in
the gestures and the speeches of her relatives and friends.

Two full-length plays followed these shorter ones. "In-
heritors" (1921) was particularly ambitious, since it endeavored to tell the history of three generations of people
in a Middle Western community, and incidentally to
criticize certain elements in the society of the present
day. In "The Verge" (1922) Miss Glaspell returned to
material more central to her nature, though not necessarily more central to her ideas, which have always been
radical by the current definition of that term. The heroine

of this her greatest play is Claire Archer, whom her family believes to be on the verge of insanity, but who considers herself to be on the verge of sanity. A talented and highly strung woman, she becomes depressed by the monotony and meanness of life and endeavors to break through its bonds into the "outside"—a significant word always in Susan Glaspell—where life is absolutely new and real. The action of the play can scarcely be summarized in view of the fact that it is so rapid, nervous, intellectual, and extremely subtle. But it can be safely stated that human nature has seldom been subjected to a closer and more intensely imaginative scrutiny than it is here. The most interesting of Susan Glaspell's later plays is "Alison's House," which won the Pulitzer Prize for 1930. It deals with Emily Dickinson [1] and the twin mysteries of her life: her love and her poetry. The biography of Emily Dickinson has been a hunting-ground for gossips ever since her death; Miss Glaspell is neither a gossip in this case nor a dogmatist concerning her subject's "secret." She is as usual a sensitive and intelligent playwright, and she leaves Emily Dickinson the fine poet she was, with reasons for her reticence and with a permanent distinction of soul.

O'Neill 1888–   In Eugene O'Neill the American drama has unearthed its first indubitable genius of great scope. Within the space of a few years, and while he was yet a young man, he poured out in rapid succession dozens of strong and impressive plays, destroying the manuscripts of many which he did not like and preserving the best of the others in print. In fertility, in power, in variety, he has had no rival on the American stage—or, as was indicated by his receipt of the Nobel Prize in 1936, on the contemporary world stage.

Born in New York, O'Neill was early presented with

[1] For Emily Dickinson's poetry, see pages 7–9.

experiences of value to a future playwright. He traveled with his father, who was a notable actor; went to college for a year; worked in New York at various jobs; learned to think for himself, and incidentally to think radically; prospected for gold in Honduras; read Joseph Conrad and shipped for South America; went on to Africa; returned to New York to a still more varied career as actor, business clerk, and newspaper reporter; contracted tuberculosis and while he was recuperating took up the writing of plays; and after joining his forces with the Provincetown Players settled down to a busy life of authorship. His work so far bears the imprint of all this rough experience. The materials with which he deals are often elemental; he treats them frankly and completely; he is not afraid of violence, nor does he shrink from lurid contrasts. But what is more essential to an understanding of his success, he possesses a rich and bold imagination, and he reproduces human speech with an unexampled fidelity.

His first two volumes contained one-act plays of life in New York or upon the sea. "Thirst" was crude in most of its elements, but any careful reader might have seen in it the promise of a surprising and vigorous talent. "The Moon of the Caribbees" included six brief plays about sailors in southern waters, reveling in their uncouth utterances and striking to the depths of their wayward passions. "Beyond the Horizon" (1920), a full-length play which had a long run in Broadway theaters, first brought O'Neill to anything like popular attention. It is concerned with the lives of two brothers, one of whom, Robert Mayo, gives up his dream of exploring the world beyond the horizon which bounds his father's farm, and the other of whom, Andrew Mayo, leaves the farm where he naturally belongs to embrace the sea-career which had been planned for Robert. The maladjustments incidental to these errors of judgment make up the tragedy of the piece. The dialogue in many places is over-vivid, and the action borders on melodrama at times; but the play as a whole has the supreme quality of being absorbing; the characters, whatever they say or do, are important. "Anna Christie" (1922), O'Neill's next successful work, followed the fortunes in New York of Chris Christopherson, a Scandinavian-American seaman, and his daughter Anna. O'Neill here made use of experiences which he had along the waterfront, and the relations between Chris and his unhappy daughter he developed with great understanding mingled with deep sympathy. "Diff'rent" took for its theme the abnormal psychology of a woman starved for love. When Emma Crosby at forty-seven fell strangely in love with her worthless young nephew, Benny Rogers, she was called upon by her creator to act and speak in a way to strain the credulity of a theatrical audience; but that credulity is never snapped. Emma remains a pitiful figure through her squalid tragedy, and Benny takes his place as the first of O'Neill's characters to speak with a perfect and terrible naturalness. "The Straw" had for its setting a tuberculosis sanitarium such as O'Neill had known. In the love of two patients there, Eileen Carmody and Stephen Murray, the playwright reached to regions of suffering and passion which made many persons in his audience uncomfortable—so unaccustomed were they to passages as thoroughgoing and uncompromising as these.

With "The Emperor Jones" (1921) O'Neill struck out in a new direction. The play is expressionistic in form and spirit. In eight brief scenes the audience witnesses the swift disintegration of courage in the heart of Brutus Jones, a negro who has made himself emperor of an island in the West Indies. The natives have risen against him, and in unwonted haste he flees with his revolver toward the borders of his empire, hoping on the other side of some woods to find means of escape to the United States. Throughout the play the tom-tom of the angry natives beats with a sullen and maddening regularity. Throughout the eight scenes Jones finds his fright increasing, until at last in panic he is afflicted with visions of his own past and the past of his race, and wastes his ultimate bullet upon a phantom which he sees under a tree only a few paces from the point he had originally left. He has walked in a circle, and his fate now awaits him at the hands of his bitterest enemies—his own people. The technic of the play was new and surprising; the atmosphere was rich and terrible. A new chapter in the history of American drama was written in a single evening. O'Neill soon followed "The Emperor Jones" with another and even more startling play in eight expressionistic scenes. "The Hairy Ape" (1922) is charged with criticism of modern society. Yank Smith, the vast, brutal hero of the piece, is a stoker on an ocean liner. The audience sees him at his work, heaving like some unheard-of beast and exhorting his mates to keep the pace that he has set them. It seems to him that he is at the center of life. His effort makes the ship move; he "belongs," whereas the silly passengers up on deck do not. "Every ting else dat makes de woild move, somep'n makes it move. It can't move without somep'n else, see? Den yuh get down to me. I'm at de bottom, get me! Dere ain't nothin' foither. I'm de end! I'm de start! I start somep'n and de woild moves!" But through a series of circumstances he loses his confidence in his own importance on the ship, and when New York is reached he sets out in a pathetic search for "the real ting." Inspired by his contempt for society to join the Industrial Workers of the World, he finds upon going to their headquarters that they are not the revolutionaries he has thought them; they do not belong either. He is thrown in jail, where he is christened the Hairy Ape by other prisoners. He is released, wanders about more and more lost in his mind, and finally lands at the zoo in front of the gorilla's cage. At least he will be at home here—he and the animal can "belong" together. He forces his way into the cage; the gorilla seizes him and crushes him to death; he ends a mystified failure. The world means nothing. O'Neill was severely criticized by the contemporary press, not only for the ideas in "The Hairy Ape" but for the violent language in which they had been expressed. But the play had its effect; for those spectators who were without bias it was evident that a great writer was coming to his maturity; it was certain that the native drama would not be quite the same again.

In two later plays O'Neill has explored still further fields, furnishing additional data by which his view of life may be defined. "All God's Chillun Got Wings" is concerned with the theme of miscegenation, or marriage between two persons of different race. A white woman, rejected by her brutal white lover, marries a negro whom she has known since childhood. Her love for him, which flourishes under the ostracism the act brings upon her, is curiously mingled with a fear, only half understood within her own mind, lest he come to seem her equal. Actually a superior man, he is ambitious to become a lawyer, but fails at several bar examinations. She is both happy and unhappy over these failures, which progressively wreck him; until after the final one both husband and wife are reduced to a state of hysteria bordering on madness, and the play ends in frustration. In "Desire Under the Elms" the playwright returns in a measure to the material of "Beyond the Horizon." The scene is a New England farm, and the theme is the gradual disintegration of hope and strength in a family which too long has lived a sternly repressive, laborious, home-keeping life. All the industry and virtue in the world cannot save the old man who is the protagonist of the piece from an eventual despair which makes him shake his fist at God the ill-contriver and arch-blunderer.

Beginning with "The Great God Brown" in 1925 O'Neill went through a period of experimentation in dramatic techniques. In his case it was more than experimentation; it was exploration, and the motive was a desire to extend dramatic form so that more could be said in it than was being said in the conventional play. There is always an intellectual and moral urge behind O'Neill's devices, and that is why they are interesting. "The Great God Brown" was distinguished by the use of masks for all of the leading characters; these were put on and taken off at will, and they changed as the play proceeded. They represented fear or repression in their wearers, and either conscious or unconscious deception. The hero, William A. (Billy) Brown, wears no mask at first because he is a simple, frank, athletic youth with no need of one; but he assumes one as his life becomes complicated with those of Dion Anthony and his wife Margaret. Dion, a cynical and brilliant fellow, has worn a mask from the beginning; and the one worn by Margaret increases in strangeness with her husband's nature. There is only one person in the play, Cybel, who can see behind the masks; so it is she in whom the vision of the playwright resides, and it is she alone who approaches greatness. "Lazarus Laughed" (1926) was an experiment for O'Neill in that it was lyrical in its form; it is a series of choruses rather than a drama of the familiar sort, and the subject of these choruses is a certain mysticism concerning death. Lazarus laughs upon being raised from the dead because the experience has taught him that there is no death: the self forgotten, there is neither end nor beginning, and hence there is no need to fear death. His laughter, growing contagious, spreads even to the Emperor Caligula—who, however, because his power depends upon men's fear of the death he can inflict upon them, has Lazarus killed. But the most famous of O'Neill's experiments is "Strange Interlude" (1927), which has been one of the most successful of modern plays. Its device is the "aside," or the monologue in which an actor, talking to himself, distinguishes for the audience between what he says and what he thinks—or what he would say if he were being candid. "Strange Interlude" is chiefly the story of Nina Leeds, who accepts her old suitor Charlie Marsden only after a hysterical life the source of which is her shock upon hearing of her first lover Gordon's death in France. It is a long and involved story, but the most remarkable thing about it is still the method of its interior dialogue: the exclamatory monologues, spoken often at great speed, which only the audience hears.

"Dynamo" was interesting in 1928 because it showed O'Neill moving in the direction of a religious theme. Reuben Light, son of the Reverend Hutchins Light, repudiates his father's God for the God of Electricity and is sacrificed by this new God after he has tried in its name to slay his love for Ada Fife. O'Neill took a still further step in "Days Without End" (1933), whose hero, John, struggles against his former self—objectified on the stage as a man visible only to him—until when the struggle seems hopeless he wins it at last before the Cross. O'Neill's silence after this play might seem to indicate that he found in religion a way of quieting the loud questions which hitherto had disturbed him, and which he had written plays in a vain attempt to answer. A year before, however, he had written in "Ah, Wilderness!" his only free-hearted comedy, dealing affectionately with memories of high school days and puppy love. And two years before, in 1931, he had produced his maturest drama, "Mourning Becomes Electra." It is a trilogy, translating the Greek story of Agamemnon's family into nineteenth-century American terms; and it is perhaps O'Neill's masterpiece. In the first play, "Homecoming," General Ezra Mannon returns from the Civil War to be murdered in his New England house by his wife Christine, who in his absence has fallen in love with Captain Adam Brant. In the second play, "The Hunted," his daughter Lavinia and his son Orin avenge him by killing Brant and driving Christine to suicide. In the third play, "The Haunted," Lavinia and Orin return from a tour of the world to settle down and marry two old friends of the neighborhood, but they cannot do so because the past thrusts itself into their lives and warps them; Orin commits suicide, and Lavinia is left alone in the great house to die when her time comes. This is clearly the story of Agamemnon, Clytemnestra, Electra, and Orestes,[1] with Brant taking the part of Aegisthus. But the handling is modern, American, and O'Neill. Psychology is its equivalent for Fate, and the punishment of the children is more than what is ordinarily called conscience. Orin's hallucinations tell him among other things that Lavinia is his mother; at other times his feeling towards her is that of a lover; and she is elaborately analyzed as a "case." The success of the play, however, does not depend upon such an interpretation. Its action in itself is simple and ordered; its outline is large; its humanity is impressive. O'Neill,

[1] For the treatment of this story by Robinson Jeffers, see page 56.

experimenting with every known device, had hit upon
the best of them all : he had imitated a classic.

Howard
1891–   Another prolific playwright who has been a
mainstay of the professional theater is Sidney
Howard. He is an uneven artist, and only a few
of his plays have survived their seasons, but those which
have done so are distinguished by a clarity and a directness
which indicate in their author a positive and disciplined
talent. "They Knew What They Wanted" (1924) is built
around the figure of Tony, an Italian-American farmer in
California who wants a wife at fifty and thinks he has
secured one by correspondence. But in his innocence he
has sent her instead of his own likeness a photograph of
his young friend Joe; so that when she arrives to be married she is sorely disappointed. The marriage takes place,
but it is Joe's child who will be born; and the climax is
the scene in which Tony learns that this is true. Meanwhile Amy has learned to love Tony, as anybody would,
since he is one of the most robust and irresistible of stage
Italians. The suspense and the solution are both of the
highest dramatic effectiveness, as is always true of Howard's plays at their best. He is again at his best in "Ned
McCobb's Daughter" (1926), whose heroine, Carrie Cal-
lahan, represents the New England character on its most
admirable and stubborn side; her virtue is tough enough
to stand many knocks, and indeed it gets many knocks,
for her husband George comes near being absolutely contemptible. The contrast between them is highly lighted and
perhaps excessive; but Howard deals always in hard, clear
lights and shadows. His "Yellow Jack" (1933) makes an
exciting play out of medical material—the experiments in
Cuba in 1900 as a result of which it became known that
yellow fever is communicated by mosquitoes. Such subjects can be sentimentally handled, since in this case four

soldiers were to offer their lives as possible sacrifices; but Howard once more was hard and clear, as he was the next year when he assisted Sinclair Lewis in the dramatization of "Dodsworth."

Anderson 1888–   Maxwell Anderson rose to special prominence at about the same time with Sidney Howard.

After producing several plays of unequal worth, he collaborated with Laurence Stallings in 1924 upon the best of all war plays, "What Price Glory." Its force was astonishing at the time, and little or none of that force has been lost from it since. It is among other things a triumph of language. Captain Flagg, Sergeant Quirt, and the girl Charmaine over whom they perpetually fight take the leading parts, but no less important are the soldiers who hang about headquarters and indulge their genius for tall, racy, American talk. The talk makes the play, and indeed Anderson has always been notable for his contributions to dramatic style. In "Elizabeth the Queen" (1930) and "Mary of Scotland" (1933) he attempted something like a restoration of Elizabethan blank verse. His verse, which alternates with prose in the dialogue, is not an imitation in the feebler sense of the term; it is rather an adaptation to modern stage needs, and audiences have judged it successful, though it is undistinguished considered merely as verse. Its merit, that is to say, consists partly in the fact that it makes few demands upon the ear, and to the eye seems often to be no more than prose arbitrarily printed as lines. A better example of it is found in "Winterset" (1935), Anderson's contribution to the literature of Sacco and Vanzetti, and one of the most important of contemporary plays. It was in fact his second contribution, since in 1928 he had collaborated with Harold Hickerson in producing "Gods of the Lightning," whose two heroes, Macready and Capraro, are labor leaders "framed" to appear guilty of a payroll robbery. The treatment in the earlier play is pedestrian and propagandist, whereas "Winterset" enriches the subject by moving it forward in time. Mio Romagna roams the world in search of the true criminal in whose stead his father Bartolemeo had been unjustly executed. He finds him in the house of Garth Esdras, whose sister Miriamne he falls in love with; but to this house also comes the judge who had sentenced Bartolemeo, and whose mind has become deranged by years of brooding over the suspicion that he had been wrong. The situation is packed with the richest possibilities, and Anderson has realized them in his tragedy—for the end is tragedy. Nor does his verse, even though it entirely misses greatness, fail him here, for with its aid he finds the poetry which underlies this human predicament as it does any other.

Kaufman 1889– The name of George S. Kaufman has seldom appeared alone on the title-page of any play, and much that he has written in collaboration with others has been of only transient significance. But his name stands for a quality which would be precious in the theater at any time. He has a genius for the ineffably comic, he is a master of silly satire, and he is the funniest playwright of his time. "Beggar on Horseback" (1924), freely adapted from the German in collaboration with Marc Connelly, was a satire upon success in the form of a story about Neil McRae, a musician, whom only a dream saved from marrying the wrong girl—that is to say, the rich one. It is the dream that makes the play: a dream in which Gladys Cady's family join with a host of other improbable persons to cavort extravagantly through Neil's mind as he sleeps, and to provide a set of symbols which still do duty in the American drama whenever this delightful piece of significant nonsense is remembered. "The Butter and Egg Man" (1925) was among the first of many romances about the "show business" which held the New York stage in the twenties; it led the way both by its roughness and by its sentiment—a combination which Kaufman finds it difficult along with his audiences to resist. In 1929 came "June Moon," in which the collaborator was Ring Lardner, and in which the ridicule was directed at the commercialized popular song. The next year "Once in a Lifetime," by Kaufman and Moss Hart, made unmerciful fun of Hollywood and its illiterate moving-picture producers. And two political extravaganzas written with Morrie Ryskind, "Of Thee I Sing" (1931) and "Let 'Em Eat Cake" (1933), irreverently brought down the house with laughter at Congress, the Supreme Court, and America's political parties. Whatever Kaufman has touched has become comic under his hands—broadly so, and yet, because his touch is true, complexly and sometimes finely so.

Behrman 1893– Another kind of comedy is represented by the plays of Samuel Nathaniel Behrman, who has not been prolific but who has wielded the brilliant knife of analysis in every piece he has offered his select public. He writes intellectual or "high" comedy, and he is true to his tradition in that he places the mind of a woman at the center of every situation. "Biography" (1933) is in this sense typical of him, for Marion Froude, the painter who is its heroine, is superior in civilization both to Richard Kurt and to Leander Nolan, and finally must reject them both because they are incapable of understanding the love of tolerance which has distinguished her whole life and made it free. She is more or less repeated in Lady Lael Wyngate, the heroine of "Rain from Heaven" (1935), who is the only one of several persons in England prepared to sympathize with or penetrate the mind of Hugo Willens, an exile from Germany and a victim of its anti-Semitism. Leonie Frothingham in "End of Summer" (1936) is so far untrue to type as to know less about certain modern matters than her daughter Paula and Paula's radical young friends;

yet Leonie has many of the attractions of Behrman's ideal woman, wit and beauty and ease being among these attractions. The women of "The Second Man" (1927) are perhaps subordinate in interest to its hero, Clark Storey, an author who has somewhere within him a second man too cynical and critical for any wholesome purpose. But the heroine of "Serena Blandish" (1928) more than makes up for the interruption. Serena, who is taken by Behrman out of an English novel, is one of the most delicately constructed figures in modern comedy. The play, like the novel, deals with "the difficulty of getting married," and is among other things a satire upon the modes of society. But it is also a touching and amusing character study, and Behrman's name may well last longest in connection with it.

The Group Theater and Others As time has gone on in the American theater history has repeated itself. The revolution of 1915 having become a success, a certain stagnation threatened to occur; and shortly after 1930 a new set of stage societies, "little theaters," and dramatic "movements" came into existence for the purpose of keeping the theatrical ventilating system at work. Such upsurges are always necessary, and the experiment has proved salutary in the present instance, especially since an outlet has been provided for the expression of more or less "leftist" ideas to which the commercial stage is either hostile or indifferent. But the urge to modify the theater has not always had a political or economic bias. There is little in common between the Federal Theater, the Theater Union, the Labor Stage, the Mercury Theater, and the Group Theater beyond a conviction that freedom and flexibility must once more be fought for and achieved. That they have achieved this freedom is attested by their success with the public. The latest "new" drama has unquestionable vitality, and the public goes as eagerly to some of its out-of-the-way haunts as it does to the once prosperous palaces on Broadway.

Odets
1906–

Because it has sponsored the plays of Clifford Odets the Group Theater is the most important of the organizations in question. Odets is frankly concerned with a social theme, the decay of the middle class; but his handling of this theme, a familiar one since 1929, is superior to that of his colleagues in that it has depth and color, and above all realism. His dialogue burns with a fervor which seems to belong to those who speak it rather than to him who wrote it. The characters of Odets, in fact, rarely have his vision of society and therefore seem not to know of his existence. They are usually very much wrapped up in their own desires and affairs, which they take with a fanatical seriousness even though there is little meaning in them. They are the symbols of a class whose members are just beginning to know that they are bewildered, but who for that very reason redouble their efforts to exist according to their original plan. Odets underlines the irony of this, but he does so with a loving, almost heartbroken sympathy. His characters, in other words, are not naked symbols; they are painfully real human beings. "Awake and Sing" (1935) takes place in a Bronx apartment in New York, and its action centers about Bessie Berger, whose failure to understand the predicaments of her daughter Hessie and her son Ralph—predicaments for which there seems to be no assignable cause except that time is passing in the world and a new society is getting ready to replace an old one—tragically increases as the play goes on. Bessie is strong and faithful, but these virtues are of little avail at a time when decay is setting in from invisible sources. Later on in the same year Odets produced in rapid succession two brilliant pieces of dramatic journalism: "Waiting for Lefty," which explains the necessity for a taxi strike, and "Till the Day I Die," an exposure of the repressive measures taken by the Brown Shirts of Germany against the Communists. Both are brilliant, and both were successful even with spectators who did not share the author's politics. But Odets returned in his next two plays to his original theme. "Paradise Lost" (1936) deals once more with the confusions and only half-realized defeats of a middle-class family. The Gordons and their connections do not know yet what is the matter with them: why they are not as happy as they expected to be, or why the world about them is not quite the world they have always said it was. The theme is perhaps overstated by Odets, who handles more convenient material in "Golden Boy" (1937). Joe Bonaparte, a young violinist who is set upon becoming free through success, chooses the quickest way, which for him is prizefighting. He marches to a championship at the expense of many loyalties and decencies, realizing shortly before his death that his brother Frank, a labor organizer, has achieved a richer freedom by fighting with millions of comrades rather than for himself alone. The point is clear, but as usual Odets has made it through living people. The people of "Rocket to the Moon" (1938) are more important than any point, since the play is directly concerned with the passion of love—again in a middle-class setting, but with less emphasis than before upon the familiar class doctrine. Always, however, he has been concerned with people. His doctrine has lent him fervor and direction; his natural gifts, which are extraordinarily high, have kept his eyes upon the human creature as he walks and talks.

CHAPTER IV

ESSAYISTS

A GENERAL introduction to the literature produced in the United States since 1890 must leave out of the account many writers who have set forth opinions or who have discussed topics which their age has thought important. Some of these writers, such as philosophers, historians, critics, have been too technical to be included among essayists at large; others, such as journalists, have been temporary or local in their concerns; others, such as reformers and crusaders, have expressed themselves without paying any heed to the graces of expression; still others, with all the graces, have simply had nothing memorable to say. The eminence of this or that man in public life may have led his words to be taken for more than they were worth. The degree to which another has dissented from prevailing modes of thought may have given him the look of a distinction which he does not really possess. Moreover, since any generation tends to listen more understandingly to its publicists than to its artists, and to forget them more speedily, the current value ascribed to a given writer does not bear trustworthily upon his chances for survival. It happens that the past four decades or so have seen the rapid development of opinion in the United States on almost every topic, and that consequently a very large number of essayists have been called into action to resist, mirror, or encourage the changes going on. Among these it is not only difficult to say which ones will continue to be interesting;

it is also difficult to say which, in the perspective of time, will turn out to have been typical. A few, however, may be chosen as unavoidable figures in an age crowded with candidates for the choice.

Muir 1838–1914 One of these unavoidable figures is that of a man who had little to say on the specific issues of his age and who was not even born in the United States. But no naturalist is ever untimely, since the background of nature against which men live changes so little that it furnishes a perennial standard by which to measure human change; and Americans in general have so newly come from Europe that a man born there may become as genuinely an American as if he were a native. John Muir, who came from Scotland, is almost certain in the long run to seem a more penetrating interpreter of nature in America than the native-bred John Burroughs. Muir was a creature of the natural world, and he took the continent for his home. From Wisconsin, where the family had settled, he tramped to Florida, and then went on to California. Up and down the long Pacific Coast, from Alaska to Mexico, he spent the rest of his life, writing his best books about the Sierra Nevada mountains. His Calvinistic upbringing and his university studies had done nothing to tame his restless spirit. Though part of the time he had a house to go to, he was most comfortable in the wilderness. A vast energy drove him. He went toward the things he wanted with the directness of an eagle. He no more suffered from the need of society than a bear. Alert as a fox, he was forever on the lookout for all that went on, and he managed to be present at the most unusual happenings out of doors. He knew how to fend for himself in dangerous situations. Willing to kill another animal if he needed it for food, he nevertheless lived at peace with animals and seems to have been accepted by them. At the same time, he was a man, constantly drawing conclusions from his experiences, adding wisdom to his instincts, setting down, at intervals, the records of his adventures for others to read. What sustained him through all this was, apparently, more than curiosity; it was ecstasy. Eager as a child, he burned with the continuous excitement of an untiring poet.

Though Muir was not primarily a writer, and published little till late in life, it is of course through his books that he reveals whatever is known about him and the things he saw. "The Story of My Boyhood and Youth" (1913), "A Thousand-Mile Walk to the Gulf" (1916), "My First Summer in the Sierras" (1911), "Travels in Alaska" (1915), make up a more or less connected chronicle which is enlarged by other books not so clearly in the main line of his existence but hardly less personal. Taken together, they present an amazing variety of life. As botanist, zoölogist, geologist, Muir made important observations, but he was less a cool scientist than a seer hot upon the trail of the secrets of the earth. To accompany him is to put off the burdens of civilization and to go back to primitive conditions in which man lives in nature without feeling obliged to dominate or exploit it. Those conditions Muir describes in rich and picturesque detail. He seems to have studied every flower or tree or mountain-peak or waterfall or bird or beast till he was as familiar with it as with his own hand; yet his account never suffers from monotony, so brightly does it move and so vividly does it communicate its enthusiasm. When he brings human beings into his picture, he reports their appearance and their behavior with the same interest as he feels for the non-human citizens of his world. He is dramatic because he deals little with still life, and much with movement. Desiring to get a better knowledge than he has of the effects of wind upon a tree, he climbs a spruce in a mountain gale. "Never before did I enjoy so noble an exhilaration of motion. The slender tops fairly flapped and swished in the passionate torrent, bending and swirling backward and forward, round and round, tracing indescribable combinations of vertical and horizontal curves, while I clung with muscles firm braced, like a bobolink on a reed." If this seems a characteristic thing for Muir to have done, so does his account of it seem characteristic of his writing. He has no dead levels of narrative or description. He is precise to the verge of wit, as in his note on the voice of the Douglas squirrel: "His musical, piney gossip is savory to the ear as balsam to the palate; and though he has not exactly the gift of song, some of his notes are sweet as those of a linnet—almost flute-like in softness; while others prick and tingle like thistles." More often, however, Muir strikes the note of rapture and so lifts himself above dullness. In any but a traveler of extraordinary fire and passion, this rapture could have become now and then mere sentimentalism. With Muir it never does. He takes his readers actually with him to his peaks, as when he says: "Come with me along the glaciers and see God making landscapes."

Howe
1854–1937
Another writer of the period, like Muir, was late in making his full influence felt, but not because he wrote of wild nature or wrote rapturously. Edgar Watson Howe was the persistent upholder of the common life, the convinced defender of common sense against all idealisms. He began his career with a novel, "The Story of a Country Town" (1883), a full generation back. The powerful story of a prairie Othello, it incidentally accused the Kansas village in which its scene was laid of practising the vices of idleness and wastefulness and intemperance and stupidity, and this at a time when most rural novelists inclined to the idyllic. Later, Howe made himself the apologist of the virtues of industry and frugality and temperance and contentment. These, of course, he did not regard as minor virtues, since they seemed to him to be involved in the essential facts of human life. "Those facts

are, in brief, that a man would rather live than die; that he keeps himself alive by work; that he works best when he is working for himself; that the best society is that in which the most men work best." Why, if these things are true, do men act as if they were ashamed to admit them and prefer to talk about the vaguer aspirations of the higher life? The evidences contradict such talk. "In theory," says Howe, "it is not respectable to be rich. In fact, poverty is a disgrace." Somebody, he believes, should have the courage of his convictions and stand up for prudence, no matter what the idealists claim.

Such doctrines might have made Howe blind to beauty and tenderness and heroism if he were less humane. As it is, they did little more than make him wittily sensible, within his range, in his comments upon the behavior of mankind. "The Anthology of Another Town" (1920), which at once continues the subject of his own first book and answers Edgar Lee Masters's "Spoon River Anthology," may be said to belong to fiction rather than to comment. Its stories of men and women, however, are told hardly so much for themselves as for the ideas they illustrate. Howe is simply a wise observer letting his memory run through the history of the town and proving that life can be simple, that people do not need to be tortured with complicated problems. With humor and irony, he strips away the mists in which so many human actions and motives are wrapped. The way to arrive at some understanding of humanity, he hints, is not to look at it as it seems to be behaving at some remote point. It must be studied in the examples actually under the student's eye. Before learning about man, it is first essential to learn as much as possible about men.

Howe contrived to irritate a great many readers who do not like to use their naked eyes as much as he does. Optimists took so little comfort from him that they charged him with being sour and harsh. A more accurate charge would have been that he moved about, intellectually, within limits past which his imagination was not sufficient to carry him. That, however, is true of all but the greatest minds. Howe's limits must be taken into account. He lived in the tradition of the old-fashioned America, not in the tradition of a cosmopolitan culture. But within his limits, he is master, and he is so astute that persons of his disposition everywhere are likely to agree with him. Moreover, he has remarkable gifts in the art of making statements with edge and clarity. His "Ventures in Common Sense" (1919) is not a treatise, or even a group of essays, but a collection of aphorisms upon the homely qualities of life, all of them taken from the monthly magazine which he wrote himself on his Kansas farm. Few men have written more pungently than he does in such sentences as these : "The people are always worsted in an election"; "The long and the short of it is, whoever catches the fool first is entitled to shear him"; "Poets are prophets whose prophesying never comes true"; "A loafer never works except when there is a fire ; then he will carry out more furniture than anybody"; "With women, men are the enemy; I suppose they abuse them as a nation abuses a people with whom it is at war, with old stories told in other wars"; "There are no mysteries. Where does the wind come from? It doesn't matter : we know the habits of the wind after it arrives." Wisdom as hard and sharp as this defies contradiction and resists time.

Neither a passion for external nature nor a loyalty to blunt prudence characterizes Henry Adams, but a boundless intellectual curiosity and a profound culture. Belonging to a family which has been, on the whole, the most eminent family in the United States, he was one of a group of three brothers who in the latter part of the nineteenth century set out to question the legends which had grown up about certain phases of the national past and who may be said to have initiated the period of

**Adams
1838–1918**

self-criticism through which the country has been passing
since then. As teacher, editor, novelist, and historian, Henry
Adams felt that he had failed because he had had no considerable visible influence upon his age, and so settled down
in Washington as a kind of anonymous adviser to statesmen. Not until the twentieth century did he publish the two
works by which he is chiefly known and which are among
the most impressive and distinguished of American books.

"Mont St. Michel and Chartres" (1904) and "The Education of Henry Adams" (1906), great as they are in themselves, were conceived by Adams only as parts of a still
vaster work which, if any man could complete it, would
constitute a history of human energy. Adams had become
more and more dissatisfied with the modern world as he
saw it, and it is against the background of this dissatisfac-
tion that his two masterpieces must be studied.

Adams's discontent with the generations through which
he happened to live grew out of his failure—for which he
did not blame himself—to discover any single meaning in
their multiplex activities. As student, as diplomat, as traveler, as book-reviewer, as professor, as historian, as novelist, as philosopher, he had observed the world in more phases
than most persons are permitted to observe it in, and the
conviction had grown upon him that there was no formula
by which it might be summed up; there was no purpose, no
faith, no ideal, no illusion even, holding it together. At any
given moment the life of man will seem complex and confusing enough to an imaginative man, and Adams was by
no means the first of his kind in the history of thought.
Indeed, his particular complaint is a common one to-day, as
it was throughout the nineteenth century. But few men
have been so profoundly concerned as Adams was, and few
have pursued their researches into the infinite data of history with as much learning and patience and humor—for he
was richly endowed with the faculty of irony. It happened

that at Harvard he had been professor of medieval history, and it was in the course of his medieval studies that he became acutely aware of an age long past when society had been welded into an intellectual and emotional unity of the sort he would have liked to find informing his own age. This was the age of religious faith in Europe whose monument now is the series of beautiful and great cathedrals extending from England to Italy. Although Adams was in no orthodox way a religious man himself, he yet was in tendency a mystic, and his mind leaped at once to embrace a time when so far as he could see all men thought and felt alike. He decided, then, to write two books, one on the age of faith and one on the age of unfaith, which should serve as points to mark the direction which future history, either his own or somebody else's, would have to take.

"Mont St. Michel and Chartres" took its name from two cathedrals in France which Adams, quite characteristically, selected as symbols of the century which produced them. The book, however, is more than a description of two buildings—though among other things it is that. It is in effect an examination into the soul of the twelfth and thirteenth centuries as it expressed itself in architecture, art, literature, and theology. And it is a glorification in particular of a civilization which could attain an "intensity of conviction never again reached by any passion, whether of religion, of loyalty, of patriotism, or of wealth; perhaps never even paralleled by any single economic effort, except in war." Were it not, he says, that "the feebleness of our fancy is now congenital, organic, beyond stimulant or strychnine, and we shrink like sensitive-plants from the touch of a vision or spirit," we should have no difficulty in conceiving the Virgin, for instance, as what she was once, an object of worship. Not that Adams was asking for the artificial restoration of a dead faith; he simply was recording his perception that over several centuries man—not through his own fault, either—had lost unity. As an impartial historian Adams was bound to conclude that unity had "turned itself into complexity, multiplicity, variety, and even contradiction. All experience, human and divine, assured man in the thirteenth century that the lines of the universe converged. How was he to know that these lines ran in every conceivable and inconceivable direction?"

In the "Education," under the guise of an autobiography, Adams offered a picture of the modern world across which the lines of life "ran in every conceivable and inconceivable direction." The book is profoundly pessimistic, and the pessimism is all the more impressive because the author seems to know so well what he is talking about. The subject-matter is always his own experience, but the implication is that this experience must be typical. Adams represents himself as seeking in politics, in society, in universities, and in the industrial world a clue to the meaning of contemporary existence, and never finding it. The politicians, both abroad in the embassies and at home in Washington, could not prove to his satisfaction that they knew what they were doing or why they were doing it; society was decidedly ill at ease under his scrutiny; in the universities the teaching of such a subject as history was chaotic; in the world of machines there was visible power—witness the great dynamos exhibited at Chicago and Paris—but power without direction or significance. In the end Adams could only despair; standing quietly to one side, he could only sketch the history of a vast decay the cause for which neither he nor any one else might understand. His life, passed in a questioning age, concluded with a question so large that it may never receive an answer so long as there are men concerned to consider it.

Santayana 1863– The same period which produced Henry Adams produced George Santayana, who more systematically, if less picturesquely, studied the entire problem with which mankind is faced. At first a poet [1] and a critic of the arts, he later extended his inquiries. The world, he saw, was full of tumbled ideas about which no one could be sure that they were true, and of tangled instincts of which no one could be sure that they were authentic. Man seemed to be an animal who had raised himself a long way from his earlier status, but who still had in himself old passions and prejudices which had never been civilized. If he was to go further, he must review his course and learn in what directions and by what methods he had advanced. Santayana therefore undertook to write the epic of the human mind, from its first dim moments of independent consciousness to its eventual moments of pure, detached intelligence. He saw his epic as a kind of tragicomedy, through which man struggled against heavy odds and many defeats to what it was hoped would be a happy ending. This epic tragicomedy, which appeared in five volumes, is called as a whole "The Life of Reason" (1905), and is one of the memorable books of the age.

The book, though beautifully written, is difficult reading for most laymen, because Santayana had to take a great many things into account in his record. He could not make it a mere melodrama. However clearly he himself might see the thread of his plot, he could no more do justice to it by a simple poetic narrative than a botanist could do justice to a field of flowers by describing his sentiments about it without mentioning a single flower by name or distinguishing accurately among the odors and colors to be noted in it. A philosopher, like a botanist, has to be analytical and precise. Santayana had consequently to make his work as exact as a treatise. At the same time, since he was dealing with matters about which the imagination must be drawn upon for some of the evidence, he was obliged to make his work, in a

[1] For his poetry, see pages 5–6.

sense, a poem. The natural result has been that certain of the experts have found "The Life of Reason" too poetic for their taste, and certain of the amateurs have found it too scientific. This is regrettable, for the outline of history which the book presents is profound, shrewd, stirring, and lovely. Going back to the Greeks, and disregarding most of the systems of thought which have flourished since Aristotle, Santayana proceeds on the assumption that "everything ideal has a natural basis and everything natural an ideal development." Human life, as he sees it, exhibits human nature in pursuit of ideal desires. By and during the pursuit the brute impulse toward reproduction is turned into tender love, blind industry is turned into creative art, tribal gregariousness is turned into enlightened society. This much he studies in his first two volumes, "Reason in Common Sense" and "Reason in Society." In "Reason in Religion," "Reason in Art," and "Reason in Science" he studies what he considers the three principal elements of the ideal life. Religion is the quest of good; art is the effort to embody beauty; science is the method by which the turmoil of facts is reduced to meaning.

Santayana has since protested that he never meant his epic to imply that the pursuit of the ideal is a constant element in mankind, and bound to prosper. He thought that some aspirations have been reasonable and some have been mad. Indeed, he wrote occasionally as if he were an ambassador to the American barbarians, sent from the Mediterranean to point out to them the tradition of Greek freedom and Roman pride and Catholic patience. Many American traits he did not like; to some he was blind. Perhaps, however, a certain narrowness in his conception helped him to be more bold and positive than he would otherwise have been, and thus helped him to carry out his noble design without hesitating too long over the details. Undoubtedly he came after the World War to question whether the life of reason is not a much more sporadic thing than he had once believed, and to wonder whether he might not as well have called his book "The Romance of Wisdom." The new system of philosophy which he has begun to expound since the war takes into account many elemental instincts which he would once have dismissed as too remote from the reasonable to be included in his record.

It is almost certain that the American chapter of Santayana's career, signalized by "The Life of Reason," is closed, but it is still too early to estimate the work upon which he is now engaged. As a citizen of the world he has written some of the most penetrating and beautiful commentaries which have ever been written upon the United States. In "Soliloquies in England" (1923), the fruit of his residence in Oxford during the war, he has come nearer than elsewhere in his work to the concerns of daily life. Though he would like best to have been born in ancient Greece, he found in England a kind of modern compensation. "What I love in Greece and England is contentment in finitude, fair outward ways, manly perfection and simplicity." Greece failing him, he felt for a time in England able to live comfortably in the broad stream of the life of reason. Thus at ease, he turned his eyes upon the outward ways of the island and produced the charming book which first made the general public aware how eminent and witty an essayist he could be in his lighter hours. He who had been recognized as the best stylist among the philosophers turned out to be the best philosopher among the stylists. And his reputation steadily increases, now that he lives in Paris. America did not please him, and he cannot be called a representative of its national spirit; but in America he nevertheless became a poet and a philosopher. And it was America at a certain stage of her emotional development that he remembered in the novel, "The Last Puritan," with which he became a popular author for the first time in 1936.

The Younger Generation The second decade of the twentieth century, which saw the beginnings of a new activity in poetry, fiction, and the drama, saw the rise of what came to be known as the Younger Generation. The term was always vaguely applied. No group had taken it as its official name, and yet something fairly definite was meant by it. Strictly speaking, of course, every new generation is younger than its predecessor, and is more or less in revolt against it. But the Younger Generation seemed to its elders to have a concerted policy of revolt. In a sense it did, though there had been no deliberate conspiracy. Ever since the end of the past century a numerous body of critics had been accusing the nation of arrogance and complacency, supineness and corruption, in public and in private life. So long as the elder generation, however, had the reins in its hand, it could claim that it was doing as much as could be done. The war, with its terrific disorder, served to discredit, in part unjustly, these who were in power. No one, even boys and girls perceived, could have done worse. Consequently they had a better excuse than ever for demanding that they be allowed a larger freedom. Perhaps they did not so much take this freedom as talk about it. The difference was considerably a difference in candor. At any rate, youth found a voice such as it had never had in the United States before. Rebellion began to be regarded not as wild oats but as heroism. Moreover, it was rationalized by persons of notable intelligence. In this the younger writers took the lead. There had actually been an interregnum in the national literature, presided over by remote or mediocre or timid spirits who all of a sudden seemed hopelessly ineffectual. No wonder they were jostled aside by the more brilliant and outspoken poets and novelists and dramatists and essayists who succeeded them.

**Bourne
1886–1918**
Perhaps the first influential leader of the new movement was Randolph Bourne, whose "Youth and Life" (1913) raised a standard about which numerous followers rallied, disagreeing often in detail but agreeing in the main principle. Bourne, born in New Jersey, attracted national attention while he was still in college by the smooth maturity of his style and the challenging boldness of his ideas. He held that men get most of their ideas in their youth, that they feel most vividly and live most experimentally then, and that therefore youth ought not to be so dominated as it is by age, which may be merely presuming upon a greater quantity of experience, whereas only a finer quality could warrant such a domination. He saw youth as the creative ferment of life, as the element which pours into life the strength and courage by which it is enabled to move. Consistently with this, Bourne saw human existence as a sort of drama in which hopeful youth is pitted against cynical age. Being very young, he gave his sympathies unmistakably to youth's side; but he was too mature to be satisfied with the wild gestures of rebellion. He formed the conception of a league of youth, which should bring together into united effort the many impulses of discontent which he saw stirring all about him. That league, he hoped, would overcome inertia and eliminate waste and waken aspiration and set originality free and increase diversity and in the end arrive at a more fruitful order of life.

In another age his doctrine might have been dismissed as utopian. As it was, the war in Europe gave an unanticipated emphasis to the program which he advanced. The old order was obviously breaking down. The question rose whether it would not have to be rebuilt by some such guild of the future as he had thought about. His premature death, and his unpopularity during the war which he never approved or excused, cost him much of the credit which he probably deserves. Others expounded his ideas and carried on his revolt. "Untimely Papers" (1919) and "The Evolution of a Literary Radical" (1920) were published posthumously. Already he is more or less a legend to many persons who have not even opened his books and do not know that they contain all the germs of the new spirit. But even a casual examination will prove that those germs are there. Touchingly prophetic, Bourne felt the coming struggle before it had become evident to less subtle observers. During his brief, vivid life he managed to utter some significant reflection upon almost every topic which vitally concerns the age. He wrote of religion, the state, property, the arts, education. This last especially interested him. He believed that education was the key to the great change which he guessed to be imminent. In particular, he was interested in American education, for though he was often abused as unpatriotic, he was full of that higher patriotism which leads a citizen of a country to insist upon talking about its ultimate good when the majority is too full of the country's immediate problems to take long views. Bourne studied the traditional culture of America with an acid scrutiny, but so did he look eagerly for all the signs that a fresh, genuine culture was rising upon the ruins of the Americanized Europeanism which had prevailed in the United States ever since its colonial days. Uncompromising as he was in his scorn of whatever seemed to him dead, he was equally uncompromising in his demand that whatever seemed to him alive be allowed to live with as little hindrance as possible. The fragmentary nature of his surviving work should blind no one to the essential unity which it had as well as the penetration and charm which explained at the time its power over other spirits.

Brooks
1886–
Born in the same year with Bourne, and in the same State, Van Wyck Brooks shared his insights and in fact anticipated some of them.

Brooks's fifth book, "America's Coming-of-Age" (1915), was not an announcement of our maturity, as the title might indicate, but an analysis of our society in the light of a conviction that maturity had not yet come. Another volume, "Letters and Leadership" (1918), continued the analysis unsparingly; and two works on nineteenth-century literary figures, "The Ordeal of Mark Twain" (1920) and "The Pilgrimage of Henry James" (1925), studied in historical perspective the inadequacies of American culture—the stiffness, the ignorance, the frontier narrowness, and the lack of grace. If Brooks was sometimes humorless in these studies, particularly in that of Mark Twain, he nevertheless was often right; and in the book on James he invented an excellent method of presenting his material, for he assembled it out of James himself, skilfully drawing out his author to express his predicament as only he had known it. He repeated the method in his "Life of Emerson" (1932), though now a new note had crept into his criticism. Emerson was treated with unqualified admiration as a representative of the first and for Brooks the last integral culture America has had. Brooks's writing became warmer and finer, though it had been fine before; and he was now ready to commence the history of American literature of which the first volume appeared in 1936 as "The Flowering of New England (1815–1865)." This is his most popular and in many respects his best book. It is filled with an infectious enthusiasm for New England life and letters before the Civil War; it is rich in details and sensitive in the arrangement of these; and again it employs the method of direct quotation for the purpose of bringing the subject close to the reader. From having been America's most surgeon-like critic he has become the best admirer of America's best spirits, and "The Flowering of New England" promises to stand for a long time as an expression of the national ideal.

Compared with Bourne and Brooks, Henry
Mencken Louis Mencken seems rough and violent. He is
1880– essentially a satirist, bent upon destroying cant
and ridiculing stupidity and assailing dogmatism wherever
he finds them. A native of Maryland, where he still lives,
he has held himself not only outside of literary cliques but
outside of the Anglo-Saxon traditions of Boston and New
York, an uproarious Ishmael of letters. His early studies
were in Shaw and Ibsen and Nietzsche, whom he labored
to make more widely known in America. Like those men
in their various countries, Mencken found life around him
tame and sentimental, and he undertook to sting it into
activity and sense. Being in several respects an excellent
scholar, he worked for years upon a bulky treatise, "The
American Language" (1919), in which he argued that the
common speech of the United States is very different from
the classic idiom inherited from England, and implied that
American literature must consequently be as different from
the English classics which it has often been satisfied to
imitate. Primarily, however, Mencken has been a journalist, not saving up his utterances for systematic books but
flinging them off in newspapers and magazines, keeping up
a running commentary upon the news, and pointing a
satiric finger at all the follies which have come within the
range of his immense curiosity. With George Jean Nathan
he has compiled "The American Credo" (1920), which
lists nearly a thousand vulgar beliefs which his countrymen, he maintains, generally hold. Above all, in the six
series of his "Prejudices" (1919–1927) he has played the
stream of his comedy upon the age with a variety and gusto
unmatched among his contemporaries.

What first strikes the readers of Mencken is his seeming impudence. He dares, indeed he delights, to ridicule the
most respected figures. He sees nothing sacred in presidents

or bishops or magnates, but mercilessly makes game of them whenever they furnish him the opportunity by being pompous or affected or dull. Furthermore, he does not respect the common run of men any more than he does their leaders. He sees them as full of stupidity and, what is worse, full of pretenses. He bursts into laughter at the platitudes they like to hear, at the cheap books and plays and newspapers they enjoy, at the tawdry ritual of their clubs and societies, at their superstitions and their enthusiasms. The idea of democracy seems to him a dogma which can hardly be accepted by any enlightened mind. In the place of kings, he thinks, democracy has raised up demagogues; in the place of experts, it has raised up charlatans. For all demagogues and charlatans he reserves his most vigorous contempt. Above all things Mencken admires knowledge, expertness, courage, independence. When he sees these traits at a disadvantage in a community because the majority does not have them and is in fact afraid of them, he is filled with rage that true excellence should thus be submerged. Quantity does not make up to him for lack of quality. And if it irks him to see the race led by men who are not really superior, it irks him still more to see the superior members of society obliged to live unknown unless they are willing to pretend agreement with popular prejudices. He himself does not pretend. He speaks out continually in behalf of excellence and intelligence. His disposition, however, inclines him away from tragic attitudes. He is a comic prophet. Instead of shedding philosophic tears over his age, he points an ironic finger and shouts with mirth.

It must not be forgotten that critics of much the same disposition have existed in every American generation, protesting against the tyranny of the majority and demanding that minorities be given a hearing. Mencken thus continues a line already established in the native tradition. Outside of America, it may be suspected, he would be lost. He enjoys the spectacle of the swarming republic, and has never been tempted to escape from it to different lands. Moreover, he writes in the idiom of his country, not in the smooth international idiom employed by many of his bitterest antagonists. He is racy and daring; he indulges himself to the limit in the native habit of hilarious exaggeration; he is as definitely a product of American culture as Mark Twain. As a historian or as a critic of his age he leaves a good deal to be desired, and an increasing awareness of this has at last diminished his audience. But it remains true that comedy has rights which may not be taken from it. Without it, institutions come to regard themselves too seriously, and habits of thinking and feeling settle into a slavish routine. Comedy by its irreverence brings them to judgment. Those things which cannot endure laughter generally deserve to perish. Those which can survive it are generally better off for having been tested by its gay assaults. In any case, the existence of comedy is proof that the minds of men are not struggling for mere survival, but still have the superfluous strength which enables them to play lightly over the surface of their fates.

In his later days it is the scholar in Mencken who has been most active, producing books of a solidity which his once great popular audience would scarcely have been prepared to recognize. "The American Language" has been revised three times since 1919, the fourth edition in 1936 being not only a much larger but a much better book. The first edition was impressive and influential, but the work has now become standard. The same compliment cannot be paid the contributions which Mencken has made to political theory in "Notes on Democracy" (1926), to comparative religion in "Treatise on the Gods" (1930), and to ethical speculation in "Treatise on Right and Wrong." Yet these books are more sensible than many on their respective subjects, and they are orderly examinations of relevant facts and ideas.

**Krutch
1893–**

With the passage of time and with the rise of new talents Mencken lost some of his excuse for satire, at least in the tone he tended to maintain. A different sort of audience altogether greeted Joseph Wood Krutch's "The Modern Temper" in 1929—an audience equipped to think, and an audience familiar with current ideas. Krutch was interested neither in American intellectual manners nor in the diverting spectacle of man at work and play. The essays which made up his book were metaphysical, at least to the extent that they considered in general terms the ground and genesis of contemporary mental attitudes, American or otherwise. They were also historical, for the development he traced was from the optimism of the Renaissance, when man first became free to think about himself, to the present when his thoughts about himself seem not to be giving him pleasure. In science, literature, psychology, and ethics Krutch traced a trend toward despair which seemed in his view already to have reached bottom. The chapter which provoked most discussion was perhaps "The Tragic Fallacy," where he explained the decline of tragedy not in literary but in intellectual and social terms; tragedy is possible, he said, only when man is believed to be great, and now that man despises himself it has become impossible. "The Modern Temper" was widely praised and as widely deplored; but the point is that there was an audience ready for its brilliant analyses and its sober periods. Krutch has made contributions to other fields of criticism, literary, dramatic, and political, and "The Modern Temper" is by no means his only significant book. It is the one most germane to the present chronicle, however, and it still stands as a symbol not only of its decade but of American capacity for really serious reflection.

Peattie 1898–   An important tradition in American letters was revived in 1935 by Donald Culross Peattie's "An Almanac for Moderns." This tradition was established by William Bartram and Henry David Thoreau, and was carried on by John Burroughs and John Muir. It is the tradition of "nature-writing," and as the form of its expression changes with each generation, so a change has come in with Peattie. His "Almanac" is, as its name suggests, a survey of the natural happenings of a year; there are three hundred and sixty-five short essays on a great range of pertinent themes. Sometimes the subject is the coming of a bird back from its winter home; sometimes it is a plague of seventeen-year locusts; sometimes it is the swarming of elementary life in pond waters; and sometimes it is the birthday of a great naturalist—Thoreau himself, or perhaps Linnaeus the great Swedish botanist, Peattie's hero among all naturalists. But always the point of view is modern. Nature has ceased to be a personal or benevolent deity; it is life in any of its pressing forms, whether seen under a microscope as it prepares to attack a rival form of life, perhaps the human race, or seen in the great sky at night. The dimensions of the universe have enormously increased since nature-writing first became popular, and man occupies a less cozy nest than he once did. Peattie writes in steady consciousness of this, and yet without panic or despair. The world for him is still beautiful and exciting, and his book says so by its very style, which is brilliantly concise and suggestive. In 1937 he followed the "Almanac" with "A Book of Hours," which has twenty-four chapters for the hours of the day. Again Peattie revealed a vast range of knowledge and feeling; and again he proved himself one of the most attractive of contemporary prose writers in the English language. He has written a number of other books, but these two most conveniently represent his special usefulness and his special talent.

Eliot
1888–

The prose of T. S. Eliot has been as influential as his poetry.[1] It has taken the form of literary criticism, but the term literary criticism should be conceived here in its broadest aspect, as he has conceived it. In certain respects he has carried on the tradition of Matthew Arnold in England, for Arnold was much more than a mere judge of literature. He was a judge of manners and thoughts as well, and rightly considered that his function had something to do with furthering the cause of civilization. Eliot's "The Sacred Wood" (1921) was an unusual volume of critical essays in that much of its space was devoted to the questions, what is criticism for, and what kind of person is the best critic? He suggested that criticism is the art which keeps us aware of the highest standards that have ever been stated, whether now or in the past; and that the more critics we have the more familiar with these standards we shall be, even though most critics will be second-rate and do no more than keep a "current of ideas" somehow flowing. Eliot himself went on in "The Sacred Wood" to examine a few authors— Blake, Dante, Marlowe, Shakspere, and others—in the largest possible perspective; and in his later volumes he has never abandoned that perspective. His "Selected Essays" of 1932 has been an education for many readers, not only in literary matters but in literary manners and a point of view. Having a long perspective and being interested only in excellence, Eliot can write in a style devoid of flourishes, special appeals, and suppressed poetry. He seems dry and cold at first, but further reading reveals in him the passion which consists with seriousness, good faith, and a

[1] For his poetry, see pages 48–49.

love of the best things for their own sakes. He seems already to have made a place for himself among the permanently readable literary critics.

PART TWO

ENGLISH LITERATURE

CHAPTER I

POETRY

WITH the death of Tennyson in 1892 there passed a great generation of English poets whom it is the custom to call Victorian, because their careers were spanned by the reign of Queen Victoria. Their number included Browning and Rossetti, who already were dead, and Swinburne and Morris, who had ceased to write poetry. But these four were not so distinctly outlived in 1892 as Tennyson seemed in certain minds to be. The new generation of poets —the poets of the eighteen-nineties—were not so much inclined to reject the rugged realism of Browning, the estheticism of Rossetti, or the Greek and medieval programs of Swinburne and Morris as they were to turn their backs upon the purely English qualities of Tennyson. Tennyson, because his poetry for years had seemed an expression and a defense of comfortable, middle-class sentiment, was taken as the perfect type of the thing known for various reasons as Victorianism, and it was from his example that the younger poets consciously or unconsciously revolted.

The Eighteen-Nineties The last decade of the century was marked by intense intellectual activity, not only in poetry but in art and philosophy. Many new reputations were made as it were overnight; the restlessness of the time was equaled only by its fertility and its originality. Most of the experiments in poetry, being alien to native tradition, were not popular in the sense that Tennyson had been popular. French ideas and forms of verse were eagerly cultivated, and old-fashioned readers complained that no

one was left to speak to or for them. The reproachful terms
"decadent" and "fin-de-siècle" (end-of-the-century)—both
derived from France—were hurled at the new generation
by those who believed that the nineteenth century had already spent its force. It is true that no poet of Tennyson's
dimensions had arisen to take his place. The phrase "minor
poet" came properly into currency because there were so
many versifiers of slight though real genius. Yet, looked at
from this distance, the eighteen-nineties were by no means
decadent in the sense that they betrayed a diminution of
power. The typical spokesmen of the decade were sophisticated, exquisite, and perhaps affected, but they were
strong in that they broke the ground for the poetry that
was to come after them in all its vigor and variety.

Wilde
1856–1900

The name "decadent" was more specifically
and perhaps more justly given to a group of
effete and exotic poets who were bent upon destroying as swiftly and as insolently as they could the old
proprieties which they considered hostile to the free spirit
of their art. They set themselves resolutely against popular
sentiment, determined to live their own lives and write only
to please themselves. In the face of the contempt of a
majority of English readers, they continued in their chosen
course, and though their careers in some cases ended unhappily, they succeeded in writing poetry which by its
beauty and intensity will long outlive the memory of their
lives. Oscar Wilde, their most conspicuous member, was
greater as a dramatist [1] and a wit than as a poet, but he is
the most famous of the poets who embraced the doctrine
of "art for art's sake" and seriously cultivated their own
temperaments in disregard of what ordinary people might
think or say; and he was the author of "The Ballad of
Reading Gaol," one of the best-known poems produced in
his generation. Abhorring the simple and the natural, he

[1] For his plays, see pages 245–249.

urged his contemporaries to experiment with new sensations and to study art instead of nature. "Nature imitates Art far more than Art imitates Nature," he said. But curiously enough his best poem is a simple and pathetic commentary upon human nature. A term of imprisonment which he served toward the close of his life was the inspiration for "The Ballad of Reading Gaol," in the true and unaffected stanzas of which he paid a touching tribute to a fellow-unfortunate.

> I never saw a man who looked
>   With such a wistful eye
> Upon that little tent of blue
>   Which prisoners call the sky,
> And at every drifting cloud that went
>   With sails of silver by.

Dowson
1867–1900

Ernest Dowson, like the rest of the "decadents," spent the whole of his literary life in London, drinking bitterly of the experience which was to be had among the less fortunate inhabitants of that complex city. He derived his sophistication not so much from an esthetic creed as from his own poverty, disease, and dissipation, which, though they alternated with happier moments, finally prevailed and brought about his death. The total bulk of his poetry is small, and even of that only a small portion is now much read; but this portion belongs with the most tuneful of all English verse. Dowson, perhaps because of the incessant pain which he bore, was a person of singularly clear spirit; and as an artist he was master not only of meter but of the plaintive note which he was so well able to sing. His best-known poem, "Cynara," expresses in perfect music the longing he felt for a return to a simpler and more innocent existence than that which the streets and cafés of London made possible. It might be taken as the cry of a whole generation who had suddenly thirsted for a new life but who had drunk too eagerly at the beginning.

> Last night, ah, yesternight, betwixt her lips and mine
> There fell thy shadow, Cynara! thy breath was shed
> Upon my soul between the kisses and the wine;
> And I was desolate and sick of an old passion,
>   Yea, I was desolate and bowed my head:
> I have been faithful to thee, Cynara! in my fashion.

Catholic Poets   Far removed from all the rest were two Roman Catholic poets, Francis Thompson and Alice Meynell, who continued a rare friendship as long as both of them were alive. Unlike as they were in temperament and expression, in intensity of religious experience they were equals. Thompson was always oppressed by poverty and disease, so that most of his work was done in physical as well as intellectual misery. The finest of his simpler poems, "Daisy," closes with the stanza:

> Nothing begins, and nothing ends,
>   That is not paid with moan;
> For we are born in other's pain,
>   And perish in our own.

He wrote some songs of love and nature, but his most characteristic work was done in elaborate and mystical odes, the language of which, since it had so much that was difficult to express, is often very involved. In "The Hound of Heaven" he records his mystical experience with God, whom he represents as pursuing him forever until he submitted and became one with Him. The first stanza contains some of the most ambitious lines in English poetry:

> I fled Him, down the nights and down the days;
> I fled Him, down the arches of the years;
> I fled Him, down the labyrinthine ways
> Of my own mind; and in the mist of tears
> I hid from Him, and under running laughter.
>   Up vistaed hopes I sped;

And shot, precipitated
Adown Titanic glooms of chasmèd fears,
From those strong Feet that followed, followed after.
But with unhurrying chase,
And unperturbèd pace,
Deliberate speed, majestic instancy,
They beat—and a Voice beat
More instant than the Feet—
"All things betray thee, who betrayest Me."

The career of Alice Meynell was more peaceful, and this peace is reflected in her singularly pure and perfect poems. In her best piece, "The Shepherdess," the chasteness of her spirit and the delicacy of her art can most easily be studied:

She walks—the lady of my delight—
A shepherdess of sheep.
Her flocks are thoughts. She keeps them white;
She guards them from the steep;
She feeds them on the fragrant height,
And folds them in for sleep.

**Kipling
1865–1936**
While poets like these were exercising their brilliant though narrow talents, other and larger voices began to be heard from without. From far-away India as early as 1886 a young Englishman by the name of Rudyard Kipling had sent to London a volume of "Departmental Ditties," and that volume had taken the country by storm. In 1892 he sent "Barrack Room Ballads," which multiplied his vogue, and he continued for two or three decades to be the most popular of living English poets.

The causes for his popularity were numerous. In the first place, he blew like a fresh and distant breeze upon a public which had had only refined and philosophical poetry to occupy itself with—poetry which demanded the subtlest faculties for its appreciation. This poetry had been the product of a highly experienced and rather weary age, and it was essentially aristocratic in tone. It concerned itself with artists and mystics, with precious and pessimistic souls. Kipling came along with his hardy, practical songs about common men and common deeds. He wrote a language which everybody used. He was not ashamed of slang; he liked to mention ugly, familiar objects. And whereas the poets at home had experimented with fine and difficult rhythms, he was content with a bold mechanical singsong which could escape nobody. He was not over the average person's head, and he went with the current of everybody's blood.

Another reason for his immediate acceptance by the public was that he offered himself at a time when the spirit of imperialism was growing rapidly and many people were eager to know more about the Queen's dominions beyond the sea. Kipling, as the titles of his first two books indicate, came with tales of soldiers in foreign service, and by 1900 he had given complete expression to the martial temperament. He was proud to be writing of strong men for "a sheltered people." "Fuzzy-Wuzzy" and "Gunga Din" were tributes paid to two heathen soldiers in spite of the fact that one of them was an enemy and the other only a ragged water-carrier. And there were many other aspects of soldier life which Kipling could treat. There was the rough humor of the practical joke; and there was the melancholy of men who, content as they might be to serve the queen in India or Africa, often thought with stoic sorrow of their exile from home.

Even the spirit of imperialism, of which Kipling is often called the poet laureate, he presented on its darker as well as its brighter side. "The White Man's Burden" was a reminder that the business of controlling alien populations may be sad and difficult, and "Recessional," in 1897, was a powerful rebuke to those who took England's responsibilities as a guardian lightly, or who assumed too readily that supremacy must always be hers.

God of our fathers, known of old,
  Lord of our far-flung battle-line,
Beneath whose awful Hand we hold
  Dominion over palm and pine—
Lord God of Hosts, be with us yet,
Lest we forget—lest we forget!

The tumult and the shouting dies;
  The Captains and the Kings depart:
Still stands Thine ancient sacrifice,
  An humble and a contrite heart.
Lord God of Hosts, be with us yet,
Lest we forget—lest we forget!

Far-called, our navies melt away;
  On dune and headland sinks the fire:
Lo, all our pomp of yesterday
  Is one with Nineveh and Tyre!
Judge of the Nations, spare us yet,
Lest we forget—lest we forget!

If, drunk with sight of power, we loose
  Wild tongues that have not Thee in awe,
Such boastings as the Gentiles use,
  Or lesser breeds without the Law—
Lord God of Hosts, be with us yet,
Lest we forget—lest we forget!

For heathen heart that puts her trust
  In reeking tube and iron shard,
All valiant dust that builds on dust,
  And guarding, calls not Thee to guard,
For frantic boast and foolish word—
Thy mercy on Thy people, Lord!

The final reason for Kipling's fame, outside of England
as well as there, was that his sentiment and his "philosophy"
made a broad and obvious appeal. Americans might not
be capable of caring very much about England's part in
the Indian Mutinies, the Boer War, or the World War—
all of which Kipling celebrated—but they were only too

ready to respond to a maudlin poem like "Mother o' Mine"; and the majority of people everywhere agreed with the opinions expressed in argumentative pieces like "The Conundrum of the Workshops," wherein the popular attitude toward art was defended. The severe critics say that Kipling is a vulgar poet who will cease to be read when the issues he treats are no longer important, and when the more superficial of current emotions are dead. This for the most part is true. Many lesser-known poets will outlive him because they are subtler and profounder. But it will never be possible to deny his tremendous personal force.[1]

Housman
1859–1936

In 1896, just ten years after the appearance of Kipling, another and very different poet appeared who was recognized at once as a classic. A. E. Housman's "A Shropshire Lad" contained only sixty-three short poems, and for twenty-six years the public had nothing else from his pen. In 1922, however, came forty-one "Last Poems" which followed the others as naturally as if all had been written together; in 1936, the year of his death, "More Poems" were published by his brother Laurence; and now that their author's whole mind has been offered to the world, he can be discussed as if he actually were a classic.

Housman is indeed as firmly established as he would be if his books had been written in Greece or Rome. His subjects are often the same melancholy ones that occupied the other poets of the eighteen-nineties—the shortness of life, the frailty of beauty, the cruelty of time—but he stands detached from his period because of his invariable excellence and because of the timelessness of his style. His poems also are pastorals—concerned with lanes and brooks and lads and lasses; while there is much unhappiness in his voice, it is a calm, clear voice, and there is no trace of the mod-

[1] For his prose fiction, see pages 197–201.

ern fret which is heard in the works of his metropolitan contemporaries. His landscape and his mood are universal, as those of the ancient Greek lyric poets were universal; and this is not altogether an accident in view of the fact that he was a classical scholar, a well-known professor at the University of Cambridge, most of whose time was spent in editing and examining the great literature of the past.

Housman's style is so light and sure, and his stanzas are so perfectly finished, that a reader is likely at first to miss the meaning and the passion behind them. There is a great deal of both meaning and passion. The poet's consciousness of the ravages which time makes in youth and love has brought an ache into his soul which does more than inspire a commonplace complaint. It is almost intolerable for him to think of the friends he once had, or the places he once dwelt in; but he must write about them because the memory of them presses upon him continually.

> With rue my heart is laden
> For golden friends I had,
> For many a rose-lipt maiden
> And many a lightfoot lad.
>
> By brooks too broad for leaping
> The lightfoot boys are laid;
> The rose-lipt girls are sleeping
> In fields where roses fade.

A good many of the poems are concerned with soldiers who have left their farms and gone off to be killed. But where Kipling was blustering and patriotic when he treated of soldiers, Housman is softly ironic. He knows only too well that the lives of his young men have been wasted, and the pity of this waste is strong throughout his work. Irony also compels him at times to tell the strict truth about battles. In one poem, for instance, he represents a fighter as keeping his position in the lines not because he is brave but because he knows he must die some time, and if he dies in battle he will have the best possible funeral at home. But the subtlest expression of Housman's pessimism comes in those poems which declare the futility of thought. If thought could make life better, it would be well; but it only confuses the thinker further.

> Could man be drunk for ever
>   With liquor, love, or fights,
> Lief should I rouse at morning
>   And lief lie down of nights.
>
> But men at whiles are sober
>   And think by fits and starts,
> And if they think, they fasten
>   Their hands upon their hearts.

This is not gay, as may at first appear, but immensely bitter.

Housman has added to English literature a beautiful and classical note of elegy. He has also contributed a few ballads which hold their own with the famous established ones. Those who are acquainted with the old British ballad called "The Wife of Usher's Well" will recognize a certain resemblance in the following, particularly in the last two stanzas, wherein the speaker runs over in his mind the familiar details of home which he is about to lose forever.

> Farewell to barn and stack and tree,
>   Farewell to Severn shore.
> Terence, look your last at me,
>   For I come home no more.
>
> The sun burns on the half-mown hill,
>   By now the blood is dried;
> And Maurice amongst the hay lies still
>   And my knife is in his side.

My mother thinks us long away;
   'Tis time the field were mown.
She had two sons at rising day,
   To-night she'll be alone.

And here's a bloody hand to shake,
   And oh, man, here's good-bye;
We'll sweat no more on scythe and rake,
   My bloody hands and I.

I wish you strength to bring you pride,
   And a love to keep you clean,
And I wish you luck, come Lammastide,
   At racing on the green.

Long for me the rick will wait,
   And long will wait the fold,
And long will stand the empty plate,
   And dinner will be cold.

Even with that resemblance, the poem is original and great because it is the sincerest and most concentrated utterance of a rare, accomplished spirit.

"More Poems," the volume left for posthumous publication, was impressive for its consistency with its predecessors. No modern poet has struck so high an average as Housman; none of his pieces is bad, and most of them are good. And many of them are little masterpieces.

Alas, the country whence I fare,
   It is where I would stay;
And where I would not, it is there
   That I shall go for aye.

And one remembers and forgets,
   But 'tis not found again,
Not though they hale in crimsoned nets
   The sunset from the main.

There is Housman still magical with rhyme and idea; and there he is still preoccupied with the theme of death. In a lecture published in 1935 under the title "The Name and Nature of Poetry" he made it clear that poetry for him had never been a matter of the intellect merely. "The intellect is not the fount of poetry," he said. It is something more "physical" than that, a "secretion," something which "sets up in the reader's sense a vibration corresponding to what was felt by the writer," something which in his case had bubbled up at certain moments rather than come as a result of taking thought. The essay is a perfect statement of the quality to be found in his own poetry. For that poetry is spontaneous if any ever was, and the response of any reader is as immediate.

Almost at the end of the nineteenth century, **Hardy** one of its greatest novelists decided to abandon **1840-1928** fiction for poetry. Thomas Hardy published his first volume of verse, "Wessex Poems," in 1898, when he was fifty-eight years old; after which he published seven others, all of them with characteristic titles: "Poems of the Past and Present," "Time's Laughingstocks," "Satires of Circumstance," "Moments of Vision," "Late Lyrics and Earlier," "Human Shows," and "Winter Words." These books, issuing from the West-of-England country which Hardy had made so famous by his Wessex novels, gradually awoke London and the world to the realization that he was the most distinguished of living English poets. There can be little question that he is the most interesting writer whom the present chapter is called upon to discuss.

Readers of his novels will understand why the titles of his poetical works were characteristic. "Wessex," "Past," "Circumstance," and "Vision" were fundamental words in Hardy's philosophy; they were the keys to his great temperament. The words "Wessex" and "Past" remind a reader how restricted Hardy was to a single and long-inhabited locality. He chose both in his novels and in his poems to confine his gaze to objects and people in one part of the world, because he considered, and quite rightly for him, that human nature could most profitably be studied in the simplest and oldest terms, on ground which had been trod by many generations of men and women in only slightly different ways. Once he was invited to the United States, but declined for the reason that America did not seem to him to be old enough or to have suffered enough changes of human fate.

> My ardors for emprize nigh lost
> Since Life has bared its bones to me,
> I shrink to seek a modern coast
> Whose riper times have yet to be;
> Where the new regions claim them free
> From that long drip of human tears
> Which peoples old in tragedy
> Have left upon the centuried years.
>
> For, wonning in these ancient lands,
> Enchased and lettered as a tomb,
> And scored with prints of perished hands,
> And chronicled with dates of doom,
> Though my own Being bear no bloom
> I trace the lives such scenes enshrine,
> Give past exemplars present room,
> And their experience count as mine.

The word "Circumstance" calls up the whole structure of Hardy's philosophy, which is often called pessimistic, but which is more than that because it penetrates beyond the point where life can be declared either good or bad. He pondered long upon the fact that man is to some extent a misfit in the universe—that nature is neither able nor willing to grant him all of his desires, which have developed in him from a source which no one knows anything about. In one of his earliest poems, "Hap," he reflected upon the callousness of chance.

> If but some vengeful god would call to me
> From up the sky, and laugh: "Thou suffering thing,

Know that thy sorrow is my ecstasy,
That thy love's loss is my hate's profiting!"

Then would I bear it, clench myself, and die,
Steeled by the sense of ire unmerited;
Half-eased in that a Powerfuller than I
Had willed and meted me the tears I shed.

But not so. How arrives it joy lies slain,
And why unblooms the best hope ever sown?
—Crass Casualty obstructs the sun and rain,
And dicing Time for gladness casts a moan. . . .
These purblind Doomsters had as readily sown
Blisses about my pilgrimage as pain.

In "God-forgotten" he represented God as being quite unaware that the earth still exists at all.

I towered far, and lo! I stood within
The presence of the Lord Most High,
Sent thither by the sons of Earth, to win
    Some answer to their cry.

—"The Earth, sayest thou? The Human race?
By me created? Sad its lot?
Nay: I have no remembrance of such a place:
    Such world I fashioned not."—

—"O Lord, forgive me when I say
Thou spakest the word and made it all."—
"The Earth of men—let me bethink me. . . . Yea!
    I dimly do recall

"Some tiny sphere I built long back
(Mid millions of such shapes of mine)
So named. . . . It perished, surely—not a wrack
    Remaining, or a sign?

"It lost my interest from the first,
My aims therefor succeeding ill;
Haply it died of doing as it durst?"—
    "Lord, it existeth still."—

And in many narrative poems, which incidentally take a place among the most successful in the language, Hardy showed human beings in the grip of relentless fortune, tricked and betrayed by indifferent Nature. "The Curate's Kindness," for example, is the story of an old man who was congratulating himself upon having been sent to a different part of the workhouse from that which his wife would inhabit, but who by the well-intended meddling of a sentimental curate was assigned to quarters with her—whom he long had hated.

The word "Vision" is a word which Hardy had every right to use, for the eyes with which he looked at the world were the deepest of this generation—they were the eyes of the mind. In "Drummer Hodge" he sends his thought to the other side of the earth, where an English soldier, killed in the Boer War, sleeps this sleep:

> They throw in Drummer Hodge, to rest
>   Uncoffined—just as found:
> His landmark is a kopje-crest
>   That breaks the veldt around:
> And foreign constellations west
>   Each night above his mound.
>
> Young Hodge the Drummer never knew—
>   Fresh from his Wessex home—
> The meaning of the broad Karoo,
>   The Bush, the dusty loam,
> And why uprose to nightly view
>   Strange stars amid the gloam.
>
> Yet portion of that unknown plain
>   Will Hodge for ever be;
> His homely Northern breast and brain
>   Grow to some Southern tree,
> And strange-eyed constellations reign
>   His stars eternally.

And in "The Fallow Deer at the Lonely House" he exhibits his singular power of realizing other eyes than his own.

> One without looks in to-night
>   Through the curtain-chink
> From the sheet of glistening white;
> One without looks in to-night
>   As we sit and think
>   By the fender-brink.
>
> We do not discern those eyes
>   Watching in the snow;
> Lit by lamps of rosy dyes
> We do not discern those eyes
>   Wondering, aglow,
>   Fourfooted, tiptoe.

The mere fact that Hardy had a philosophy does not explain his power as a poet. His pages are thick with atmosphere, his vocabulary is very rich with old and mysterious words, and his meter, while rugged, is always strong and expressive of more than merely words can say. His philosophy alone might have paralyzed his tongue, and made it seem useless to speak or write. As a matter of fact, his dramatic [1] and lyrical genius had driven him to create hundreds of immortal scenes and situations in which he could not have participated. His warm, full nature compelled him even at times to sing joyful, reckless songs, to celebrate a happiness which he personally could not share.

> Let me enjoy the earth no less
> Because the all-enacting Might
> That fashioned forth its loveliness
> Had other aims than my delight.
>
> About my path there flits a Fair,
> Who throws me not a word or sign;

[1] For his dramatic work, see pages 275–279.

I'll charm me with her ignoring air,
And laud the lips not meant for mine.

From manuscripts of moving song
Inspired by scenes and souls unknown,
I'll pour out raptures that belong
To others, as they were my own.

And some day hence, toward Paradise
And all its blest—if such should be—
I will lift glad, afar-off eyes,
Though it contain no place for me.

**Bridges
1844–1930**
One more English poet had made his reputation before the beginning of the twentieth century, and that was Robert Bridges, poet laureate. Like Hardy, he was already advanced in years when in the eighteen-nineties he collected and published several volumes of his "Shorter Poems." They proved him to be a graceful and genuine lyric poet, and he continued to hold the respect of younger writers. But while he was an accomplished and serious workman, and an able student of the art of verse, he had little of the force which distinguishes the men who have since achieved prominence. A few of his gentle love-lyrics will survive, and devoted readers will not cease to praise the technical skill with which he has imitated the movements of external nature. Here, for instance, is the beginning of his excellent poem called "London Snow":

When men were all asleep the snow came flying,
In large white flakes falling on the city brown,
Stealthily and perpetually settling and loosely lying,
    Hushing the latest traffic of the drowsy town;
Deadening, muffling, stifling its murmurs failing;
Lazily and incessantly floating down and down.

And there are those who maintain that his long posthumous poem, "The Testament of Beauty" (1929), has greatness

in it; though another view of it is that it meanders rather
flatly through the subject of man. It is a philosophical poem
in four parts—"Introduction," "Selfhood," "Breed," and
"Ethick"—and it can be said to follow the Platonic lead
in its discussion of love, truth, and beauty. Sometimes there
is a touch of humor, as in the passage on the epicure:

> In such fine artistry of his putrefying pleasures
> he indulgeth richly his time until the sad day come
> when he retireth with stomach Emeritus
> to ruminate the best devour'd moments of life.

And there is always urbanity, always a tempered and well-
bred wisdom. But the interest of the poem may never become more than an interest in its line, which, from the
sample seen above, will appear to have solved the problem
of the hexameter in English; for it has six stresses, and
these fall naturally where the accent of the sense deter-
mines.

Hopkins
1844–1898
It may be that Bridges will longest be remembered because he first made known the poetry of
Gerard Manley Hopkins. Hopkins was a Ro-
man Catholic priest whose death in 1898 was noted by no
student of poetry because his contribution to the art had
been as obscure as his life. But one of his friends had been
Robert Bridges, and in 1918 the poet laureate published
"Poems of Gerard Manley Hopkins" with a preface which
discussed the technique of those poems. The volume gradually won its admirers, though a second edition was not
necessary until after Bridges's death, in 1930. Since then
the name of Hopkins has grown rapidly important, and
there are those who call him the greatest English poet of
the late nineteenth century, and indeed one of the great
English poets. He has influenced almost every young poet
in England since 1920, and his fame seems secure. He is
discussed here not because he wrote within the limits of

this work but because the circumstances attending his discovery have made him to all intents and purposes a contemporary.

Discussions of him usually devote more space than is needed to the oddities of his technique, and particularly to the "sprung rhythm" concerning which Hopkins himself wrote a brief essay. The rhythm to which he refers has been used by every poet who was more than a counter of syllables, and indeed is the rhythm, as Hopkins points out, of common speech; also of nursery rhymes, most music, Greek and Latin poetry, and all early English poetry. It is the rhythm which comes after or builds upon the mechanics of meter. Hopkins in using it was merely reverting to the great tradition of metrics—a tradition, truly enough, which was little understood in his time. Its importance in his case is that it permitted him to say all that he wanted to say in the accent of passion which was natural to his very highly organized mind.

His great subjects are the beauty of the world and the glory of God. His celebration of neither thing is conventionally pious; rather it skirts the edge of error because of the force with which the subject is felt. But error is in most cases avoided through the sheer power of Hopkins to convince his reader that the passion laboring to express itself is authentic. When he wants to say that no matter how "seared" the world is with trade, no matter how "bleared, smeared with toil," a "dearest freshness deep down things" restores it to its original purity, he can end a sonnet with two bold lines:

Because the Holy Ghost over the bent
World broods with warm breast and with ah! bright wings.

The "ah!" is so far from being a syllable to fill out the last line as to be indeed the great word of the whole sonnet. It is both a sound to be heard and an invitation to look and see the virginal loveliness of creation. The vision and its effect on the poet are both there, and with a wonderful brevity. The touch is characteristic of Hopkins everywhere, whether he is tortured by doubts of his own spiritual health, as in the sonnet which he ends by praying God to send his roots rain—the imagery of drought is traditional among all mystical poets—or whether he is looking with delight at things of the earth, including human figures, which have given him delight. There is the poem "Pied Beauty," to "dappled things"; there is the panegyric on Felix Randal the farrier; and there is the requiem for the great English musician Henry Purcell, dead two hundred years before Hopkins. Nowhere is Hopkins slack, sluggish, or commonplace. That is the chief reason that he has acted as a kind of electric charge in the minds of his poetic heirs. Whatever their religion or their politics, they have combined their voices in paying homage to the most valuable teacher who has survived for them out of the past century.

Masefield 1874–   John Masefield's career is one of the most interesting of the century. Born in 1874, he was trained for a sea life while still a boy, and sailed to many parts of the world with no thought that he should ever be a writer. It was in America that he began to read the older English poetry and decided to emulate it. He has told the story himself in the preface to his "Collected Poems": "I did not begin to read poetry with passion and system until 1896. I was living then in Yonkers, N. Y. (at 8 Maple Street). Chaucer was the poet, and the *Parliament of Fowls* the poem, of my conversion. I read the *Parliament* all through one Sunday afternoon, with the feeling that I had been kept out of my inheritance and had then suddenly entered upon it, and had found it a new world of wonder and delight. I had never realized, until then, what poetry could be. After that Sunday afternoon, I read many poets (Chaucer, Keats, Shelley, Milton, and Shakespeare, more than others) and wrote many imitations of them. About a year later, when I was living in London, I wrote two or three of the verses now printed in *Salt Water Ballads*. For the next few years I wrote little. I wrote the rest of the verses in *Salt Water Ballads* in about six weeks, at Christmas time, 1901, in a London lodging." "Salt Water Ballads" was not the volume which made him famous, although it is now much treasured by his admirers for a few admirable lyrics which it contains, such as the magical piece called "The West Wind," beginning

> It's a warm wind, the west wind, full of birds' cries;
> I never hear the west wind but tears are in my eyes.
> For it comes from the west lands, the old brown hills,
> And April's in the west wind, and daffodils.

The book which definitely marked his arrival, and which as much as any other single book brought on the modern revival of poetry in England, was "The Everlasting Mercy," written rapidly under great excitement in 1911 and published immediately in a magazine. It began on a brand-new note:

> From '41 to '51
> I was my folk's contrary son;
> I bit my father's hand right through
> And broke my mother's heart in two.
> I sometimes go without my dinner
> Now that I know the times I've gi'n her;

and it sustained that note through a long narrative of the conversion of Saul Kane after his life of violent sin. In the bluntest and most realistic terms the reader is told of Saul's fighting and carousing at a public house until the entrance of Miss Bourne, a Quaker whose Christian spirit suddenly communicates itself to him and sweeps him into ecstasy.

Readers were instantly stirred by this uncouth yet beautiful poem to a consciousness of the possibilities for real poetry that existed in modern life and modern speech. Here was a thrilling story told in rattling rhymes; here was the English language put to a fresh use. Masefield quickly followed "The Everlasting Mercy" with three other narratives equally good, "The Widow in the Bye Street," "Dauber," and "The Daffodil Fields." The first continued in a realistic vein, being the story of a young Shropshire man who was brought to destruction by a wicked woman; but with the second Masefield departed into a new field, the sea, and while he was still vulgar enough in places, he developed a power of description such as none of his contemporaries has yet equaled. "Dauber" describes the difficulties of a boy at sea who wanted chiefly to paint the water, but who was forced to work at the sails like the other men until during a storm he was knocked to the deck and killed. One stanza inspired by the storm will convey some notion of the deep music and the furious movement of the poem.

> All through the windless night the clipper rolled
> In a great swell with oily gradual heaves
> Which rolled her down until her time-bells tolled,
> Clang, and the weltering water moaned like beeves.
> The thundering rattle of slatting shook the sheaves,
> Startles of water made the swing ports gush,
> The sea was moaning and sighing and saying "Hush!"

"The Daffodil Fields" was almost too melodramatic in plot to be effective, but it again gave proof of Masefield's surpassing gift for lovely language; and it helped to consolidate his position as the most commanding of the younger English poets.

From 1913 to 1919 he composed little poetry other than a collection of distinguished philosophical sonnets and a number of fine, reflective poems of a personal nature. He returned to narrative poetry in 1919 with "Reynard the Fox," a story of a fox-hunt told from the point of view of the fox, and in many respects his most engaging work. After this came "Right Royal," a tale of horseracing, and other narratives which cannot be described at length. It is on these longer poems that his reputation will probably rest, though his lyrics are of a rare quality and his sonnets are among the best of the century. His greatest achievements have been the revival of the honorable art of narrative poetry and the reinvigoration of a language that had begun to grow pale. In spite of his frequent roughness and superficiality, a reading of his pages will make it clear how forceful and moving he is, and how rightly he deserves to be ranked among the most ringing of English versifiers. In 1930, upon the death of Bridges, he was appointed poet laureate.

The Georgians   In 1912, a year after the publication of "The Everlasting Mercy," a collection of contemporary verse was published with the title "Georgian poetry: 1911–1912." Its purpose was to make better known the work of several poets whose volumes had recently appeared, and its success was so great that two years later another collection was published. Through five such anthologies the word "Georgian" came to have a meaning over and above the original one, which had simply to do with the fact that the poets concerned lived and wrote in the time of George V. "Georgian" grew to be the name of a specific group of writers, and it was believed to denote a definite quality. There may be doubt as to the literal accuracy of this, for many different kinds of poetry were represented in the various volumes of the series. At any rate, by "Georgian" was generally meant something not very different from "Caroline." Georgian verse was usually flawless in form. The poems were short, and often they were composed upon pastoral subjects, or upon love. Their prevailing temper was sweet and ingenuous, and their music was of the most delicate sort.

**Davies
1870–**

The best of the surviving Georgians is William Henry Davies. Davies was a common laborer and a vagabond in America and elsewhere until in 1905 he settled down in London and wrote a slender volume of poems which he printed at his own expense and sent to various prominent authors for criticism. One copy came to Bernard Shaw, who later said that he had not read three lines before he knew he was reading poetry. Davies has published many other slender volumes since that time, and in none of them perhaps is there a page whereon one cannot find poetry. The reason lies in Davies's very simple and honest soul, and in the extraordinary gift he has for describing the ordinary things he sees. He makes no claims to profundity.

> I hear men say: "This Davies has no depth,
> He writes of birds, of staring cows and sheep,
> And throws no light on deep, eternal things—"
> And would they have me talking in my sleep?

He is content to look at the world with his own clear eyes, and if it only contains the usual number of birds and cows and trees and pretty women he must be happy. He of course does not render the world as most people see it. For him it is uncommonly definite and bright. He sharpens every object with his gaze.

> I look on Nature and my thoughts,
> Like nimble skaters, skim the land.

> Then—like a snail with horns outstretched—
> My senses feel the air around;
> There's not a move escapes my eyes,
> My ears are cocked to every sound.

And he can make the most trivial things important by his method of mentioning them:

Oft have I seen in fields the little birds
    Go in between the bullock's legs to eat;
But what gives me most joy is when I see
    Snow on my doorstep, printed by their feet.

He recalls the Caroline Robert Herrick when he praises
the simple life, as he often does.

My walls outside must have some flowers,
    My walls inside must have some books;
A house that's small; a garden large,
    And in it leafy nooks.

A little gold that's sure each week;
    That comes not from my living kind,
But from a dead man in his grave,
    Who cannot change his mind.

A lovely wife, and gentle too;
    Contented that no eyes but mine
Can see her many charms, nor voice
    To call her beauty fine.

Where she would in that stone cage live,
    A self-made prisoner, with me;
While many a wild bird sang around,
    On gate, on bush, on tree.

And she sometimes to answer them,
    In her far sweeter voice than all;
Till birds, that loved to look on leaves,
    Will doat on a stone wall.

With this small house, this garden large,
    This little gold, this lovely mate,
With health in body, peace at heart—
    Show me a man more great.

But Davies is in no sense merely another Herrick. He is
altogether Davies by virtue of the unique charm of his
imagery and his versification. He can furnish delight to

his contemporaries out of none other than his own art and his own experience.

De La Mare 1873– Walter De La Mare is often mentioned in company with Davies. He too is a fine and charming workman, but the impression he makes is fainter and more effaceable. He is most widely known for his children's verses, which have taken him into the nursery and in turn have taken the children into fairy-land. He has an older audience, however, in those who are captivated by such poems as "The Listeners." This brings a reader's mind to the edge of that mysterious other-world which De La Mare delights so much to let his mind play upon.

"Is there anybody there?" said the Traveller,
    Knocking on the moonlit door;
And his horse in the silence champed the grasses
    Of the forest's ferny floor;
And a bird flew up out of the turret,
    Above the Traveller's head:
And he smote upon the door again a second time;
    "Is there anybody there?" he said.
But no one descended to the Traveller;
    No head from the leaf-fringed sill
Leaned over and looked into his grey eyes,
    Where he stood perplexed and still.
But only a host of phantom listeners
    That dwelt in the lone house then
Stood listening in the quiet of the moonlight
    To that voice from the world of men:
Stood thronging the faint moonbeams on the dark stair,
    That goes down to the empty hall,
Hearkening in an air stirred and shaken
    By the lonely Traveller's call.
And he felt in his heart their strangeness,
    Their stillness answering his cry,
While his horse moved, cropping the dark turf,
    'Neath the starred and leafy sky;
For he suddenly smote on the door, even
    Louder, and lifted his head:—

"Tell them I came, and no one answered,
  That I kept my word," he said.
Never the least stir made the listeners,
  Though every word he spake
Fell echoing through the shadowiness of the still house
  From the one man left awake:
Ay, they heard his foot upon the stirrup,
  And the sound of iron on stone,
And how the silence surged softly backward,
  When the plunging hoofs were gone.

War Poets The Boer War left little mark on English poetry outside the pages of Kipling and a few narrow patriots. But the World War, touching in one way or another the mind of every man, provoked many different kinds of utterance, and created not a few new reputations. The established poets, almost without an exception, expressed themselves in characteristic veins. Kipling celebrated the prowess of the British fleet; Hardy and Masefield, with varying degrees of insight, sang the pity of the slaughter. In addition, at least two new poets were born from the conflict.

Brooke 1887–1915 Rupert Brooke had been one of the originators of the Georgian series; in the volume for 1911–1912 he had appeared as an exceedingly clever and spirited young poet, with a gay love of natural beauty and a promise of ability in satire. His name, however, did not make a wide impression until 1915, when the world suddenly was presented with a group of sonnets which he had written upon entering the army, in whose service he died at Scyros. Immediately these sonnets were in all British and American newspapers and magazines, and the name of Rupert Brooke became the universal synonym for radiant, martyred youth. Perhaps it is still impossible to assign them their true value; there can be no doubt that they are expressions of a winning, spontaneous soul. In the following tribute to "The Dead," for instance, can be felt a joyful vigor which more than relieves the subject of its melancholy:

> These hearts were woven of human joys and cares,
>   Washed marvellously with sorrow, swift to mirth.
> The years had given them kindness. Dawn was theirs,
>   And sunset, and the colors of the earth.
> These had seen movement, and heard music; known
>   Slumber and waking; loved; gone proudly friended;
> Felt the quick stir of wonder; sat alone;
>   Touched flowers and furs and cheeks. All this is ended.
>
> There are waters blown by changing winds to laughter
> And lit by the rich skies, all day. And after,
>   Frost, with a gesture, stays the waves that dance
> And wandering loveliness. He leaves a white
>   Unbroken glory, a withered radiance,
> A width, a shining peace, under the night.

Owen
1893–1918
Rupert Brooke at the beginning of the war sang with the enthusiasm of excited youth. Four years later, a group of disillusioned and bitter youths wrote satirical verse not only against the war in which they had fought but against all wars. Siegfried Sassoon and others aroused a wide and occasionally an indignant interest by their poems exposing the unmitigated horror and ennui of frontline life. Many of these poems have not survived as poems, though they still are impressive as documents. But those of Wilfrid Owen may outlast Rupert Brooke's, for they are more than protest; they are poetry. They were posthumous, for Owen had been killed in battle in 1918. Their editor was Siegfried Sassoon, who wrote a preface warning the reader that he would hear assonances and dissonances instead of perfect rhymes, and reprinting at its close a manuscript which Owen evidently had intended as his own preface. Owen assured the reader:

> Above all, this book is not concerned with Poetry.
> The subject of it is War, and the pity of War.
> The Poetry is in the pity.

Yet the poetry has proved that it exists in itself; were it otherwise, the pity would not have been so powerfully expressed.

> If you could hear, at every jolt, the blood
> Come gargling from the froth-corrupted lungs
> Bitten as the cud
> Of vile, incurable sores on innocent tongues—
> My friend, you would not tell with such high zest
> To children ardent for some desperate glory,
> The old Lie: Dulce et decorum est
> Pro patria mori.

"It is sweet and right to die for one's country." Owen's voice seemed to be repeating the famous words hoarsely from his grave, and of course ironically. The assonances and dissonances of which Sassoon spoke helped to achieve this note of hoarseness, which has not yet ceased to sound in poetry that concerns war. They are devices common in good poetry, but Owen made a special use of them. For he had a special thing to say.

**Graves
1895–**
One of the unsentimental war poets was Robert Graves, who passed an even harsher judgment on the years 1914–1918 in an autobiography to which he gave the title "Goodbye to All That" (1929). Immediately preceding the war, however, and for a few years after, Graves was characteristically Georgian; the volumes "Fairies and Fusiliers," "Country Sentiment," and "The Pier-Glass" provided excellent examples of the neat, pleasant poem then in demand—in his case with the addition, to be sure, of wit and sometimes of mockery. Although "Neglectful Edward" is an exercise in imitation of the old ballad dialogue, it is gay and modern; and " 'The General Elliott' " asks whether a soldier whose face swings on a tavern sign

> died for England's pride
> By battle, or by pot.

As time went on and the Georgians became old-fashioned, Graves put them behind him and began to write a much more complicated kind of poetry. Collecting his verse in 1926, he suppressed a number of "anthology pieces" and emphasized the metaphysical strain which had crept into his work. In place of singing and dancing stanzas there were stanzas as grave, and as distinctly in the manner of the new hero Donne, as the following from the poem "Pure Death":

> This I admit, Death is terrible to me,
> To no man more so, naturally,
> And I have disenthralled my natural terror
> Of every comfortable philosopher
> Or tall dark doctor of divinity:
> Death stands again in his true rank and order.

A still later phase revealed him as one of the most "difficult" of all modern poets, and as one of the most brilliant; though latterly his poems have been published by private presses and have had limited circulation. His energies in recent years have also been given in part to a series of historical novels dealing with the times of Claudius, Roman emperor between Caligula and Nero.

Auden and Spender In the early thirties of this century, just a decade after T. S. Eliot had risen to power as a poet in England, literary history turned another corner and a pair of new poets ascended to the first position. Not that they were or are better poets than Eliot, whose qualities remain what they were; but it was they whom it grew fashionable to read, discuss, and imitate. They came in with the times. Eliot had spoken for a decade of despair; they, at the very time that Eliot was seeking and finding refuge in religion, sought and found another refuge in radical politics. As vigorously as Bernard Shaw in the nineties they set out to attack the middle class; with the difference, though, that they wrote not as Socialists but as sympathizers with the Communist faith. Contemporary

England appears in their poems and plays—for they have assisted in the drive to restore poetry to the stage—as a dying or dead world which still goes through its motions but does not understand why it does so, or what the meaning of any fact is. Amid the machines and symbols of a new age, and in spite of the pressure of economic realities, it tries to live the life of the past and in doing so only presents the spectacle of a twitching corpse. Stephen Spender and W. H. Auden were students together at Oxford, and the poetry they wrote both then and afterwards coupled their names in the public mind, though the resemblance between them is slight. Spender's most effective mood is elegiac, as when in "The Pylons" he reflects that England, once built of stone, is now being rebuilt in steel and copper:

> But far above and far as sight endures
> Like whips of anger
> With lightning's danger
> There runs the quick perspective of the future;

or as when in "New Year" he broods on the work time is doing—building a new world

> Where scythe shall curve but not upon our neck
> And lovers proceed to their forgetting work,
> Answering the harvests of obliteration.

In the poem beginning, "I think continually of those who were truly great," he names no poets or prophets of the past, for it is not their individualities that matter either to them or to us; they signed the air, he concludes, not with their names but "with their honour," for their only desire was to make the world free. Auden's mood, far from being elegiac, is explosively and impudently bright. He is playful, daring, nimble of wit and careless of where his arrows fall. He has been the more prolific of the two, and steadily has emerged as the more interesting, at least to his strict contemporaries. He is certainly the more difficult to read. His medley of prose and verse, "The Orators," is a satire of considerable proportions and with a powerful sting, but it leaps so nervously from theme to theme, from idiom to idiom, that few have followed it to its end—which is not especially different from the end arrived at in the verse play "The Dance of Death." The play begins with an announcer declaring to the audience : "We present to you this evening a picture of the decline of a class, of how its members dream of a new life, but secretly desire the old, for there is death inside them. We show you that death as a dancer." And it ends with Karl Marx entering to pronounce death by liquidation. Not that Marx enters solemnly. The comic talent of Auden strikes in all directions, including that of his own faith; he is not doctrinaire so much as restless, and impatient to remove all those restrictions upon human life, including even "material facts," which threaten contemporary man. His short poems have been many and various, and frequently puzzling; but it is interesting to note that the volume "On This Island" concerns itself largely with love, the dedication reading :

> Since the external disorder, and extravagant lies,
> The baroque frontiers, the surrealist police;
> What can truth treasure, or heart bless,
> But a narrow strictness?

The names Auden and Spender have separated themselves from each other gradually, and new names have been added to the list of radical poets demanding attention in contemporary England. And it is clear that Auden stands at the top of this list. But the pair of young poets who ushered in the tradition will continue to be remembered as a pair while the tradition maintains its supremacy.

CHAPTER II

PROSE FICTION

THE novel had held a high place in English literature for more than a hundred years before 1890, and it is easy to exaggerate the amount of change which took place about that time. The main outlines of the form had been traced in the eighteenth century; there had been much intensive cultivation during the nineteenth; and these two centuries bequeathed to the twentieth a heritage which it was difficult to improve upon. Besides this native tradition, however, there were certain foreign influences which considerably modified the English novel about the end of the nineteenth century. French fiction taught intensity and form, objectivity, and artistic control—qualities which English fiction had always needed. Russian fiction did not teach form to the English in any narrow sense, for by the strictest criterion it was formless; but it greatly enlarged the prevailing conceptions of the limits of the novel, and it explored vast sections of human nature hitherto unentered. English fiction profited by all these types, and in the light of them the more intelligent public demanded better writing. But the novel had so sound and rich a national history that much which was purely British remained unaltered. Throughout the period now under consideration Thomas Hardy, though his work as a novelist was nearly finished by 1890, and had been done in the native tradition, has generally been regarded as the greatest novelist of the age, particularly for the unity of his place, tone, and ideas.

Moore
1852–1933

There is no unity of place, tone, or ideas in the novels of George Moore. Their only unity lies in their excellence, for in their various ways they are all the work of a master story-teller and a master stylist who never anchored himself in any portion of the world for long, but drifted with the tide of his own irresponsible thoughts and chance desires. Born in Ireland, he was privately educated by well-to-do parents who when he was twenty permitted him to go to Paris for the finishing touches. He stayed there ten years, and completely surrendered to the fascination which French literature had for him. His work for a long time after his return showed the effects of this residence abroad, and even to-day some readers find his genius more Latin than English. Certainly no English writer ever achieved the same quality of beauty as is to be found in his prose. He left a record of the ten years in a youthful book, "Confessions of a Young Man," which announced rather stridently his esthetic creed; he was to live purely for his art, subordinating fortune, fame, comfort, and morals if need be to the one thing worth serving, beauty. He lived in England until the opening of the new century, writing some of his most important books there; then in 1901 he suddenly discovered Ireland, and returned to associate himself with the leaders of what is called the Irish Renaissance. The attempt to repatriate himself was not altogether successful, as he showed in a long and mocking autobiography, "Hail and Farewell" (1911–1914), which made clear once and for all how little fit he was to embrace a nationality. After ten years he ceased to think of Ireland at all, and the remainder of his career was devoted to producing lengthy and exquisite books in the various moods that visited him.

The novels which Moore wrote in England after his return from France were prevailingly realistic, after the French mode of Flaubert and Zola. They were entirely objective in their treatment of poverty, sin, and misery; some readers have found them callous, and have been outraged at the spectacle of a writer proceeding heartlessly to appropriate the unhappiness of others for the purposes of his art. Whatever Moore's inward thoughts may have been, it is certain that his art was excellent. He painted several pictures from life which will endure as long as literal truth is interesting.

"A Mummer's Wife," the first of these, is the story of a provincial woman who falls in love with a traveling actor and runs away with him. Her efforts to accommodate herself to the life of the troupe with which she goes from town to town are no sooner successful than she undergoes a series of misfortunes and begins a decline which in the end reduces her to the most sordid stages of hysteria and alcoholism. The lazy, obese lover who charms her and arouses her insane jealousy is presented in full detail, and the successive steps in her own downward progress are marked off with a superb craftsman's skill. Only "Esther Waters," published ten years later in 1894, is superior to this among all of Moore's early books. It is his masterpiece in realism, and indeed one of the best of English novels in any class. The heroine, a servant, may have been derived in idea from French fiction, but as she develops it is obvious that she comes straight from the life which Moore observed—he says in another connection, as a matter of fact, that conversations with his housekeeper furnished much of the material for Esther. The background of race-track life was also familiar to Moore at first hand, for he had been brought up in Ireland in the midst of much talk about betting on horses. The betrayal of Esther by her lover William, the birth of her child in London and her difficulties with it there, her desolation until she finds a kind mistress, the reappearance of William and the marriage of the two under happy circumstances, William's illness and his resumption of his gambling habits and his death, and Esther's return to the country-house where she first served—all this happens with the utmost naturalness, so that the persons of the story, and particularly Esther, exist for the reader and elicit constant sympathy. The author himself, obeying his artistic creed, refrains at all times from expressing pity or moral disapproval. It all happened; therefore he puts it down.

After Moore abandoned Ireland as a faith, he produced three books of fiction differing very widely in theme. "The Brook Kerith" (1916) retold the story of Christ as Moore's unreligious eyes saw it. He accepted an old legend to the effect that Jesus survived the cross, and showed him back in the peaceful shepherd life from which he had come to declare himself the Son of God. He now repents of that madness—for so it seems to him—and wishes to live the rest of his life in personal charity and philosophic calm. He has not the slightest desire to convert the world, and deprecates the ambition of Paul to go forth and harangue the world into worship of him. The flowing beauty of the writing did not prevent an outcry being raised from those readers who interpreted Christ's life differently. Moore had been attacked on many previous occasions for what was called his immorality, and this was the last straw. He announced that he would write henceforth only for men of letters; after 1916, accordingly, his books appeared under the protection of a private imprint. "A Story-Teller's Holiday" is a collection of limpid and candid tales; "Abelard and Heloise" (1921) is a long rendering of the famous history of the medieval monk and the woman he loved.

Moore was very far from being a profound writer; he contributed no ideas, and he cannot be said to have had insight to a remarkable degree. In addition he was capricious, arrogant, vain, diffuse, and often indecent. But he had the great merit of being able to write prose as fine as lace and as swift as water; and he remains one of the most charming story-tellers of modern times.

Barrie 1860–1937   Sir James Matthew Barrie's career as a writer of fiction ended with the nineteenth century. After 1900 he gave all of his attention to the drama.[1] But the sketches and novels which he published before that year laid the foundation for his literary fame, and some of them make up the most important work of any kind that he did. The scene of his best fiction is invariably Thrums—this name he gave to his native village—and its inspiration is the memory of younger days.

"The Little Minister" was Barrie's first novel to strike a large public favorably. Partly by its own vogue and partly because it was skilfully dramatized by the author, it is today perhaps the best-known story that has to do with Thrums. The love of Gavin Dishart, the little minister, for Babbie, the pretty "Gipsy" who flitted into his sober life from a neighboring town, is treated in the vein of purest romance, as are the betrothal of Babbie to Lord Rintoul, the Gipsy marriage of Gavin and Babbie, and Rob Dow's sacrifice of his life in the flood at the end of the book. There is melodrama in many places, and an old-fashioned kind of stage-romance. But the story is excellent, and the people interesting.

Barrie struck deeper in the two novels which, taken together, comprise his masterpiece. The Thrums sketches were chiefly pathetic and picturesque. "The Little Minister" was chiefly exciting as plot, since the real identity of Babbie was not disclosed until late. But "Sentimental Tommy" (1896) and "Tommy and Grizel" (1900) deal with fundamental phases of human nature. The first takes the hero and heroine through childhood, and the second shows their mature love. Tommy begins his career in London, with his

[1] For his plays, see pages 267–271.

dying mother and his sister Elspeth. After the death of the mother the children are removed to Thrums, where Elspeth enters upon a devout and sisterly existence that rarely is interrupted by excitement or romance, and Tommy meets Grizel, the young daughter of a queer "painted lady" on the outskirts of the village. The rest of the history is concerned with the relations between these two remarkable persons.

Tommy is called sentimental before it is known that the root of his human shortcomings lies in his being an artist. He is a born writer, but this means that he sees double— sees not only a world of people but sees this world with himself prominently in it. Never until his last day can he be sure that he feels anything unselfishly. Charming as he is, there is much of the pretender about him. He cannot resist indulging in what he knows to be heroics, in doing and saying things simply for effect. He is never wholly convinced that he loves Grizel as much as he likes to think he does. In brief, he is not the single-souled man who ought to be the hero of a romantic novel. Grizel on the other hand is all that is implied in the words "single," "faithful," "passionate," and "proud." She becomes a profound woman, impatient at first with the sentimentality of the boy whom she loves in spite of her will to remain independent, and at last completely humble before him. This surrender of herself is more than Tommy can bear, since he understands it to be something deeper than his own feelings. His promise to marry her he cannot keep when the time comes for action, and there is a spell of intense pain for her while he retires to London. After more tragic passages he returns to find her out of her mind, and marries her in this condition. Upon her recovery the two live serenely together for a few years, until his death during a moment of infidelity. She continues in love of him forever, forgiving him all of his failures to be the man she would have liked him to be, and preferring to think that he had never been more than a gifted boy.

"Tommy and Grizel," in which most of the action just described takes place, is poignant and true, and genuinely dignified by the tragedy which it so competently analyzes.

Kipling
1865–1936

Although Rudyard Kipling's fiction is undeniably of a higher order than his poetry,[1] the same difficulties stand in the way of a final judgment upon it. The difficulties are chiefly two, one having to do with the philosophy behind the work and the other having to do with questions of art. The philosophy is so agreeable to some critics and so disagreeable to others that practically all of them are blinded to the intrinsic merit of Kipling as a writer. The philosophy, or to be more accurate the attitude, of Kipling is generally conceived to be a brutal one, favoring hardness and force, contemptuous of the refinements of civilization, hating peace, extolling war, and recommending a discipline of life that includes all the experiences which in cant usage are called manly. The art of his stories also finds the critics in violent disagreement, for it likewise savors of hardness; it is called conceited, smart, smug, and cheaply knowing—the art merely of a glorified journalist, a supreme reporter.

The opinions of professional critics are in a sense irrelevant, since the lay public continues to delight in Kipling without reference to formal judgments. His books, it is believed, are read by more people both in and out of the English-speaking world than those of any other contemporary British author. Yet even these popular readers do not present a united front against the warring critics, for Kipling developed many new sides of his character and his art, and in consequence he has many audiences who in a manner never mingle and agree concerning his work as a whole. He has a separate audience of children, and he has audiences of adults who like variously his stories of military India, his stories of civilian and native India, his stories

[1] For his poems, see pages 163–166.

of the supernatural, his stories of England and America, his stories of occupations and machines, his stories of the spirit.

There can be no question that his career was one of the most brilliant in literary history. Born in Calcutta, he was taken to England when a child, educated there, and sent back to Lahore at seventeen, to become famous throughout India before he was twenty. In two years more he was famous throughout the English-speaking world. He traveled around the globe, married an American woman, lived four years in Vermont, and then returned to England, where his subsequent life was comparatively uneventful. He made a phenomenal reputation by twenty-five; he had done nine-tenths of his best work by thirty-five; at forty-five he had to all appearances retired.

His first volume of stories, "Plain Tales from the Hills" (1888), fascinated its English audience, as it had its Indian audience, by a remarkable freshness and crispness then unfelt in contemporary literature. It exploited a new subject-matter, Anglo-Indian life, and got much of its effect out of the spectacle of two entirely different civilizations mingling for a practical end in a distant and interesting place. There was no sentimentality about either the East or the West; there was no romanticizing of the native and no fatuous glorifying of the alien. It was clear that the author considered the British superior to the Indians, but he made them out on the whole to be a hard lot. He dealt with the simplest yet the strongest themes—love, death, dissipation, jealousy, sin, pride, and disease. He was terse, sardonic, and often cynical; he took always an indifferent observer's point of view. He sprinkled his pages with epigrams that astonished the reader by their sophistication. And more important yet for his success, he gave the impression of being a complete authority on the life that he described. It seemed, and subsequent books proved that it was true, that he had an indefinite number of stories yet to tell, that these were only a sample, chosen out of a store too rich to measure. The next volume made a departure into rough humor which was immediately labeled American and considered to derive from Mark Twain or Bret Harte. "Soldiers Three" (1888) brought to birth Mulvaney the Irishman, Ortheris the cockney, and Learoyd the Yorkshireman. These three musketeers fought, drank, talked, swore, and laughed their way quickly into fame; they still are the foundation of their creator's popularity among all readers who are most attracted by his rougher surfaces. Other collections followed, sometimes at the rate of more than one a year, displaying Kipling invariably in new guises, but consistent with all that had gone before in the brilliance of their technic. As he gradually abandoned India for a wider world of people and things, he became more practised in the art of reporting. He had a boundless curiosity, an unquenchable thirst for facts; in a few weeks, or perhaps from a single conversation with one who knew, he could pick up enough details about a nation, a trade, a ship, a locomotive, or a school to make himself seem an authority. Also he carried over from his later Indian work a capacity for tenderness, so that he was able eventually to treat of subtler emotions, and even to suggest ideas beyond the ordinary range.

The most famous of all the short stories is "The Man Who Would be King." It is no less compact than elaborate; without the closest attention to each detail the reader becomes lost in the maze of adventures that befall the two heroes, Peachey Carnahan and Daniel Dravot. These rogues push into the interior of Asia and pass themselves off as rulers and gods to a remote tribe. But there is a mutiny at last, and the retribution visited upon the pretenders is as horrible as any of the horrible things in Kipling; Dravot is dropped to his death from a rope-bridge overhanging a deep valley, and Carnahan, after torture by crucifixion, is sent stumbling home with his partner's head in his hands. It is a ghastly but engrossing tale, drawn against a thoroughly savage background and rendered credible through the energetic art of its author. "The Brushwood Boy," in many respects the most beautiful story from Kipling's hand, tells of a boy and a girl who in their separate parts of the world dreamed a twin-dream, and only upon meeting as lovers identified each other. Even a profounder love-story is "Without Benefit of Clergy," again with an Indian background—the story of John Holden's life with the native woman who bore him a son and who, after the child's death from fever, died in an epidemic of cholera declaring her belief in one God: John Holden. Kipling treated of machines and builded things with still another kind of affection. ".007" is the story of a great locomotive on the night of its first thrilling run through strange space, and "The Ship That Found Herself" so far personifies a vessel as to describe the voice which she learned to use on her first voyage across the Atlantic.

Kipling from the start was deeply interested in children. The two "Jungle Books" (1894–1895) scarcely need discussion, since they are almost universally read and enjoyed. Their boy-hero, Mowgli, reared in the jungle by wolves and acquainted at first hand with all the beasts—the elephant, the python, the monkey, the tiger, and the cobra—is learned in a kind of life which cannot but appeal at some time or other to every one. Kipling's imagination was never more cleverly in command of its material; for the time being the jungle-beasts are the only creatures that dwell on the earth. The "Just-So Stories" facetiously make plain to younger readers how the elephant got his trunk, how the rhinoceros got his wrinkled skin, and how the cat came to walk "by his lone" at night. They are masterpieces in their vigor and invention; though the author occasionally breaks the rules of the game by smiling over the child's shoulder at an adult by-stander.

Of his novels "Captains Courageous" is largely a report of the life led in dangerous waters by the fishermen off the Newfoundland coast. The hero, an American boy who falls from a translantic liner and is rescued by a party of these men, is little more than a figure designed to hold the chapters together. But the reporting is superb. "Kim" appeared in 1901, in Kipling's thirty-sixth year, and it is by many admirers called his greatest book. The hero, like Mowgli, has two strains in his education, though his adventures are all among more or less civilized men. His real name is Kimball O'Hara, and his father was an Irish soldier in India, but his skin is as black from the sun as any Hindu's, and his mind is wholly made over into an Oriental thing. He is a gentle and resourceful boy, of genuine spiritual distinction, and destined to many wanderings; for he takes up with a benign old priest from Tibet, Teshoo Lama, and goes with him on a religious search, at the same time that he becomes engaged with members of the Secret Service. The picture of India is one of the most elaborate ever executed by a western writer between the covers of an imaginative book. "Kim," not only for that reason but because it expresses most sides of Kipling's nature, may outlive many of his slighter works; it may come in time to represent the best of him that is worth preserving.

Conrad
1857–1924
Although Joseph Conrad, like Kipling, first appeared before the public as a writer of tales about far-away places, he had a different kind of tale to tell, and he began under totally different circumstances. He was anything but a prodigy. Kipling at twenty-one was publishing "Departmental Ditties"; Conrad at twenty-one did not know the English language. He was born in Poland in 1857, and his name was Teodor Josef Konrad Karzeniowski. At seventeen he left school to go

to sea, and four years later reached England, which he immediately admired so much that he shipped on a British vessel as ordinary seaman, learning the new speech rapidly and becoming a master in the English merchant service by 1884. After ten years of service in various parts of the earth he resigned, being then thirty-seven, and offered a novel, "Almayer's Folly," to a London publisher. It was accepted and it seemed to the reviewers when printed so interesting a study of life in the Malay Archipelago that Conrad was at once hailed as the Kipling of that locality. He was hardly that, as will later be seen, but his success among discriminating readers was assured, and thenceforth he lived altogether on land in the profession of author. For the first ten years he dealt almost exclusively with the sea as he remembered it from his twenty years of experience upon it. His memory intensified a fascination that he had always felt in the element which is most free if most terrible among the forces of the earth, and these early books are his best, because the most passionate. In the succeeding period he tended to set his scene on land, or at the sea-board; the ocean gradually withdrew from his work until it appeared only now and then as a beautiful reminiscence. Latterly he told stories of England, France, Russia, Italy, South America, and Africa.

The sea purely as an element was not treated by Conrad more than a few times, for his interest was first and last in human character. But the series of "memories and impressions" published as "The Mirror of the Sea" records many aspects of his imaginative experience with great waters, and one story, "Typhoon" (1903), is a complete study of a storm which assailed the vessel of Captain M'Whirr off the coast of the Malay peninsula. Here Conrad's narrative method can be observed to excellent advantage. Detail is piled upon detail in the most careful manner. First the captain is sketched—matter-of-fact, unimaginative, stubborn, and contemptuous of all the signs which are pointing to the approaching monster. The barometer falls at an amazing rate. The sea smells strangely, and has a new color. Clouds appear in ominous formations; there is an unholy calm; then wind and water rush full upon the ship. The author's problem now is to control himself so that the height of his expression may not be reached too soon. Conrad accomplishes this difficult technical feat; time and again the whole fury of the typhoon seems to have been felt, yet there is more and worse coming. At last the vessel arrives safely in port, though it is ludicrously damaged, and the prosaic captain proceeds in his old mood, which for that matter has never been interrupted by the crisis just passed.

Conrad came as closely in "Typhoon" to his ideal of fiction as he came anywhere. What that ideal was he often tried to make clear in essays or autobiographical passages. He emphasizes the importance of the five senses as mediums through which to render his effects. "My task . . . is, by the power of the written word, to make you hear, to make you feel—it is, before all, to make you see. That—and no more, and it is everything." He strenuously directs his aim to "the plasticity of sculpture, to the color of painting, and to the magic suggestiveness of music—which is the art of arts." He is scrupulous to the point of laboriousness. He wishes to tell everything precisely as it happened, and to do this he is convinced that it is necessary to find "the right word," as Flaubert in France had tried a generation before to find it. "Give me the right word and the right accent and I will move the world." When he says that fiction is "an imaginative and exact rendering of authentic memories," he is underlining the second adjective. Given extreme seriousness and sincerity, a man of these convictions will write with difficulty, and the impression of strain is strong over all of Conrad's work. This is only partly the result of his having learned English late. He deliberately complicates his artistic problem, and writes in a manner frankly modeled at times on that of Henry James, who was a close friend of his in England.

The foregoing applies even more definitely to his studies of human character, which aspire to a subtlety and a complexity never dreamed of by Kipling, for instance. "What is a novel," Conrad asks, "if not a conviction of our fellow-men's existence strong enough to take upon itself a form of imagined life clearer than reality . . . ?" His conviction concerning his fellow-men's existence is that it is predominantly a tragic one. When he has not shown men struggling blindly against unguessed odds, and he has liked to show this in the case of the unimaginative Englishmen whom he so much admires, he has painted men at full length in the torment of psychological dilemmas. It is "the capacity for suffering," he says, "which makes man august in the eyes of men." Conrad's attitude in such cases is strictly that of an observer—compassionate, to be sure, but philosophically detached. He views the individual man as philosophers have always tended to view him—as a lonely soul, striving in a close envelope of unfriendly facts to maintain his pride, his sense of self, his very existence. In "The Nigger of the Narcissus" (1897) he describes a ship moving off from shore as being like a planet that swims into infinite space, ringed by horizons that may never be attained. A ship is as personal a thing as a man; both feel, in proportion to their capacities, the largeness and darkness of the universe.

The disadvantages for Conrad's art of seeing men like this are that he courts obscurity and that he deals with mental problems which for many intelligent readers of an opposite persuasion do not exist, and so cannot be made to seem important. But the great advantage is that he hereby sees men intensely, notes their every speech and gesture, and desires to create them so that they will shine steadily in any observer's gaze. His great characters have a solidity and a luminosity which are directly enhanced by the dark seas of uncertainty surrounding them. The most famous is the hero of "Lord Jim" (1900), who is ceaselessly tortured by the ambition to retrieve an error in his past which has undermined his self-respect. Another is the Nigger of the Narcissus, who faces death from disease with a set of subtle faculties never perhaps quite comprehended by the reader, as they never are by the other men on the ship. Another is Almayer, who at every turn is weaker than Nature. Another is Nostromo, who although powerful is conquered by a silver-mine. Another is the hero of "Youth," confronting failure with an indomitable brow. Captain Whalley, in "The End of the Tether," can never be forgotten by one who has seen him as Conrad meant him to be seen—an old man crouching at the head of the vessel whose command he will not relinquish although he has gone blind. So Captain Lingard moves as an unapproachable figure through several novels; so Heyst, in "Victory," is eternally separate even from the woman whom he has taken to an uninhabited island to love; so Captain Falk, in the story to which he gives his name, hungers forever dumbly for the possession of Hermann's niece.

It is for the creation of such personalities as these, as well as for his luxuriant descriptions of nature on land and sea, that Conrad wins respect from other novelists who can appreciate his craft. Whether he will long have a large popular following is a question harder to decide. He presents many difficulties, in his involved and self-conscious style for one thing, and in his highly intricate manner of narration for another. He is so bent upon completeness and verisimilitude in the rendering of an episode that he insists upon giving it through the mouths of numerous witnesses brought for the purpose upon the scene. His narrators, indeed, sometimes get in the way of the story; the device which they represent becomes a mannerism. But with all his difficulties he is a conscientious and skilful artist; his sincerity, his poetry, and his massive reality can never be denied.

Wells 1866– A younger man who appeared on the literary scene at about the same time with Conrad was destined to a very different sort of career. Herbert George Wells began by writing tales of pure wonder and ambitious fancy, but he early developed an interest in man as a gregarious animal, and for years his ruling passion has been sociological.[1] The novels on which his reputation is chiefly based have been anything but patient, laborious structures of mingled realism and romance, as Conrad's novels are; they have been rapid, discursive, provocative studies of definite contemporary problems; they have dealt with "ideas."

Wells's life up to the time that he became an author is variously reflected in his works. Born the son of a small shopkeeper, who failed, he spent some years with his mother at a country-house where she was housekeeper. Later he was a discontented clerk until sixteen, when the reading which he had energetically been doing at spare moments enabled him to become a teacher at a grammar-school. He obtained a scholarship in a scientific school in London, and there he studied the subject which he has always considered the most important of all, biology. Graduating with honors, he was for a time tutor, lecturer, and journalist, until in 1893, at the age of twenty-seven, he became sure that he would be a writer, and settled down in London to a long and busy career.

He has written in a preface to a novel by one of his contemporaries who is noted for his objectivity: "I have no use at all for life as it is, except as raw material. It bores me to look at things unless there is also the idea of doing some-

[1] For his essays, see pages 288–292.

thing with them. . . . In the books I have written, it is always about life being altered I write, or about people developing schemes for altering life. And I have never once 'presented' life. My apparently most objective books are criticisms and incitements to change." This in the main is true, but it does not sufficiently account for the short stories and the scientific romances which Wells wrote during the first ten years of his literary life, and which in the spontaneity and exuberance of their imagination are more pleasing even to-day to some readers than his more serious, more responsible works.

The short stories are rapid, ingenious, and exciting, and they show the young author, under the influence of the scientific speculations his studies had led him to indulge in, exceedingly expert at slipping his readers off the ordinary plane of living into an altogether different one where new laws operate and all objects have a strange, clear look. It is this power to conceive another world, and what is more to describe it, which has made of Wells a dreamer of Utopias and a reformer of the contemporary mind. But in these earliest works he is free from any other purpose than to perfect himself in "the jolly art of making something very bright and moving." He lets his mind play free among miraculous and often horrible things. In one story an orchid reaches out tentacles and sucks the blood of its sleeping owner. Another studies the psychology of fear; a skeptical man left alone in a room supposed to be haunted is reduced almost to insanity merely by the regular going out of the candles which he has set in various places. A crystal egg in a shop window is found to be a lens through which the inhabitants of Mars examine the earth. A naturalist in Madagascar digs up the vast egg of a prehistoric bird from the warm sand where it has lain for centuries, and in the full heat of the sun it hatches. A teacher of chemistry is blown into the fourth dimension by an explosion in the laboratory, and when he returns he is a reversed man; his right hand is the left, as it would be in a mirror. So on through five fascinating volumes in which so far there are few hints of the reforming spirit.

It was in the course of the writing of his scientific romances that Wells discovered and applied his gifts for conceiving better societies than the present one. Even these books—particularly the early ones—are inspired principally by a delight in sheer invention. "The Time Machine" tells of a marvelous contrivance able to convey its passengers not through space but through time. The narrator and the inventor, quite characteristically for the coming Wells, decide to go forward rather than backward; so with very little delay they find themselves in the year 802,701 A. D. The only change which has taken place on the earth is that the two classes of society, the leisured few and the laboring many, have proceeded in their differentiation until one is a race of delicate, mindless creatures inhabiting the surface of the globe and the other is a race of bestial cannibals who come up when necessary from their homes underground and feed on their aristocratic victims. "The Island of Doctor Moreau" is a grisly account of a scientist who has withdrawn to a remote place and there is bloodily vivisecting the lower animals in a more or less successful effort to hasten evolution and turn them into men. "The War of the Worlds" describes an attack upon the earth by superhumanly intelligent creatures shot in steel bombs from Mars. "The War in the Air" and "The World Set Free" demonstrate the devastating qualities of war in the distant future. "The First Men in the Moon" contains a picture of the moon drawn in the light of the surest scientific knowledge. There is purpose in each of these books, but there is even more purpose behind "In the Days of the Comet," which tells how men suddenly were cured of the shortsightedness and the intellectual debility which now make of society so muddled and unhappy a thing.

From what has been said so far it might be deduced that the novels of Wells are deadly in their seriousness. As a matter of fact, they are replete with wit and spirit; they have established their author as one of the humorists of his day. Observation of actual life authenticates most of the pages; houses, streets, schools, laboratories, and country landscapes are presented in lively detail; and the characters, though many of them are not altogether successful to the extent of being made to live outside the books for which they were created, are interesting and brisk. The talk is in almost every case wonderfully eloquent. Wells himself writes with a flow hardly equaled by any contemporary; he knows how to make his people speak forever without being dull. He has mastered the vernacular of his time as few others have mastered it; the most picturesque of slang is sure to be found somewhere in his narrative, and the most familiar attitudes are faithfully expressed.

His earliest realistic novels treated of scenes and experiences that he himself had known, though with interesting differences. "Love and Mr. Lewisham" takes a young man through the assistant-mastership of such a grammar-school as that in which Wells had first taught and to a course in science in London. But instead of graduating him with honors, it gets him married to a poor if attractive girl who by her dependence upon him distracts him from his intellectual duty and ruins his career. The book is a brief against premature marriage, as well as a reminder that there are several things in life as important as love—work, thought, ambition. But it is also a cleverly documented report upon the state of the middle classes intellectually and emotionally. It is one of Wells's first books to attempt a demonstration of how pathetically common the life of common people is. Middle-class language, furniture, dress, education, religion, morals, are mercilessly hit off; a rather seedy society looks at itself in this mirror. "Kipps" comes at the same truth from a different angle. The hero is a draper's clerk, as Wells had been, and the story deals with his failure to make any real use of the twelve hundred pounds a year which he suddenly inherits. He thinks to rise in society and marry well, but he gives up and marries a servant girl when he realizes that society cannot accommodate itself to rapid changes, or that if it could his pitiful middle-class culture would not support him even among the false comforts of the well-to-do. Wells permits himself at the end to blame his hero's fiasco on "the ruling power of this land, Stupidity." "The History of Mr. Polly" again has for its hero an insignificant draper. But nothing happens to Mr. Polly except that he wearies of the dinginess and pettiness of his business and wanders off to indulge his love of beauty and quaintness in a wider world. His quest comes to naught because the world is not hospitable to such spirits—seeing in them, Wells implies, only their foolishness and not their virtue of mind and temperament. This novel, delightful as it is in its irresponsibility and gaiety, declares itself near the end as a sermon against the prodigality of a society which wastes such excellent human material as Mr. Polly vainly offered. It is also an exposure of the humbug of business; but "Tono-Bungay" (1909) is more distinctly and more powerfully that. "Tono-Bungay" is in many ways the best of Wells's novels, as it is probably his most popular. It is another picture of society in the process of wasting its material because it does not know how to direct its energy. Miriam, a fine and original woman, comes to nothing. George Ponderevo, the hero's uncle, throws away his vigorous if vulgar life making a huge fortune out of a worthless patent medicine called Tono-Bungay. That he loses it at last is not so important as that he prostituted his strength to advertising, publicity, pretense, and meaningless enterprises. Wells was one of the first to ridicule at close hand the shoddy psychology of modern business, and to indicate that it is rendering a once beautiful world less fit to live in. The gusto of "Tono-Bungay" is enormous; the eloquence is overwhelming; the reporting of contemporary talk is well-nigh perfect.

Since 1909 Wells has tended in his novels to treat more specific issues than those of middle-class life and the psychology of business, although he has not failed in any case to relate these to the general social problem. Indeed, he has become increasingly discursive with time, so that whole chapters may be little more than essays or debates on economics, politics, or the position of woman, and the bearings of such questions on the general happiness of the race. "Ann Veronica" introduces into fiction a certain type of modern woman who has since grown very familiar. Ann tires of the stuffy air in her commonplace father's household and, throwing over a condescending male of the town who wishes to marry her and "protect her," goes to London to make her living with her brains. She studies biology, falls in love with a young scientist who already is uncongenially married, and lives with him frankly until his wife is no longer an obstacle to their marriage. Her coolness and intelligence brought a freshness into contemporary studies of women, and she has many imitators in the novel. "The New Machiavelli" exposes the confusion and cynicism of twentieth century politics. "Marriage" deals more maturely with the problem that was considered in "Love and Mr. Lewisham." A scientist who marries after a beautiful courtship finds that social life interferes with his work, so takes his wife to Labrador where they come to an understanding of the things which they consider important. The author implies that in such a helter-skelter existence as is led to-day by even the best people there is too little time for self-scrutiny or for differentiation among ideals. "The Passionate Friends" shows a rare love between two high-minded persons put to death by the prejudices of a thoughtless society, and more particularly by the brutal possessiveness of a conventional husband. A similar husband is attacked in "The Wife of Sir Isaac Harman." "The Research Magnificent" has a title as well as a theme entirely characteristic of its author. Wells's mind has ever been conducting passionate researches into life, hoping against hope that some formula could be found whereby men and women could learn to live "nobly and thoroughly." Such is the hope of the hero in this case; but the conclusion is that the search is long and hard in the present world.

Since "The World of William Clissold" (1926), a two-volume novel which was more discussion than story, Wells's vogue as a writer of fiction has rapidly declined. "William Clissold" was substantially a failure, in spite of the excellence with which many subjects were treated in its pages; and its successors have tended to be trifles, fantasias, or extravaganzas. "Star-Begotten: A Biological Fantasia" (1937), for instance, shows its author returning to his original medium, the scientific miracle. But he has returned with a difference; the old zest is gone, and the old fineness of fancy.

Bennett
1867–1931

The names of Wells and Bennett are often coupled in discussions of the modern novel, yet the two writers had little in common beyond the fact that both were modern, unsentimental, brisk, witty, and realistic in their descriptions of middle-class life. Arnold Bennett came like Wells from a commercial world and a commonplace atmosphere, and like Wells he exploited those beginnings in his fiction. At bottom, however, his attitude was widely different from that of any other British novelist of the first rank. He had none of the philosophy or the romance of Hardy, none of the estheticism of Moore, none

of the sentimentalism of Barrie, none of the conscious viril-
ity of Kipling, none of the musing over destiny and personality of Conrad, and above all none of the critical passion of
Wells. He was to all appearances perfectly satisfied with
the life that he saw; he saw it with the shrewdest and clearest eyes of his generation; and he presented it in terms of
the sanest realism.

Bennett had an uneventful, workmanlike career. Born
in one of a group of pottery-towns which he was later to
make famous as the Five Towns, he early received a multitude of impressions which doubtless he never dreamed
would work themselves into fiction. He went to London
University, returned shortly to spend four years in the
law office of his father, practised a little journalism in
the office of a local newspaper, became restless, and went
to London again, where the call of journalism became
stronger than that of the law. He did not begin to take
himself seriously as an author until 1893, when he sold a
story, and he achieved nothing like success until several
years after that. In the meantime he was an indefatigable
reader of English and French literature, and he tried his
hand at nearly every form of composition—book reviews,
articles, sketches, and stories. He went to France in 1900
for a visit which lasted eight years, and there settled down
to the composition of his initial series of books.

It was not at once that he developed to the full his
technic for reporting the Five Towns. Having determined
to make his living by authorship, he turned in these early
years to whatever was most profitable, and this meant
then, as it has meant on various occasions since, sensational fiction of no very high order. Bennett classed the
novels which he wrote under this impulse as Fantasias.
They are exceedingly clever, as all that he writes is; but
they are distinguished by no genuine imagination, and
they are often lacking in the fine sensibilities which set

his superior narratives apart in a type of their own. The scene is usually London, and the action is likely to be violent or fantastic. Ghosts, coffins, robberies, and murders, with all the other trash of terror-stories, are handled with real but shallow ingenuity. Perhaps the best single example is "Buried Alive," which has fewest of the crude elements just enumerated. It became widely popular, and was dramatized by the author for a still greater audience under the title "The Great Adventure." It is the story of Priam Farll, an eminent English painter who so dislikes publicity that when his valet dies he allows the police to think that he himself has died, thinking thus to escape attention disguised as the valet. While the supposed Priam Farll is being buried with honors in Westminster Abbey, the real Farll buries himself in London, marries the woman who had been corresponding with the valet through a matrimonial bureau, is confronted by the valet's deserted wife, and finally gives himself away through his inability to keep from his easel. His pictures are sold, identified as Farll's, and eventually used as evidence of his existence. The book is smart, inventive, and glib; but there is none of the human nature in it which Bennett was to document so carefully in his works of permanent value. In the composition of it Bennett was never restricted to facts, whereas his true forte was facts; he wrote the most profoundly when he kept his observation under the strictest control, when he struggled with the most stubborn, the most unpromising, the dullest material.

In an early autobiographical work, "The Truth About an Author," Bennett analyzed the more serious problems of fiction which he wished to solve. He made clear in the first place his indebtedness to French realistic fiction, the detachment of which he always emulated. But more important than that, he formulated a philosophy of the commonplace. He spoke of "that intense and unoriginal humanity that distinguishes all of us." The two adjectives are of equal significance, "unoriginal" referring to the human traits which literally everybody has observed, and "intense" implying that in the right hands those traits may be raised to a high place in the imagination. He wished to see "the usual miraculously transformed by Art into the Sublime." Critics of Bennett have tended to emphasize his preoccupation with the usual and to forget that his transformation of it was miraculous. "I am so morbidly avaricious of beauty," he went on to say, "that I insist on finding it even where it is not." This did not mean that he was to gild the more vulgar aspects of human life with false or romantic prettiness; it meant that he was to see the truth with so just and open an eye that it would assume the beauty which pure truth always wears. Fortunately he was equipped with "an omnivorous and tenacious memory"; he was not to forget the most trivial gesture that his gaze had ever caught, even in the years of his boyhood. And as if to guarantee the modernity of his work, he prophesied that he would take "a malicious and frigid pleasure in setting down facts which are opposed to accepted sentimental falsities." He was to be as free from illusion as Bernard Shaw, though incidentally he was never to wage war for definite ideas of philosophy and conduct.

In addition to all this, Bennett happened to be the possessor of a quality which has been of the utmost value to him as a realist—humor. He was one of the most original humorists of his day, and his humor, being original, was also of course unique. It was a direct result of his honesty in scrutinizing both himself and others. Indeed, his observation seems usually to have begun with himself. There is no evidence that he ever had illusions about himself, and he refused to have illusions about other people. He was acquainted with all the little vanities and pretenses and exultations of the purely private self—the innumerable emotions which are never confessed and seldom even recognized. His heroes and heroines are all egotists of one sort or another, as human beings in general are; that is, they are self-centered, proud of their triumphs, unaware of being really heroic but willing to take the credit for being so, watchful for advantages which they can take over the world, intelligent though not always clear-headed, imperfect, decent, and ordinary. In following their thoughts as well as their actions the reader becomes peculiarly their friend because he knows them to be like himself, and incidentally he is surprised to find that any one else knows him so well.

Even among the Five-Town novels there is a division to be made on the ground of merit. All are excellent in their way, but some are lighter than others. "Denry the Audacious," first published in England as "The Card," contains some of Bennett's most easy and charming humor. Denry the hero is a young man of no particular distinction who by mere luck and nerve blunders into one success after another until he reaches the loftiest position conceivable by a Five-Townsman: he is elected mayor. His adventures are exquisitely funny for the most part. Bennett seems constantly to be making sport of him, yet he likes him, and the reader likes him, because he is unable to predict his own successes, and is ingenuously delighted with them when they come. Bennett implies by this or that ironic parenthesis that the mayorship is not the highest reach of human happiness in his personal estimation, and that the people of the Towns are most of them stupid and vain; yet he at no time abandons himself, as Wells would have done and indeed did do in "Tono-Bungay," to a sermon against the insufficiency of the commercial ideal. This is the way that people behave, and that is enough for Bennett. "Helen with the High Hand" is even more irresponsible comedy. It is the story of a clever young woman's conquest of her old uncle, whose household she has entered in spite of a family feud that has long separated them, and whom she finally induces by her extremest blandishments to take a larger house which she likes better. The incidental comment of Bennett upon the motives and processes of his people is deliciously illuminating. The reader temporarily feels himself to be a specialist in human nature, and congratulates himself upon his ability to see through the externals of conduct. All he needs to do, of course, to disabuse himself of this notion is to close the book and try his luck with new people. Others of the minor Five-Town novels are more serious. "Anna of the Five Towns," one of the first and best, tells a quiet and tragic story of a woman who is loved by two men and is forced to accept the stronger but less likable one. Certain sordid aspects of pottery life are touched upon, and in particular a miser is introduced with great skill. Bennett was always interested in misers, as many French novelists are; they afforded him scope for his calculating, refined genius; he loved to trace their stinginess through every picturesque if forbidding step. Later on, "Riceyman Steps" furnished another instance of his power in this direction. "Whom God Hath Joined" is concerned with the tragedy of divorce as it affects family relationships in Staffordshire. And quite incidentally it contains a number of sentences expressive of Bennett's unique attitude toward the materials of his fiction. "These people are the most commonplace people on earth, but they touch me profoundly," he says; and he speaks of "a strange, overpowering, mystical sense of the wonder of existence" in the presence of the flattest provincials. Bennett also wrote a number of short stories upon his favorite themes. They are expert in their various manners, but on the whole he is more impressive when he is covering a larger canvas;

reality requires a great deal of room in which to be felt, just as long experience is necessary before one can claim to know life.

Bennett's supreme novel of the Five Towns is "The Old Wives' Tale" (1908). This is his masterpiece, and it is one of the most interesting books of the twentieth century. It is a very long and detailed account of the lives of two sisters, Constance and Sophia Baines, daughters of a small draper in Bursley. Constance leads a comparatively humdrum existence at home, growing up, marrying, and being left alone at last with her placid thoughts. Sophia has more exciting adventures. She runs away with a cheap scalawag to Paris, is deserted there on the eve of the siege by the Germans in 1870–1871, establishes a boarding-house which makes her a good living, and finally comes home to spend her old age with Constance. Bennett's point of view throughout this epic of the commonplace is never explicitly stated, but it is clearly not satiric, as Wells's might have been. Neither on the other hand is it sentimentally sympathetic. He is profoundly interested in the two women, and as they approach death he is respectful. But the plain truth —which he trusts to be beautiful—is his chief concern at all times. He pours between the covers of the book the richest observations he has been able to make of the five towns which he names, somewhat differently from the atlas, Bursley, Turnhill, Hanbridge, Knype, and Longshaw, with Oldcastle as an occasional sixth. And in addition he lavishes his powers of interpretation upon the figures and the souls of his two heroines. He tells in a later edition of the novel how he happened to create Constance and Sophia. He was in a restaurant in Paris one day when he saw a plump old lady of no particular distinction get up from her table and trudge away, dropping a few bundles as she did so and being much embarrassed at the laughter of the smarter girls who frequented the place. He was moved to the reflection that at some time in this creature's life, and to some few friends, she had been attractive and important; and he immediately set about filling in an imaginary life for her and for a sister whom he added to make the picture complete. The result, after several years of labor, was "The Old Wives' Tale." The story, when it is not laughable or pathetic or bustling with action, is impressive in the way it rounds out the meaning of existence. All life, including the reader's life, takes on a significance not perhaps deeper than that which it essentially has, but not, certainly, shallower.

Although "The Old Wives' Tale" is generally conceded to be Bennett's chief work, it has a close rival in a series of four novels dealing with the lives of Edward Clayhanger and Hilda Lessways. "Clayhanger" (1910) takes the ordinary if sterling hero through a rather dreary childhood which ends with the breakdown of his father, an old printer; through his arrival at manhood and a kind of success; through his love for the strange and passionate Hilda; through his engagement to her; and finally through the disappointment of his life when she without so much as a warning marries another man. "Hilda Lessways" (1911) tells the same story from the heroine's angle, explaining her forced marriage to the bigamist George Cannon and preparing for her eventual freedom when she can marry Clayhanger. "These Twain" (1916) analyzes in brilliant detail the more or less petty difficulties of their married life together and creates the character of George, Hilda's son by Cannon. In the fourth novel of the series, "The Roll-Call," the younger Cannon practises architecture in London, wins a prize, marries, fails to advance in his profession, and when the World War happens along enlists with a sigh of relief. So much for the skeleton. The flesh and the blood of the series are more important, consisting as they do of humor and pathos, satire and sympathy, observation and creative interpretation on the magnificent scale to which "The Old Wives' Tale" has accustomed the reader. There are few characters in English fiction so well known to one who has met them as Edward and Hilda. When in "The Roll-Call" (1919) they come to London to assist at the birth of George's child, and George, looking out of an up-stairs window, sees their homely, faithful, provincial shoulders emerging from the taxicab which has brought them from the station, a rush of recognition sweeps over the reader as it does over the son, and life for the moment is inexpressibly enriched. Certain portions of the four novels are already classic, as for instance the account in "Clayhanger" of the decline of Darius, Edward's father; or Edward's visit to Hilda at Brighton; or the visit of both of them to Cannon in the prison, in "These Twain." But the virtue of the whole resides after all in its completeness, its soundness, and its power of convincing the reader in fresh ways that the burden of life, even of every-day life, is what Edward once called it, "exquisite."

Arnold Bennett explored a limited locality for his material, as Hardy did for his; but he did not read into that locality more than was there. Neither did he find it crying for reform, as Wells found a similar locality. If he lost poetry or piquancy by this method, he at least gained his own kind of truth. And since he tells the truth with genius, he cannot be tiresome until life itself is tiresome.

Gals- The labors of John Galsworthy were divided
worthy about equally between fiction and the drama,[1]
1867–1933 and he has readers in one department who do not know him in the other. Until 1922, when his greatest novel was completed and given to the public as "The Forsyte Saga," there was reasonable doubt as to which of his two forms he excelled in. Then it became plain that he was first

[1] For his plays, see pages 264–267.

of all a novelist; and it is hardly to be denied that in the book just named he achieved one of the three or four significant stories of the present century.

The objections to his fiction in former years were chiefly two. In the first place, he seemed to be using literature as a vehicle for moral ideas; he was didactic. In the second place, he was not vigorous and incisive enough in his narrative; instead of making his books frankly tracts, he softened their outlines with "atmosphere" and allowed his criticism of society to be muffled in a vague voice of pity and sympathy. The gentleman and the artist seemed too much mixed within him. His life was known to be comfortable and serene. He had been given the most fashionable kind of education at Harrow and Oxford, and after a trial of the law, with extensive travel for recreation, he had settled down as a country gentleman to write books. The books themselves were beautifully written; if possible too much so. Their language was exquisitely turned; they abounded in subtle descriptive passages; their sentiments were eminently humane; but they somehow lacked the final force which might sharpen them into effective masterpieces.

"Fraternity" (1908) is by certain critics declared Galsworthy's best work before "The Forsyte Saga." The dominating character is an old philosopher, Mr. Stone, who is writing an endless book on brotherly love. A beautifully minded if cracked old metaphysician and poet, he reads out paragraphs of his lone masterpiece in the quavering voice of a defeated Chorus, while beneath his very eyes, if he could but see them, tragedies and comedies are being enacted in the real world which give the lie to his speculations. Hilary and his wife Bianca are unaccountably estranged; pride and subtle incompatibilities keep them from reconciliation even while Mr. Stone declares for universal love. Hilary is drawn at the same time toward a destitute little artist's model of the lowest social class; there seems to be a possibility that the two will go away together and be happy in a simpler place; but Hilary's traditions have too strong a hold upon him, and in the end he gives up the ghost of his attachment in despair. Other members of the poorer class languish in a wretched state of being unable to help themselves; other members of the well-to-do wish to help them and never find out how. There is no fraternity, no interfeeling. All is paralysis, vain longing, incurable futility.

Galsworthy found escape from this artistic and moral Slough of Despond in two ways. He created human beings who are free because they are completely passionate, and he created others who are real because they live their lives in ignorance or disregard of philosophical problems. The best examples of the first are women, and the best examples of the second are men—particularly old men.

The women are Mrs. Bellew in "The Country House," Mrs. Noel in "The Patrician," Anne Stormer, Olive Cramier, and Nell Dromore in "The Dark Flower," Noel Pierson in "Saint's Progress," and Irene Forsyte in "The Forsyte Saga." With two exceptions these are mature women, and with one exception they are married. Their passion is by no means a plaything; it is not in the superficial sense of the word romantic. It is, Galsworthy seems to say, the fundamental thing in their lives as it is the fundamental thing in all human existence. It is the thing which redeems society from too much comfort, from too much money, from all its crueler or dingier aspects. It is the devine fire in an otherwise earthy world. With this in mind, one cannot perhaps object that the women who possess it are considerably alike. They are invariably quiet with a hunted quietness; they are soft and mysterious and beautiful; they suffer without end from the grosser qualities of husbands, fathers, relatives, and friends who set respectability above private integrity, who honor law before love.

One cannot object, that is, on the score of poetry or philosophy; but one can object on the score of fiction. This very sameness which makes a half-dozen women impressive as documents robs them of validity as characters. They are almost completely lay-figures which their creator has employed to preach a sermon on the necessity of passion. Take their passion away and little remains except a colorless, stereotyped beauty. It is not they who feel the passion in the first place; it is Galsworthy. So even they do not redeem him altogether from the charge that his fiction is more himself than mankind, more propaganda than truth. It is as if he had decided in the calm of his study that passion is important and had invented some people to put it in; not as if he had found the people first and presented them initially as people, with passion as only one, if an important one, of their qualities.

The old men of Galsworthy, however, are indisputably a triumph. They are obviously the fruit of observation, and one suspects that they are the persons whom Galsworthy has most relished living among. He understands them perfectly; he remembers even the most trivial thing that they do; they are marvels of objective and interesting reality. He has arrived at them through a prolonged study of the institution of the family. Although upon occasion he has seemed to be discussing the family as a sociological problem, he has at all times given an accurate, living picture of it; it has lived for him as people live for any first-rate creative writer—with flesh-and-blood reality. There is the Pendyce family in "The Country House." There is the Valleys family in "The Patrician." There are the four Freeland brothers in "The Freelands." Above all, there are the innumerable Forsytes in "The Forsyte Saga."

"The Forsyte Saga" grew slowly from its beginnings in the first of the three novels which compose it, "The Man of Property" (1906), through "In Chancery" (1920) and

"To Let" (1922). In the volume of nearly nine hundred pages which now contains the three there are in addition two interludes, or short stories, called "Indian Summer of a Forsyte"—one of the finest products of Galsworthy's pen—and "Awakening." The five narratives together make up an epic of truly heroic proportions, an epic of the English family; and it is one of the solidest contributions to contemporary fiction. The theme, if a theme be sought, is, as always with Galsworthy, social. The conflict of forces is a conflict between the sense of property on the one hand—middle-class materialism or British Philistinism—and the sense of beauty on the other—the free worship of beauty and love which does not count the cost, either in possessions or in social standing. The first force is represented chiefly by Soames Forsyte, a man who increasingly demands the reader's pity because of his unconquerable deficiency in the lovelier qualities of the race. He is rich, successful, and upright, but he never quite sheds the sense that he owns all that he has: whereas, Galsworthy indicates, the most precious things are common, and cannot be cornered. Soames even owns his wife, Irene; and her struggle to escape from his cold grasp furnishes the plot of the novel. She is Galsworthy's masterpiece among his quiet, soft, passionate women, and her story is the story of her loving two other men, Bosinney and young Jolyon Forsyte, until she achieves the freedom which is her necessity and her destiny. But neither the plot nor the theme is the crowning virtue of "The Forsyte Saga." That virtue inheres in its complete and permanent picture of a certain kind of life. The family which it describes is almost bewilderingly large, and it has a sufficient variety. Only Soames and Irene are uniquely one thing or another—types around which a war of forces could be supposed to wage. The rest either stand for different stages of social growth or are in themselves mixtures of many qualities. The essential fact is that they are real. They exist as acquaintances of the reader, being born, working, loving, marrying, growing old, and dying in the various houses which the reader visits so often that they become as familiar as his own. Three generations pass before the narrative is done. Perhaps the first of these is the finest in point of characterization, including as it does the six elder Forsyte brothers, James, Swithin, Roger, Nicholas, Timothy, and Old Jolyon, and the four sisters, Ann, Julia, Hester, and Susan. Old Jolyon and his line, down through Young Jolyon to June, Jolly, Holly, and Jon, will engage any one's affection. The death of Old Jolyon is told in the interlude called "Indian Summer of Forsyte," and it is one of the most magnificent deaths recorded anywhere in fiction. The old man was a ripe, confessed pagan, enjoying his money, his wine, his food, and his children to the utmost limit, and incidentally, as with all true pagans, feeling if only fitfully the urge of beauty in a wider and freer world than the one into which he had been born.

Galsworthy continued the history of the Forsytes in a sequel consisting of three novels, "The White Monkey," "The Silver Spoon," and "Swan Song." These were collected in 1929 under the title "A Modern Comedy," which Galsworthy explained in a preface by saying: "An Age which knows not what it wants, yet is intensely preoccupied with getting it, must evoke a smile, if rather a sad one." The remark indicates clearly enough that Galsworthy's sympathies are not with the period which his comedy covers. The time is 1922–1926, and for Galsworthy the England of these years has completely forgotten the art of standing still. Not only is Property gone, along with God, Free Trade, Marriage, Consols, Coal, and Caste; but there is no longer any sense that the future is predictable, or that it is worth planning for. The nation, like the rest of the world, has the "jitters." The General strike of 1926 is hostilely presented, and Galsworthy has little respect for the desires his young people are moved by—so little, indeed, that his trilogy is not finally effective either as tragedy or as comedy. Its central personage is Fleur, daughter of Soames Forsyte and wife of Michael Mont. Her libel suit against a woman who has publicly called her a snob and a lion-hunter takes up much of the space, symbolizing as it does the desperateness with which, in an age uncertain of its values, she has taken to the salon for her spirit's entertainment. But the chief action concerns her hopeless love for Jon Forsyte, son of Irene and Jolyon and husband of Anne Wilmot. Realizing that she cannot have Jon, Fleur tries to die in her father's house, but only succeeds in setting it afire so that when Soames comes to the rescue he is killed, ironically, by the fall of one of his own beloved pictures. But he has also been killed in effect by his beloved daughter. And so the trilogy ends with the death of Soames; and with the resolution of Fleur to make something out of her life yet, though Galsworthy seems unable to guess what that will be. "A Modern Comedy" has its interest, but it is distinctly inferior to "The Forsyte Saga," the materials of which he perfectly understood and loved.

In John Galsworthy English fiction possesses one of its most finished and admirable writers, but a man who has left to posterity only a few characters and a few situations sufficiently free from the peculiar problems of their day to be long worthy of acquaintance. The Forsytes are that, and some others; and they, perhaps, are enough. Most great novelists are remembered for one or, at the farthest, two or three books. Galsworthy will be remembered for "The Forsyte Saga" as Bennett will be remembered for "The Old Wives' Tale" and the Clayhanger-Lessways tetralogy.

A rival of both "The Old Wives' Tale" and **Maugham** "The Forsyte Saga" for the position of first **1874-** place among twentieth-century British novels has been written by a younger man who in no other work has approached his masterpiece. William Somerset Maugham's "Of Human Bondage" was published in 1915, during the World War, and perhaps for that reason did not produce the immediate effect upon readers which it deserved to produce. But it has stolen quietly and surely into general estimation until now there are critics prepared to call it the triumph of its generation. However that may be, it is excellent evidence in support of the hypothesis that a writer will do his best work when he is drawing upon his own experience. Maugham, who incidentally is most popularly known for his numerous witty plays, has written several novels which have been ingenious in conception and skilful in execution. But they have been based upon situations invented for the purpose; they have been significant for their art rather than for their life. "Of Human Bondage" is more than a situation; it is a life, and it is the author's life. It is perhaps the most brilliant of the many autobiographical novels which the present century has seen.

Passing notice may be given to a minor novel of Maugham's, "The Moon and Sixpence." It is his second-best book, and significantly enough it also is based upon the known life of a man—not the author in this case, but a modern French painter of genius, Paul Gauguin. Maugham's hero, Charles Strickland, happens to be an Englishman, but he pursues a career closely resembling that of a Frenchman. In middle age he suddenly abandons his business and his family for art, painting in Paris through years of cruel poverty until opportunity offers for a voyage to the South Seas, where he works on in comparative solitude until his horrible death from leprosy in a cottage whose walls he has covered with the finest, most mysterious products of his genius. The book is chiefly a study of temperament. Strickland is an inarticulate man who knows within himself exactly what he wants to do but who cannot express himself in any other medium than color and line. Outwardly he is callous to an almost fiendish degree; utterly indifferent to the claims of other people, he rides them down, snarling at those who would help him and contemptuous of those who condemn him. Inwardly he is filled with a vast desire for beauty of a sort which has never before been captured; this ideal he pursues to a more or less successful end. Maugham has employed all of his great intelligence, and not a little of his characteristic bitterness, in the account of this man dominated by a terrible purpose.

"Of Human Bondage" tells the story, with certain inevitable modifications, of the first thirty years of Maugham's life. He studied first in England and then in Germany; tried painting for a while in Paris, but gave it up; became a physician in London; and only later embraced the profession of author. His hero, Philip Carey, goes to school in England and Germany, spends futile years among the artists of Paris, returns to London for a medical training, and leaves the reader at the close to continue happily in a country practice. The greatness of the book, however, consists in two qualities which are independent of the plot. One of these is completeness in the picturization of life; the other is integrity in the presentation of a personality. Philip has a multitude of adventures, some of them fortunate but most of them wretched. The triumph of Maugham is that he has been able to render any aspect of existence which his hero has touched both interesting and important. The reader looks through Philip's intelligent and remarkably clear eyes at an English school, a German university, a colony of artistic failures in France, a dreary business house in London, the streets of London, a medical college, a hospital, and a village on the British coast. All these places, and many more, come as close to the reader as they did to Philip, and Maugham may digress as long as he likes in analysis or description; the words are fascinating because they are true. The gallery of characters is equally long and good; Philip's uncle and aunt, Miss Wilkinson, Weeks the American in Germany, Hayward the esthete, Cronshaw and Lawson the artists, Fanny Price the pathetic suicide, Mildred, the Athelnys, and Dr. South—these suffer, rejoice, and live forever. Philip himself, the personality through which the rich experience of the book is passed, learns much from the world, and teaches the reader much. The book is an intensely personal one. Philip is not in the least concerned, as one of Wells's heroes might have been, with showing the world how to live; he struggles to wrest from the world the secret of its own ways. Physically handicapped by a club-foot, he is inordinately sensitive to cruelty and disappointment; he is forced to ask time and again what life means, for there seems to be no reason in its behavior toward him. His conclusion is that life has no meaning which can be set forth in a formula; it is this for one person and that for another, but if one has lived thoroughly one's memories will shape themselves into a pattern as rich though as unsymmetrical as those patterns formed by the colors in an oriental rug. It is a wise young man who has learned this at thirty; a generous, intelligent, clear-minded, imaginative, and in no respect morbid human being. One other character in "Of Human Bondage" can scarcely be described. Mildred, the commonplace girl whom Philip so stubbornly and unaccountably loves to his loss, is unique in fiction. There seems to be no reason for her being loved; but she undeniably is, as the suffering which she contributes to Philip's sum is undeniable. She takes her important place among the innumerable facts of existence which have educated Philip in patience, in understanding, in matureness and profoundness of emotion.

Maugham's later fiction has usually taken the form of the short story, and his settings have been by preference remote—the South Seas, China, or some other region of the world where the British live sparsely in colonies and meet one another from time to time for long conversations in clubs. An atmosphere of leisure, whiskey-and-soda reminiscence, and worldly wisdom hangs over most of the volumes in which Maugham has collected his tales—usually in the number six, since they run to generous length. The action developed is likely, in contrast with this atmosphere, to be sharp and violent; Maugham wishes to be entertaining, has no illusions about the length of time these books will live, and takes care to deliver an appropriate amount of sensation and suspense in each narrative. He himself has said that his favorite story is "Red," from the volume called "The Trembling of a Leaf." It develops a characteristic irony: a sailor leaves a native girl, she marries another man, and she continues to dream of the sailor so that she cannot give her whole devotion to her husband. Years later, however, the husband sees the sailor and finds him fat, cheap, and ugly; it was for this that she had sacrificed two happinesses. Maugham's ironies are often as obvious as that, and his epigrams frequently have the same quality; though there is an unquestionable intelligence at work too, and the narrative skill is regularly high. The story "Rain," originally called "Miss Thompson," is perhaps the best known thing of its length by Maugham, since it was popular when dramatized under the later title, and since it dealt shrewdly with the psychology of repression—a favorite subject at the time. "The Casuarina Tree," "Ashenden," "First Person Singular," and "Ah King" are other volumes which have served their purpose of entertainment well, the story "Virtue" in the third of these, and "Footprints in the Jungle," from the fourth, being especially characteristic of their author's later manner. "Footprints in the Jungle" describes a couple, the Cartwrights, who have never been charged with the crime of killing Mrs. Cartwright's former husband, though they have been suspected. They have survived the incident gracefully, living now with apparently free minds; though a man who knew them at the time can remember that when Mrs. Cartwright was told of her husband's body being found, "she gave a long gasp, it was not exactly a scream, it reminded me oddly of a piece of silk torn in two." In 1930 Maugham diverted the literary public with "Cakes and Ale," a merry and satirical novel which was widely supposed to have a replica of Thomas Hardy for its hero, though the evidence for this was not complete. Even more interesting was the portrait of Alroy Kear, a literary politician who seemed to fit several figures of the time. He was sketched with diabolical accuracy, not to say malice, and the satire was salutary. Maugham's talents in this direction could have been oftener used with advantage to the cause of human decency and dignity. His review of his own career, "The Summing Up," makes it clear how highly he has always valued that cause and yet with how strict a modesty he has confined his attention to the literary craft. His candor, his intelligence, and his lack of illusion concerning himself have prevented him perhaps too often from aiming beyond his average mark; but they are attractive qualities in themselves, and few books possess them in brighter degree than "The Summing Up."

Lawrence
1887–1930
Among the younger generation of British writers who dominated the field of fiction in the third decade of the twentieth century as Wells, Bennett, and Galsworthy had dominated it in the first two decades, David Herbert Lawrence was the most powerful. His temperament was a novelty in contemporary literature, marking him as essentially of a new age, and separating him from his elders by a gulf which represented more than the World War. The war created in him the disillusion, the contempt for democratic masses, and the indifference toward all public questions which are so bitterly expressed in his pages. But the growing violence of the century found its

culmination in him, as it did in several of his brilliant young coevals. They denied the validity of all experience save that which is personal, self-centered, and free. Conventional ethics, politics, duty, responsibility do not exist in their books; only the processes of individual psychology are worth detailing; and here Lawrence spoke with authority, not only as one who had explored his own tremendous endowment of emotion, but as one who possessed the knowledge which the modern science of psychology, and more particularly of what is called psychoanalysis, had made current.

The son of a Nottinghamshire coal-miner, Lawrence after some years of teaching in London began writing novels, and his third one, "Sons and Lovers" (1913), made him immediately famous. It is in some measure autobiographical, as the hero Paul Morel is brought up among miners and sees many rough aspects of life. More important as autobiography are the experiences of Paul as a lover. These may have had little or no basis in outward fact, but they were central to Lawrence's psychology, and they were described in a manner which afterwards became proverbial in his books. Paul, like most of Lawrence's heroes, is a passionate but a baffled lover—baffled not only by the refusal of women to return his love but by his own failures to satisfy his nature completely. As many scenes of revulsion and disgust are given as of attraction or happiness. Lawrence studied more carefully than any other dead or living author the reverse side of love—the side of hate, of sudden disillusionment, of self-love interfering with love of another. Lawrence's people are stubbornly egoistic; they in no case consent to surrender their private wills; they wish always to feel themselves intact. Love is the chief enemy of self-possession; war is Lawrence's invariable theme. His masterly short stories pursue the same subject, as do several later novels. Or they pursue a kindred subject, such as the power of touch to break down the ego, which is treated in "The Blind Man," one of Lawrence's finest short stories in a volume called "England, My England" (1922).

Lawrence's death at forty-three was felt as an irreparable loss by devotees whom he had won in England and America. Increasingly restless towards the end of his life, he flung himself from one country and one continent to another in search of a formula wherewith the malady of contemporary thought—its paleness, its "whiteness," its unreality—could be corrected. He never found this formula, though his pursuit of it was so passionate and so disinterested that he assumed the proportions of a Messiah and after his death was worshiped by a sort of cult. Two of his later novels are eloquent in their employment of symbols to suggest the reservoir of power from which in Lawrence's opinion most modern people had cut themselves off. In "St. Mawr" the symbol is a horse, a great golden stallion whose eyes have eternity in them and whose wildness makes two American women, Lou Witt and her mother, his slaves forever. In "The Plumed Serpent" the symbol is borrowed from the ancient religion of Mexico. It is none other than the god Quetzalcoatl, whom certain moderns attempt to revive as a living deity. One of these moderns is an Irish woman, Kate Leslie, the heroine of the book; the others are Don Ramón and Don Cipriano, two Mexicans of extraordinary personal power who found a religion and become not only its high priests but indeed its gods. The details of this religion and its rituals are strange and rich; Lawrence never wrote better than here, even though some readers may not share his conviction, frequently voiced through the mystic utterances of Don Ramón, that the time has come for penetrating to the dark, deep, hot, flowing life at the center of the world, or that such a consummation is ever to be more than wished. At his worst Lawrence is a mystagogue; at his best he is a writer of flaming sincerity, and of an eloquence unmatched anywhere in modern British fiction.

Huxley 1894– With the rest of his generation. Aldous Huxley came to suspect the validity of the ways of life which were generally accepted during the past century but which were broken up in the turmoil accompanying the war. He saw the established virtues practised without reward and the established vices practised without penalty. He saw prudence dejected and folly triumphant. Moreover, learning confirmed him in his pessimism. History assured him that the general direction of mankind is full of purposeless drifting; science assured him that men, if more than puppets, are at best no more than animals. The mystery of life itself may possibly be discovered to reside in the atom. The mystery of character, of love, hate, ambition, devotion, may turn out to depend upon the chemical action of obscure glands. Human existence may therefore be best regarded as a dance, either a dance of life or a dance of death. Thus, indeed, the matter was regarded in Huxley's early novels and short stories. He filled them with persons, mostly belonging to a leisured class, who profess the maddest ideas and follow the most unregulated careers.

"Antic Hay" (1923) exhibits a group of smart and intellectual Londoners all contending in their different ways with the discomforts of boredom. They are not, strictly speaking, a group, for they come and go with only occasional contacts, weaving a pattern which Huxley knows is meaningless. He does not seem to be distressed by their eccentric habits. He at least allows them to say and do whatever they will, concerned himself with nothing but making an ironic comedy out of the performance. Always perfectly self-possessed, he plays his sardonic wit over his characters, finding something absurd in every step they take. Yet back of this apparently irresponsible mood of his lies something more austere. He genuinely admires the undeluded intelligence. He has a secret longing for a universe which should be orderly and just, harmonious and beautiful. Not finding it, he suffers disappointment, which imparts to all he writes that note of bitterness which is as obvious as his mirth. His bitterness gives him, as an artist, one of his chief merits. However ironically he may represent his whirling world, he holds his materials well in hand and shapes them with cutting outlines.

"Those Barren Leaves" (1925), carrying Huxley's pessimism to a point past which there was no going on, did as a matter of fact mark a turning point in his career. For his next novel showed the influence upon him of D. H. Lawrence, and henceforward he had a faith to propagate. He took over Lawrence's belief that modern man suffers from a split in his soul expressive of the duality he mistakenly emphasizes between passion and reason; and in "Point Counterpoint" (1928) he endeavored to prove by examples that men and women today are monsters either of pure passion or of pure reason. Illidge the determinist, Lord Edward Tantamount the amoral scientist, and Webley the disciple of force are monsters of rationality; Burlap the pietist, Spandrell the cynic, Lucy Tantamount the sensualist, and Walter Carling the sentimentalist are monsters of unregulated feeling. Only one person in the book, Mark Rampion, occupies both poles of the spirit at once; and he is Lawrence. Philip Quarles the novelist is Huxley himself; and it is interesting to note that in one of the passages from Philip's journal Huxley seems to be commenting on himself. Philip admits that he is not "a congenital novelist"; he can deal only with ideas and with monsters who express them, he is only an intellectual novelist. Huxley is as candid as that; his freedom from illusion extends even so far as to freedom from illusions concerning himself. "Brave New World" (1932), however, showed him carrying his method on as if it were the only one—and it is the only one available to him. The scene is a scientist's Utopia, a world of non-human perfection in which men and women live as much as possible like machines. If a specifically human state recurs in one of them he is made unconscious by a drug called soma until he has recovered a suitable equilibrium. This is all very well; but a savage from the Southwestern United States, straying into Utopia, finds its perfection intolerable and commits suicide. That is Huxley's comment on the narrowly rational ideal, as "Eyeless in Gaza," his next novel, is in its conclusion a comment on the only way out of the modern dilemma. Its hero, Tony Beavis, having exhausted the resources of sensuality, ascetic logic, and political reform, lands at last in the lap of contemplation. He discovers a discipline both of the mind and of the body whereby he can secure peace through a surrender of his self to the cause of the All. This gospel Huxley inherits from Lawrence, whose influence can therefore be seen well to have outlasted his life. Huxley, who to be sure is no "congenital novelist," and is not a natural story-teller, has nevertheless performed a certain service in his day. He has educated readers in current ideas—either converting them to his own or suggesting other and opposite ones. If he does not live as a narrative artist, he will for a long time be of historical interest because the central thoughts of his generation found brilliant expression in his pages.

Katherine Mansfield 1888–1923   Entirely apart from any intellectualist cult or current of her time, Katherine Mansfield kept herself busy for more than a decade before her death at the difficult art of short-story writing. Her endowment was natural and great; it consisted first of a warm, spontaneous sympathy with human beings in their infinite variety, and then of a bright, quick style for the expression of this sympathy. Her several volumes, published between 1911 and 1924, were collected into one in 1937;

and this volume serves to display the modern short story in its finest form. Her method was always more or less the same, though her subjects were increasingly attractive for their subtlety. An early story, "The Tiredness of Rosabel," followed a shopgirl home one evening and recorded her daydream of marrying a young gentleman who had entered the shop that day to help his fiancée make a purchase. "The Woman at the Store," three years later (1911), was an exercise in cruder colors: a New Zealand woman tells three men who ride up to her store that her husband is away sheepshearing, but that night her ugly little daughter draws a picture for two of the men which shows how the husband had disappeared—the wife had killed him and buried him with her own hands. "Ole Underwood" the next year was little more than a sketch of a sailor who, after twenty years spent in prison for killing his wife because she had been "done in" by another man, was still obsessed by the desire to kill and destroy—flowers, kittens, men, or whatever living objects came in his way. "Prelude" (1918), the longest of all the stories, reconstructed certain aspects of the author's own childhood in New Zealand, and was particularly notable for the success with which it created the child Kezia. After this Katherine Mansfield seems to have settled down to a final method; though there is no telling what further evolutions she would have gone through had she lived. The story called "Bliss" is a painfully if delicately ironic tale of a young wife who, awakened one evening to new love for her husband, and supposing that a woman who is her guest somehow shares her consequent delight in life without knowing its source, discovers that her husband has fallen in love with this woman. A pear tree which blooms in the garden is used with exquisite skill as a symbol of Bertha Young's brief bliss. "The Daughters of the Late Colonel" paints the portrait of a dead man through the influence we see he has exerted on the characters of his two spinster daughters; they have been so intimidated by him that they are now hopelessly and helplessly aflutter, even to the point of trembling with fear lest he scold them for spending so much money on his funeral. "Mr. and Mrs. Dove" is a charming if pathetic account of how Reginald, about to return to Rhodesia, goes to ask Anne for her hand in spite of his fears that she will laugh at him. She does, because she has always done so, and explains her refusal by pointing to her two doves; since she does not really love him, she says, they would be like these two rather absurd, bowing creatures who tread their perches all day and have no passion for each other. He goes sadly away, uncomplaining, until something in him makes her call him back as "Mr. Dove." "The Garden-Party" is remarkable for the amount it suggests without saying. Laura Sheridan wants her family to cancel a garden-party they are to have because a poor man lies dead in his cottage nearby. She is overruled, and actually enjoys the genteel guests who come; but later, when she goes to the cottage with a basket of food for the widow and sees the man lying dead, she has a vision of life which she can scarcely communicate to her brother who has come to take her home. Yet she does communicate it in a few broken sentences; for she has Katherine Mansfield's art of saying much in little, of speaking beautifully in a few plain words.

Virginia Woolf 1882–   Virginia Woolf, daughter of the biographer Leslie Stephen and herself a literary critic of fine distinction, has written since 1915 a series of novels whose narrative method has become increasingly complex. Mrs. Woolf's fame has grown in direct proportion to this complexity, until there are those who put her achievement above that of any living English novelist. She deserves the praise on technical grounds, for her manner has its fascinations; but her matter is of less importance than certain encomiums would suggest. It inclines to be minor, as is usually the case with a novelist whose art is so noticeably specialized. It is nevertheless fine. Mrs. Woolf's dominant theme is death, especially as it announces itself against the theme of a beautiful woman's life. Her first novel, "The Voyage Out" (1915), centered about the death in South America of Rachel Vinrace—a death which occurs just as Rachel has matured into grace and is about to marry. "Night and Day" (1919) was a not wholly successful attempt at polite comedy, but "Jacob's Room" (1922) returned to Mrs. Woolf's theme when it took for its material the life of Jacob Flanders as seen and re-membered later against the fact of his death in the war. Here for the first time Mrs. Woolf discovered her peculiar method, which is that of ellipsis and suggestion: fragments of experience, quickly rendered and loosely connected, composed into a sort of impressionist portrait. Looked at close, the canvas is all dots and strokes; at the proper distance, however, it shimmers with light and meaning. "Mrs. Dalloway" (1925) is a day in the life of Clarissa Dalloway, the day that divides her youth from her old age. Symbolic of this circumstance is the striking of Big Ben, hour by hour, as Clarissa walks through London, returns to her house, and prepares for the party that eve-ning to which her old lover, Peter Walsh, will come. Peter, arrived from India where he went after her rejection of his suit, enters her life now as a reminder of the woman she might have been had she not become the very beauti-ful yet rather inconsequential lady she is. Parallel to the story of her day runs the story of a shell-shocked soldier whose suicide is hastened by the bungling of a great doctor called to treat him. The doctor arrives at Mrs. Dalloway's party along with the other guests, and Mrs. Dalloway, hearing of the suicide, withdraws for a few moments of reverie in which she imagines herself follow-ing suit. But she returns to her guests, and the book ends at the point where Peter looks up and sees her entering the room. There is no conclusion except that Mrs. Dalloway's day is over and that she knows herself now as she has not known herself before. The work is done with the greatest delicacy throughout, as a similar task is performed in "To the Lighthouse" (1927). But the heroine of "To the Lighthouse," Mrs. Ramsay, is a well-nigh flawless woman, being not only as beautiful and graceful as Mrs. Dalloway but profound, selfless, and good in addition. The book creates her spirit in all sorts of indirect ways, but chiefly by showing a house in the Hebrides first with her as its presiding genius and then, after her death, with her only as its essential memory. A painter, Lily Briscoe, is shown at her canvas throughout, trying to catch the secret of the place; and only at the end does she understand that the wraith of Mrs. Ramsay whom she sees on the steps is the stroke which will complete the picture. Mrs. Ramsay, ideal woman that she is, is witty as well as good, charming as well as profound; modern fiction has produced few such characters, "Orlando" (1928) deserted its author's path in the direction of fantasy; its hero, Orlando, lives fluidly through three centuries of English literary history, changing his sex at thirty and changing his style at all times. The book is both a hymn to literary history and a parody of it as it is written. But in "The Waves" (1931) Mrs. Woolf returned to the path, producing now the most intricate of all her patterns. It is a riot of images derived from the sea, whose movements are celebrated in passages of italics distributed throughout the volume. Meanwhile the lives of six persons who had known one another as children—Bernard, Susan, Rhoda, Neville, Jimmy, and Louis—ebb and flow with the tide of time, through the death of their friend Percival and the suicide of Rhoda until the day when Bernard, an old man, sits and reviews the lives of all six. The coloring is more fragmentary than ever before, and this is the most difficult of Mrs. Woolf's novels to read. It is, that is to say, the one most like modernist poetry in its technique. But that is the secret of Mrs. Woolf's method. It is the method of modernist poetry. Therein lies both her strength and her limitation.

CHAPTER III

THE DRAMA

THE eighteen-nineties, which saw literature in England quickened on so many sides, saw no more remarkable change on the whole than that which took place in the drama. Here the process was not, as it was in the case of poetry, the substitution of one set of writers who were excellent for an older set who had been equally excellent; it was the creation of an entirely new excellence, almost of an entirely new art, where none had been immediately before. The stage plays of the nineteenth century had been for the most part inferior as literature; that is to say, they had little value out of the theater. They might be amusing, as many of the adaptations of French farce were, or they might be effective with the singularly unsophisticated audiences which went to see them; but their triumph was ephemeral, and they now make dreary reading when they are read at all. During the last three decades of the century W. S. Gilbert, at first alone and later in collaboration with the musician Sir Arthur Sullivan, made himself a force in satiric, burlesque comedy, but while his influence has been on the whole enormous, and his charm enduring, his name properly belongs to opera and to extravaganza. It was still possible for George Bernard Shaw, settling in London about 1880, to shake his head and proclaim that there was no living drama worthy of the name.

**Pinero
1855–1934**
     The names of only two playwrights emerge from the period before 1890. Sir Arthur Wing Pinero was prolific, and his technical proficiency

obtained for most of his plays at least a temporary popularity. He was remarkably deft at unfolding his plots, his dialogue was simply and expertly handled, and in general he exhibited a shrewd understanding of what constitutes effectiveness behind the footlights—his early experience as an actor standing him here in good stead. Almost from the beginning he exercised his hand in three types of play: the farce, the sentimental comedy, and the serious "problem" play; but he is now most important for his problem plays. In this department he came fairly close to eminence in at least three instances. In "The Second Mrs. Tanqueray," "Iris," and "Midchannel" he confined his attention to mature members of a complicated society, and studied with considerable care the tragic problems which arise out of their loves and marriages. The influence on English drama of Henrik Ibsen—to be discussed later in the present chapter—has nowhere been more pronounced than it is in the case of these three plays, all of which present practically insoluble difficulties in human relations, and each of which ends with the suicide or the ruin of the chief character. "The Second Mrs. Tanqueray" (1893), perhaps the most famous of Pinero's plays, tells the story of Aubrey Tanqueray's second marriage, the new wife, Paula, being a woman with a past which must be hidden from Aubrey's many friends, and particularly from his daughter, if the marriage is to be a happy one. The concealment, owing to a variety of circumstances, is not effected, and Paula, lacking the support which she had expected from the indecisive Aubrey, kills herself in the end to avoid further disclosure and humiliation. The tragedy in "Iris" is more definitely the outcome of character. Iris Bellamy has the fatal weakness of being unable to exist without luxury, so that when she is deprived of her fortune she cannot remain true to her impecunious lover, Laurence Trenwith, who has gone to the colonies to make a fortune for her. He returns to find her living with the millionaire Maldonado, and in the last scene both men desert her, leaving her in the depths of helplessness and despair. "Midchannel" deals with the problem of incompatibility in marriage. Zoe and Peter Blundell are two proud persons who cannot live peaceably together, Zoe being a case of modern "nerves" and Peter a conceited and possessive brute. During a brief residence in Italy she compromises herself with Leonard Ferris, and although upon her return to England she is willing to make it up with her husband, he hounds her literally to suicide, which is all the more desirable to her since her lover Ferris has been dismissed and in anger has engaged himself to an innocent girl whom both of them know.

Pinero's reputation will stand or fall by such serious efforts as these. Unfortunately, even in them he failed to show a really penetrating insight into human nature. He was willing to accept the current dogmas and prejudices of society—at least as material for drama—and although he indicated their radical injustice here or there, he by no means proved that he could see through them to motives which are universal. Compared with one who came after him—Bernard Shaw—he seems relatively feeble and unintelligent.

Jones 1851–1929   Henry Arthur Jones, like Pinero, developed in power and skill under the influence of new fashions which he himself did not invent, but like Pinero he remained a second-rate though effective writer. He also was prolific, and ranged from farce to tragedy; he also is most important for his problem plays. "Mrs. Dane's Defence" is another story of a woman who unhappily cannot live down her past. Mrs. Dane wishes to marry young Lionel Carteret, but under a cross-examination by his father she breaks down and confesses to an affair she once had on the Continent, and so is beaten. The cross-examination is ably conducted; the philosophy of life behind it is never examined. In "The Case of Rebellious Susan" a test is conducted of a wife's right to retaliate against her husband's infidelity with infidelity of her own. Another cross-examination is held, and many purely social complications arise which doubtless will be less interesting to future generations of readers than they are to this, or possibly not interesting at all. "Michael and His Lost Angel" (1896) a tragedy, is perhaps the best of Jones's plays. It recounts the struggle in the breast of Michael Feversham, a clergyman, between sacred and profane love. Both Feversham and Audrie Lesden, the pagan woman who has become infatuated with him, and with whom against his will he himself becomes infatuated, are ruined by the inhuman rigidity of his conscience, which too consistently defies nature. The play is effective theatrically rather than in any other way. The same incurable artificiality which was characteristic of Pinero operates to render this spectacle of egregious human folly in the last analysis unconvincing and without permanent significance.

Wilde
1856–1900

Pinero and Jones both wrote good plays; neither of them created good literature. A play becomes literature when it possesses, over and above the qualities which make it interesting in the theater, wisdom or beauty enough to give it validity for any reader at any place at any time. The author must have brought with him into the theater some attitude or some genius which he has developed in the larger world outside; he must seem to be a person in his own right. There is no personality in the plays of Pinero and Jones, and as a direct consequence there are no characters. Suddenly, between the years 1892 and 1895, there appeared a personality upon the English stage so distinct and fascinating that audiences were compelled to give it their attention, and playwrights were bound to pay tribute to its potency. This was the personality of Oscar Wilde, who from being an esthete and a minor poet [1] now turned to being a comic dramatist of the first rank. Wilde brought into comedy both an attitude and a gift. The attitude was one of superciliousness toward all people who are not clever; that is, toward those who do not understand that the intellect is something to play with rather than work with. It was an attitude of superiority to ordinary morality, to conventions of thought and particularly of speech, to stupidity and staleness of any kind. The intellectual atmosphere of the drama was stale; Wilde wished to energize it with wit and insolence. The gift was a gift for epigram such as perhaps no other British writer has been able to boast. It was a necessary corollary of the attitude in the sense that unconventionality of thought always encourages surprising and paradoxical speech; current platitudes are then inverted so as to confound their users and throw new light upon nature and human nature. But what is more important yet, Wilde seems to have been born with a talent for conversation. A born snob, as Bernard Shaw calls him, he was also a born wit, and the fact that he was born in Ireland may have had much or little to do with the matter. Legend has it that his own talk was even more brilliant than that of the persons in his plays. At any rate, he was stamping himself upon the drama at a time when it was devoid of anything but technical, theatrical virtue, when it was attending altogether too narrowly to situations and devices.

To Wilde at his best, situation and plot were of inferior interest, and character in the ordinary sense of that term was of no importance whatever. Like certain of the Restoration comic writers, with whom he is often compared and from whom he unquestionably derived much of his material, he demanded nothing more than that a group

[1] For his poems, see pages 160–161.

of graceful and accomplished ladies and gentlemen should
be brought together on the stage so that they could talk—
and then that they should be allowed to talk like Wilde.
With one exception he created no characters that are distinct from one another and so have existence outside the
play. His heroes and heroines are remarkably alike, and
his situations do not materially vary. The epigram was the
thing; that was his contribution and his triumph. Significantly enough, many who can repeat a dozen or more
of the witty speeches with which he sprinkled his dialogue
cannot say for certainty from which play or from which
person they come. It is the speeches alone that have existence outside the theater. Shakspere created Falstaff and a
score of other people who now march up and down the
world in full life; Wilde set loose some dozen paradoxes.
The following are examples. "Nothing succeeds like ex-
cess." "The youth of America is their oldest tradition."
"Children begin by loving their parents. After a time they
judge them. Rarely, if ever, do they forgive them." "Men
marry because they are tired; women because they are
curious. Both are disappointed." "More than half of modern culture depends upon what one shouldn't read." "Relations are simply a tedious pack of people, who haven't got
the remotest knowledge of how to live, nor the smallest instinct about when to die." "I can resist everything except
temptation." "Life is far too important a thing ever to
talk seriously about it." "As soon as people are old enough
to know better, they don't know anything at all." "It is
perfectly monstrous the way people go about saying things
against one behind one's back that are absolutely and entirely true."

Unfortunately for himself and for literature, Wilde was
not permitted to attain perfection in the form which he
had invented or revived. When he ceased writing plays in
1895 he had produced only one which was free from cer-

tain melodramatic elements which he carried over from the older tradition. He began indeed in the early eighties by writing sheer melodrama, but ten years elapsed before he made his proper entrance upon the dramatic scene with "Lady Windermere's Fan" in 1892. In this comedy Lord Darlington contains in himself the promise of the whole line of cynical wits who were to make their creator the most talked-of living playwright. His brilliance flags after the first act, however, and he gives way before a plot which carries Wilde to excesses of sensation and bathos. "A Woman of No Importance" the next year introduced the glittering figure of Lord Illingworth, who like Lord Darlington derives his cleverness from the fact that he has led an unscrupulous life and so can condescend to the proprieties. But his wickedness is rebuked in the end by the triumph of Mrs. Arbuthnot, a good and uninteresting woman whom he once wronged; and so another comedy closes on a false note. Two years later "The Importance of Being Earnest" exhibited Wilde's genius at its zenith. No serious issue is fought out in this delightfully absurd piece. The hero, Algernon Moncrieff, is a wholly irresponsible wit who indulges his captivating insolence at every opportunity and at the expense of everybody. There is the thinnest pretense to a plot, based upon the question whether Jack Worthing, who shares with Algernon the honor of being hero, is rightly named Jack or Ernest. When it is proved that his name is Ernest, and therefore that he is fit to ask for the hand of Gwendolen Fairfax, he realizes "the vital importance of Being Earnest"—not before, or for any other reason. Algernon comes as near as any of Wilde's mouthpieces to having an independent personality. His humor and his perverse charm are so real that he can legitimately be said to live.

"Salome," from which an opera was made, and which is at present one of the most widely known of Wilde's works, is the only tragedy in which he may be said to have succeeded. It is based upon the story in St. Mark of John the Baptist and Salome, the daughter of Herod. The original narrative has been elaborated by an exotic and somewhat feverish imagination, and overlaid by a rich covering of highly wrought imagery. The florid vein which can be found in Wilde's fiction appears here in all its more or less morbid strength. Beautiful, mysterious phrases hover over the unhealthy scene as if they were on wings, and the beheading of John, or Jokanaan, comes as the climax of a hectic scene. This play is one of the chief weapons in the hands of those critics who dismiss Wilde as an unnatural and pernicious writer. Wilde would gladly have accepted the charge of being unnatural, for in his vocabulary naturalness was almost synonymous with stupidity; but he would have claimed with justice that he had produced a work of strange beauty and power. Perhaps "Salome" will vie with "The Importance of Being Earnest" for the privilege of perpetuating his fame.

Shaw
1856–

At the same time that Wilde was bursting upon the British public, another Irishman was beginning to make a reputation which took longer to reach considerable dimensions but which has since grown to be the greatest of the present age. George Bernard Shaw was born in Dublin in the same year with Wilde, and came over to London at twenty not so much that he might educate himself as that he might educate England. His education at home had been chiefly in music and painting; he now was to acquaint himself with the best ideas of Europe in philosophy and sociology, and he was to preach those ideas through any medium which offered itself. Nearly twenty years passed before he found expression in the drama. Meanwhile he wrote several novels; read Henry George and Karl Marx; modified their socialistic doctrines to suit his active and independent mind; joined the Fabian Society, an organization whose purpose was to debate and disseminate the truth about the relations between the social classes; served the press in the capacities of art critic, musical critic, and dramatic critic; [1] and finally in 1892, the year of "Lady Windermere's Fan," produced his first play, which was called "Widowers' Houses."

Before Shaw's plays can be profitably discussed, his attitude, his ideas, and his personality must be defined. He brought to English comedy as much wit as Oscar Wilde was bringing, and he brought infinitely more. He brought a sense of social responsibility which was wholly the opposite of Wilde's flavor of gentlemanly nonchalance. As much as Wilde he scorned unintelligence, but the intelligence which he recommended was to be a cure for distressing evils rather than a gesture of careless contempt. He was bent upon searching with his very keen faculties every assumption and every sentiment which lay beneath contemporary literature and contemporary psychology; his comedy was aimed definitely at the destruction of a system of moral conventions which by instinct and by education he detested.

If comedy is to be properly destructive it must be informed with ideas; Shaw has fairly bristled with ideas, and most of them, by constant and brilliant repetition, he has made familiar if not acceptable to his public. Here he joins forces with Henrik Ibsen, the nineteenth-century Norwegian dramatist who had been the greatest influence in the theater of Europe for at least two hundred years. Shaw, partly by a book on Ibsen which he wrote in 1891, but chiefly by the example of his plays, has been the channel through which the intelligence and the art of Ibsen have exerted most definitely their power in the English-speaking world. Shaw derived many of his ideas from other

[1] For his essays, see pages 284–288.

sources; from Ibsen he derived the assurance that it was worth while to attempt serious and thoroughgoing analysis of society through the drama.

Shaw begins with the assumption that society is confused because it does not know its own mind. It has in reality a collective mind, but large spaces therein are blankly unconscious or else are rotten with illusion and sentiment. If society only knew it, poverty, the greatest of all crimes, could be abolished by the collective will; the mass of people included within the middle class could be leavened by honest thought and made sensible; violence and evil could be eradicated as any disease can be eradicated; the people could cease to be the victims of military exploitation, could cease to be the instruments by which any brutal leader worked his will. But though he is an enemy of violence, Shaw is the champion of intellectual and spiritual force. He despises Napoleon because he was so stupid as to have illusions about himself; he admires Cæsar because he had humor and imagination, as well as an irresistible will. Here Shaw shows the influence of Ibsen and of the Geman philosopher Nietzsche. Humility is a contemptible virtue. Ignorance is no excuse for inferiority—"hell is paved with good intentions." Nature, and the life force, are never to be denied. Morality can cease to become a dreary duty and become the privilege of spirited human beings, of supermen. Heretofore it has been possible to say of a great many persons that they were too good, meaning that they were too weak to assert themselves in a vigorous world; it ought not to be possible to be too good, for goodness is the same as strength and intelligence. Ethics may be the product of thought, and not its enemy. Morality may be based on something more permanent than the conventions of the majority; it may be the expression of those few or those many who are keenly alive, and know as individuals what they want to do. Human relations do not need to be accepted at their traditional value, especially when they work cruelty and hardship, or when they bore the best minds. It has generally been assumed that children owe obedience to parents; parents, rather, owe obedience to children, and when they are in the way with their prejudices, which are death, they should give way before the reason of the children, which is likely to be life. Society, as the followers of Marx and Darwin presume, is not mechanically regulated; it moves in accordance with the will of its most enlightened members. Literature and art suffer more than anything else from ignorance.

Both in the long prefaces which Shaw has prefixed to his plays and in the plays themselves he has endeavored to drive these convictions into the consciousness of the public. Because of his fertility and his willingness, at least in imagination, to present the other side of the case, he has sometimes seemed inconsistent; yet in the long run he has been remarkably consistent and serious, and he has impressed his personality upon all who are capable of being attracted by sheer, naked sense. He has been frankly didactic, even to the point of incurring the charge of intolerance and puritanism; he has announced himself as a foe of the sensual majority, and every sentence he has written has been stiff with impatience at anything but brains.

He has been serious. Yet the ordinary opinion of him is that he is a clown, a mountebank, a man who has nothing consistent to say and desires only to turn common sense upside down for the mystification or amusement of his audiences. Here he suffers the fate which clear and lively minds have always suffered. The lazy majority punish his unconventionality by dismissing it as funny; not understanding his meaning, or refusing to agree with it, they decide that it conceals only another paradox, or another attempt to be shocking and sensational. A case in point is his opinion of Shakspere. Shakspere is one of the "divinities" whom Shaw has tried to reduce to the dimensions of humankind, in the conviction that blind worship of anything is bad for the mind. He examined Shakspere and found that although he is an absolute master of language, of narrative, and of the music of words, he has no ideas. The greatest of poets, he is one of the least of philosophers; there is no proof that he ever really scrutinized and criticized the motives of men. The cry went up at once that Shaw had called himself better than Shakspere. Actually he had said only that his mind was better than Shakspere's, and he meant it. He was not afraid to question one of the English idols. Incidentally he has done the reputation of Shakspere a great deal of good by thus distinguishing between his content and his magic. Shakspere henceforth will not be burdened with the necessity of appearing profound, but can exert his full force as the most skilful manipulator of words and moods who ever wrote.

Shaw is possessed of the brightest wit now known to literature; he has raised more laughs both in the theater and out than any of his contemporaries. Yet even here it has not always been possible to say whether his intention originally was to be funny. Like any great comic writer, and especially Molière, with whom he is certainly worthy to be compared, he knows how to destroy error by laughter. Often, however, his comic effects are the result purely of his quickness and directness and accuracy of vision, the triumph wholly of his uncommon sense. Something which he may say with the utmost gravity will be amusing only to those who have not heard it before, or who cannot perceive its bearings; what may seem practical and simple to him will seem refreshingly absurd to slower intelligences. After that is said, nevertheless, it remains to say that Shaw has proved himself the master of most of the devices designed to elicit laughter. He has enormous gusto, he can write with unexampled sharpness and point, he can see the ludicrous side of his own case, he does not hesitate to employ the broader kind of horse-humor when he so desires, and his eloquence is irresistible.

To come to a closer inspection of his plays themselves, it is well to say first that Shaw's chief interest in writing them has been critical and psychological. He has endeavored to place his people in situations which conventional writers would treat romantically or sentimentally, and then to show them doing what normal people would do. This, as he once warned, does not mean average people. Average people would be romantic and sentimental. They would do what they had seen other people do in novels and plays. Shaw means by normal something that may be summed up as intelligent, individual, self-respecting, bold, and perhaps impudent. He means himself. If the complaint be made that he is not everybody, he admits that. If the complaint be made that he represents too few of the softer and more soothing qualities of human nature, he replies that he thinks those qualities on the whole vicious because they prevent the healthy working of the mind. His objection to the ordinary problem play, such as Pinero and Jones have usually written, is that it does not pierce far enough into convention to find the enduring springs of action. "The vapidness of such drama," he says, "lies in the fact that in them animal passion, sentimentally diluted, is shown in conflict, not with real circumstances, but with a set of conventions and assumptions half of which do not exist off the stage, whilst the other half can either be evaded by a pretense of compliance or defied with complete impunity by any reasonably strong-minded person. Nobody can feel that such conventions are really compulsory, and consequently nobody can believe in the stage pathos that accepts them as inexorable fate, or in the genuineness of the people who indulge in such pathos. Sitting at such plays we do not believe; we make believe." He gives as his own purpose in drama "the presentation in parable of the conflict between man's will and his environment." His plays are a succession of attempts to show will triumphant over weakness, intelligent hope triumphant over blind pessimism, and reason triumphant over sensual habit.

Shaw's earliest collection of plays, published in 1898, was entitled "Plays, Pleasant and Unpleasant." The "Unpleasant Plays" were "Widowers' Houses," "The Philanderer," and "Mrs. Warren's Profession." In the first a purely economic issue is presented through the person of Dr. Trench, who upon learning that his fiancée, Blanche Sartorius, derives her income from a vicious rent-system, refuses to marry her, only to find shortly after that his own income flows from the same source. He succumbs to the system, of which he is really a product, and agrees in the end to become the husband of Blanche. "The Philanderer" exposes the mock-modern man and woman to bitter contempt, and analyzes relentlessly the relations of lovers in any society. An Ibsen Club has been formed whose members are prohibited from thinking and talking conventionally; radicalism is abandoned, however, as soon as it fails to secure for its exponents the particular thing that their passions desire. The moral is not that such persons are too radical, but that they are not radical enough —that they neglect to make over their whole lives on a sensible and intelligent scheme. "Mrs. Warren's Profession" was the first of Shaw's plays to show parents in conflict with children. Vivie Warren, finding that her mother is engaged in a loathsome occupation, and resenting the fact that she is dependent upon her, throws her over and goes to seek her own fortune in London by work. In reply to Mrs. Warren's declaration of maternal love, she insists that such love in the present case is an indecent thing, and

Mrs. Warren is left exclaiming, "Lord help the world if everybody took to doing the right thing!"

Among the "Pleasant Plays," "You Never Can Tell" again attempts to dispose of the theory that there is anything sacred in the affection of parents for children, and with a good deal of levity presents the conflict in the minds of two young people between their love for each other and their self-respect. Shaw is particularly fond of strong-minded persons who resist love as long as they are able; the implication being that other concerns in life are of equal or greater importance. "Arms and the Man" is a merry account of a soldier who is so much superior to his profession as to have imagination and a sense of humor. He never pretends that he is brave, but through mere frankness and wit he manages to get what he wants; he defeats by ridicule a pompous and pretentious soldier whom Shaw represents as typical of the profession, and wins the adoration of a romantic lady through refusing to be impressed by her "noble attitude" and "thrilling voice." In "Candida" the inflated personality of the Rev. James Morell is punctured by his wife Candida's declaration at the end that he is weaker than a certain neurotic poet who also loves her, and that therefore she must send the poet away and remain at home to protect Morell. He has always thought of himself as her protector, whereas like many large men with vague ideas he is a helpless baby in the hands of a spirited and genuinely good woman. "The Man of Destiny" similarly deflates the character of Napoleon by showing him to be a man of ridiculously small vanity who no more is under the guidance of a star than the least of his soldiers is.

Shaw's next volume, called "Three Plays for Puritans" (1900), contained three attempts to correct popular misimpressions of heroic motive. "The Devil's Disciple," a melodrama of the American Revolution, rebukes those theater-goers who suppose that when a man sacrifices himself in the interests of a woman he does it always because he loves her; Dick Dudgeon offers himself to be hanged in place of the preacher Anderson because his nature at the moment prompts him to do so, and for no other reason. Incidentally there is more satire on soldiery in the speeches of the attractive General Burgoyne. "Cæsar and Cleopatra" is a vindication of the character of Julius Cæsar against the aspersions of Shakspere's Roman heroes, and a revelation of what Shaw takes to be the great man's genuine intellectual processes. Shaw's Cæsar is witty, and he never glosses over his actions with large, loose phrases designed to justify them on moral grounds. He happens to be a strong man, and his philosophy, of which Shaw approves, is to do what he likes. Most people, the implication is, are feeble because they do not know what they like. "Captain Brassbound's Conversion" is a study of the motive of revenge. Captain Brassbound, under the clever management of Lady Cicely Waynefleet, is forced to admit that his mother, whom he has been waiting years in the solitude of Africa to avenge upon his uncle, as a matter of fact was not worth avenging; and thereby is transformed from an angry, sulking simpleton to a reasonable human animal.

Shaw's first masterpiece was "Man and Superman" (1903). This play is one of the great works of the twentieth century, not only because it is a perfect expression of perhaps its chief writer, but because it contains in one form or another most of the ideas that are distinctively modern, and conveys them with unexampled brilliance. The hero is John Tanner, an impetuous and eloquent socialist who is running over with ideas about everything, from love to economics. Shaw pours himself out through Tanner and other characters, until the play becomes a veritable encyclopedia of contemporary wit and wisdom, with not a little absurdity mixed in. Tanner's chief theory, and the theory for which "Man and Superman" is famous, is that marriage is the most dangerous enemy of men. A strong man has other things to do than surrender himself to love, and particularly to a family; he must think, and he must live; he must be free. Yet sooner or later woman, whose business it is in nature to pursue him and subdue him, will prevail, and he will fall. The very life force which stimulates his intellectual ambition dictates that he shall marry and reproduce his genius. Tanner spends most of his time fleeing Ann Whitefield, who loves him and whom in spite of his denials he loves. In the end he succumbs, and the audience leaves him despairingly orating upon the misery of his fate and upon the sort of man that he hopes to remain in spite of the fact that he has been humbled. This interpretation of the relations between men and women is not original with Shaw. The shrewdest observers of all times—and Shaw must admit Shakspere among their number—have subscribed to it, and several nineteenth-century philosophers in Europe made much of it. Shaw's contribution was that of a dramatist and a humorist, and perhaps "Man and Superman" will continue to be its classic expression. In the middle of the play there is a long interlude the scene of which is hell, and the principal actor in which is Don Juan, who is only John Tanner transformed. "Man and Superman" thus connects itself with a great tradition of literature, the diabolic; and the discussion in this scene of all subjects under the sun takes its place alongside the most interesting philosophical writing in English.

"John Bull's Other Island," the next play in point of time, is a study of the English and Irish national temperaments, with the defects of both conspicuously set forth. In "How He Lied to Her Husband" Shaw tries to draw the eternal triangle according to a new geometry; he proposes to show how real people, not stage people, might act in a certain hackneyed situation. A man who has been writing poetry to the wife of another man lies when the poetry is discovered by the husband and says he does not love the wife. The husband is indignant that any man should not love his wife, and offers to fight; but on the other's assurance that he does love her indeed the husband desists and is happy. "Major Barbara" contains another specimen of Shaw's strong man in Andrew Undershaft, who, although his profession of munition-maker is distasteful to his exceedingly Christian daughter Barbara, at last convinces her that there is more life in his single will than in all of the Salvation Army, to which she has fancied herself devoted. This is Shaw's protest against weak-kneed and sentimental Christianity, and particularly against the doctrine that poverty is in any way a holy thing. "The Doctor's Dilemma" relieves Shaw of all his animus against the medical profession, which he distrusts as much as Molière distrusted it. "Getting Married" is little more than a symposium on the institutions of marriage and divorce. "The Shewing-up of Blanco Posnet" takes place in the southwestern part of the United States, and is in effect a commentary upon the fact that goodness as conventionally practised is felt to be a shameful thing. Blanco has done a difficult and noble deed in sacrificing himself for a woman and her sick child, but he has been so accustomed to despising the good people of his town that he cannot approve of himself until a crisis forces him into an admission that it is better to be a good man than a bad one. "Misalliance" and "Fanny's First Play" are pictures of the younger generation asserting itself, the second of the two being introduced and concluded by some critical dialogue which again reminds the reader of Molière, who was fond of representing the critics in conference about himself. "Androcles and the Lion" makes uproarious fun of martyrs and of all Christians whose religion does not have what Shaw would call a natural basis. The scene is Rome in the time of the persecutions, and the lion which Androcles meets in the arena, only to recognize him as the beast from whose paw he once had extracted a thorn, is certainly one of the most comical characters to be found in any English play. In "Pygmalion" Professor Higgins the philologist takes a young cockney girl into his house in order to test a theory he has that he can make a lady out of any girl by teaching her to speak like one. He does so to his satisfaction, and stops there; Shaw takes the pains to prevent him from falling in love with Liza, as any professor would have done in almost any other play.

After these plays came the World War, and Shaw, with the exception of a few "playlets," was silent until 1917, when "Heartbreak House" appeared. The piece is accurately named, for in it Shaw registers once and for all his doubts that English society will ever reach an understanding of itself; Heartbreak House is England, and attractive as many of its inhabitants may be, divinely as a few of them can talk, it is a house of cross-purposes and degenerate idleness. Shaw in this play, which he wrote at sixty, was more mellow and more amusing than he had ever been before, and in addition he was more of a poet. He has rarely been accused of poetry, but there is a surprising undercurrent of mysticism here, and there is a certain character, old Captain Shotover, who by his indefinable, gruff charm entitles the playwright to a place among the most magical members of his craft. The mark of a genuine dramatic character is that he seems to have a life independent of the author's will—that he speaks out of his own past, and creates his own future as the play progresses. Captain Shotover is such a person, and he is one of the very few of his sort in Shaw's whole work. Many of Shaw's people are Shaw himself in one form or other; Shotover is Shotover, as Falstaff is Falstaff. "Heartbreak House" is one of Shaw's best plays—perhaps posterity will find it the best of them all.

Three years later Shaw astonished the world with a play which was much the longest that he had yet composed, and much the most ambitious. "Back to Methuselah" is really five plays in one, being a survey in five settings of the development of man as a biological specimen. The first scene is the Garden of Eden where the parents of the race discover error and death, their two chief enemies. The second is England at the present time; two scientists, the Brothers Barnabas, are perfecting a philosophy which encourages them to believe that in the future men by willing it may prolong their lives to three hundred years—that being the estimate of Shaw as to the length of time which would actually be necessary for a human being to outgrow the childishness of the best civilization to date and become in any profound sense mature. In 2170 A. D. "The Thing Happens," and by 3000 A. D. England has already become an island whereon only "normal" people are allowed to live, the "short-lived" being banished to Bagdad. The "normal" people are flawlessly intelligent, and an occasional visitor from Bagdad must struggle to avoid the deepest humiliation in their presence. Finally, in the year 31,920 A. D., there are no more short-lived people. Certain incredibly wise "ancients" walk about, enjoying the world as only pure mind can enjoy it; children are hatched from eggs full-grown; there is no useless passion any more, no error, no war, no love, no sensual art. The Golden Age has arrived, and Shaw in the prospect of it is at last a happy man. The wealth and the wit of this gigantic play can only be hinted at. It disputes with "Man and Superman" and "Heartbreak House" the right to be considered Shaw's masterpiece, and it belongs without a question with the finest literature of the first quarter of the twentieth century. It is not merely a protest against the stupidity of the World War; it is an enduring protest against the indolence of the mind of man. It is the quintessence of the older Shaw, and it may turn out to be the Bible of many generations to come.

After four more years of silence so far as the stage was concerned, Shaw produced "Saint Joan" in New York, and demonstrated in a new way his ability to speak with beauty and power upon themes of universal importance to the human mind. "Saint Joan" is Shaw's version of the life of the Maid of Orleans, Jeanne d'Arc. Voltaire, Anatole France, and Mark Twain have at various times interpreted this marvelous life to suit themselves. Shaw finds in Joan a perfect expression of the protestant disposition; the disposition to think and feel for oneself, to obey one's inspiration regardless of whether or not the organization of existing society is thereby disturbed. The simple girl of medieval France who comes to court with her wonderful message is in the end crushed out of existence by church and state, neither of which can tolerate the supposition that a private person can know more than properly ordained bishops and kings. The issue is clearest in the fourth act of the play, where with a vividness and a grasp rare in English drama Shaw pits Joan against the Inquisition, met to try her for the heresy of believing that the church is not a necessary intermediary between man and God. Shaw takes pains to make the issue a real one. The officials of the Inquisition are men of intellect and integrity who sincerely feel Joan to be dangerous. Shaw makes his play, therefore, a parable of the eternal conflict between inspiration and organization, between the one and the many, between originality and conformity, between the new and the old. In addition he paints a touching and beautiful picture of Saint Joan, and he contributes to English drama one or two of its best tragic scenes.

Shaw's plays since "Saint Joan" have been called by malcontents the comedies of his dotage. It is true that they lack his earlier energy, yet they could have been written by no one else and they are not only edifying but amusing. "The Apple Cart" (1931) suggests that democracy will fail unless it learns how to distribute goods and how to select its rulers wisely. King Magnus, by threatening to abdicate his throne and make himself a candidate for Parliament, forces the prime minister, Joseph Proteus, to do what he likes. This is because Magnus happens to be a brilliant and attractive statesman; but Shaw's point is that he is therefore conspicuous in a country which does not bring its best men to the top, and that democracy is always liable to upset because sooner or later the brightest men will rule. "On the Rocks" (1933) is another political comedy. Sir Arthur Chavender thinks he is overworked as one of the King's ministers, and incidentally the scene in which he tries to remember the speech he is dictating to his secretary is one of the funniest in Shaw; but the real trouble is that he is mentally underworked. Sent to a sanatorium where he has plenty of time to think, he returns in the realization that he has never been anything but a figurehead for those who "whitewash" the slums. A Socialist now, he is put out of office, but he does not personally care. He knows that in time the fight for an equable distribution of goods will take place; and he ends with a prediction that if necessary it will be accompanied by bloodshed. "Too True to be Good" (1934) has, as always with Shaw, a serious core, but its surface in wildly nonsensical. He returns to the medical theme again, beginning with a rich young woman who is in bed because her mother thinks she is ill and because she herself has been made to think so. A monster microbe at her bedside complains on the other hand that she has given it diseases by coddling her condition. A nurse and a burglar, met in the room to rob the

young woman of her pearls, become so attractive to her
by contrast with her foolish mother that she jumps out of
bed perfectly well and runs off with them to have a pre-
posterous round of adventures. The boredom of the rich,
says Shaw, is their greatest misery, and the eagerness of
the young woman for adventure is as much a sign of this
as the illness she has been unconsciously faking. The play
runs into nonsense, but its point is consistent with every
point Shaw has ever made.

Gals-
worthy
1867–1933 The stamp of Ibsen is perhaps more obvious
on a playwright like John Galsworthy than it is
on Shaw; though it is not so deep. The plays
of Galsworthy, like the maturer plays of Ibsen, are ju-
dicial, controlled, and rather bitterly lacking in warm
humor. Shaw in many cases has let his nature run away
with him—has preached when he was morally indignant
or excited, has played the buffoon when he was in high
spirits. Nothing ever ruffled the smooth mind of Galsworthy. A highly competent technician, he usually wrote
plays which are more perfect than Shaw's; but none of
them is as great because none of them is saturated with as
important a personality.

Galsworthy was educated to be a lawyer, and there is
something legal about the extreme care with which he presented his cases. For in practically every play there is a
case. Galsworthy had a sensitive mind. He was finely
aware of the misery existing in the world, and his analysis
of its causes was generally subtle and just. But the reader
or the spectator is never permitted to forget that an analysis is going on. The playwright does not seem to be lost
in this or that person, in this or that terrible wrong. Always conscious of himself, always employing the most
excellent dramatic devices and drawing upon the most
serene sources of his intellect, he becomes impressive
chiefly for his skill. There is little abandon is his soul, and

hence there is little poetry. Ibsen in a sense was a great poet, and, contrary to the popular notion, so is Shaw. Galsworthy was a civilized man and a master of letters; he was not a force.

The ideas in his plays are simple and few. Injustice is a painful superfluity in the world, caused by blind passion and curable by reason. Justice, peace, and freedom are beautiful, and they are attainable by all who will live humanely. The perfect state would be one in which each individual was at liberty to pursue his ideal of the comely life unhampered by the jealousy or the ignorance of his neighbors. Prejudice is a detestable thing, and love—free, devoted, generous—is the profoundest of blessings. Galsworthy's method as a dramatist is to select a simple, concrete situation in life and treat it dispassionately though sympathetically in the light of these convictions. He believes that out of every truly human relationship, when scrutinized by a refined imagination, a moral rises; his aim is to imply—not necessarily to point—that moral. His sophistication as an artist saves him from being didactic or sentimental. He proceeds with admirable caution to build a structure upon the original germ of fact which shall have both significance and beauty. The very simplicity of the result is often deceptive, especially for inexperienced readers.

He did not begin to write plays until he had worked at fiction [1] for ten years. "The Silver Box" (1906), his first play, is concerned with an idea which has found frequent expression in later pieces—the idea that the justice of the world exacts a greater penalty from the poor than it does from the rich. A rich young gentleman has stolen a purse while drunk. A poor man steals it in turn while he is drunk. The poor man is sentenced to prison; the gentleman escapes with nothing worse than a scare, and the fear

[1] For his novels, see pages 220–226.

on the part of his family that there will be scandal. But Galsworthy's most famous and effective treatment of human cruelty is "Justice" (1910), in which William Falder, a lawyer's clerk, is punished out of all proportion to his crime (forgery) because his employer, James Howe, wishes to make an example of him; that is, wishes to take the sternest possible precautions against the chance that his property shall ever be tampered with again. The prison scene, with Falder pounding on the door of his cell, and the final scene, where he leaves the lawyer's office to commit suicide, are justly celebrated. Galsworthy nowhere else came so near to authentic tragedy.

Galworthy was much interested in the phenomenon of an individual crushed by the majority. Stephen More in "The Mob," like Dr. Stockmann in Ibsen's "An Enemy of the People," has taken the unpopular side in an important public issue—in this case a war. As he proceeds to defend the rights of the small nation which is being victimized by his own government, his family deserts him one by one, and the mob, after attacking him on the streets, breaks into his house and kills him. Clare Dedmond in "The Fugitive," failing to get the sympathy from her friends which she deserves in her effort to live away from her unsuitable husband, is reduced to despair and takes her own life in a mean restaurant on the day of a big race. Her predicament is interesting among other reasons for its parallel with that of Irene Forsyte, the heroine of Galsworthy's masterpiece in fiction, "The Forsyte Saga."

Among all the conflicts which Galsworthy was pained to observe in contemporary life, none was more distressful to him than the conflict between groups or classes of people. One of his earlier plays, "Strife," was concerned with a great strike which had persisted in a northern factory town for months longer than was necessary because of the stubbornness of the two men who led the opposing parties.

The war is not ended until Roberts, representing the union, has seen his wife die of starvation, and Anthony, the president of the directors, has physically broken down. Then by an irony which Galsworthy is careful not to make too apparent, a settlement is put into effect which all except the leaders had agreed upon before the personal feud began. "The Skin Game" shows two families, socially jealous of each other, fighting with every kind of weapon, scrupulous and unscrupulous, until the spirit of each is shattered and victory means nothing in either case. "Loyalties" shows two groups opposing each other to the death. When De Levis, a wealthy Jew, accuses Dancy, a Gentile, of stealing some money from under his pillow in a country-house, the club-friends of Dancy rally to his support against an alien race. De Levis, fighting for that race, pushes the investigation until Dancy's guilt is exposed, and Dancy shoots himself. It has been supposed that Galsworthy took sides in this play, but there is no evidence that he did so. He was interested merely in the deadlock, and regretful that life should be marred by passions so destructive of courtesy and truth.

Barrie 1860–1937 Nothing so solemn as a problem, whether of society or of the individual, was ever the concern of Sir James Matthew Barrie. This engaging Scotchman abandoned the writing of fiction [1] about the beginning of the present century and devoted himself to the drama, with varying success but with constant delicacy and charm. He was never accused of having "ideas," and he rarely was considered important by the more serious critics. He could never have said like Shaw, for instance, that "in all my plays my economic studies have played as important a part as a knowledge of anatomy does in the works of Michael Angelo"; or like Galsworthy that " 'The Moral' is the keynote of all drama." His ap-

[1] For his prose fiction, see pages 195–197.

parent aim was first of all to amuse or touch his audiences, and after that to play as his fancy suited him upon the minor strings of the human instrument. Few playwrights have been defter in avoiding the ridiculous, and few have shown more clearly that they were not intended for the sublime. He occupies the middle ground of sentiment rather than the upper or lower reaches of passion.

When Barrie did not definitely desert reality and enter fairy-land, as in his best-known play for children, "Peter Pan" (1904), he contented himself with decorating the fringes of human character. He exploited pathos instead of tragedy, absurdity instead of error, affectation instead of villainy. He maintained an excellent temper into which nothing morose or morbid had been allowed to intrude. He earned from almost every commentator the adjectives "whimsical," "quaint," "elfish," and "capricious," and indeed he cultivated such qualities to the point where he was dangerously near ruin on the rocks of sentimentality. But he preserved himself through an ever-present humor, which, though at times it may be trivial or complacent, was always a thing of the mind, and always something just beyond critical analysis.

Two of Barrie's most successful plays, "The Little Minister" and "Peter Pan," were dramatized from his novels —the second from "The Little White Bird." Of the others, "Quality Street" early set the tone which was to become so familiar both in Great Britain and in America. Susan and Phoebe Throssel are two timid spinsters in the time of the Napoleonic Wars who attract the attention of a gentleman, Valentine Brown, just as he is about to leave and enlist. When he returns ten years later, Phoebe, who once fancied that he loved her, has become a school-teacher, and at his first glance she seems too old for him. Piqued by his betrayal of disappointment, she disguises herself as a niece and charms him with her youthfulness, only in the end to discover that he prefers her as she really is. The author's management of the disguise, and of the ball-room scene where it is momentarily successful, carries "quaintness" to an almost objectionable limit; but wit and ingenuity prevent the whole, as often with Barrie, from becoming maudlin or embarrassing.

In "The Admirable Crichton" Barrie skirts the edge of something which in Galsworthy would be a problem—the problem of the relations between social classes. Crichton is the butler in a wealthy household whose head, Lord Loam, likes to pretend that all human beings are equal, and who accordingly once a year entertains his servants at tea. Crichton, believing firmly that such an arrangement violates the laws of nature, resists without avail until during a yachting trip the family is wrecked on a desert island and left there for two years. Now the situation is different. Now the laws of nature dictate that the most competent member of the party shall be head, and since this is Crichton he cheerfully assumes responsibility, reducing the others to the position of slaves. When rescue comes, however, and England is reached again, Crichton punctiliously restores the old balance, and life goes on as it always had. There is not a moment of seriousness in the play; all is done in the spirit of extravagant burlesque, and so Barrie evades the only charge which might be brought against him of taking society seriously.

"What Every Woman Knows" is a tribute to all plain little wives who get less than their due from their husbands. Maggie Shand is in reality the brains of her house, but John, a member of Parliament, whose pompous speeches she improves when she copies them, does not discover this as soon as the audience does. Hence the suspense of the spectators, and hence once more the emergence of obscure virtue from unlikely places. "A Kiss for Cinderella" is exactly the piece which it might have been predicted that Barrie would write, for the Cinderella legend lay always in the back of his mind. In this case a young cockney girl is allowed to dream of a paradise in which she should be a triumphant princess. The dream is made material on the stage, and proves to be as laughable as it is wistful. Barrie appeals with especial force to all who day-dream; few do not. "The Twelve-Pound Look" is unique among Barrie's plays as recalling in some measure the convictions of Shaw with regard to the position of women in society. Sir Harry Sims is a solemn, possessive husband whose first wife has tired of the routine of domestic idleness and left him to take a job as typist. She returns by chance and warns him against the possibility that his second wife shall begin to have the "twelve-pound look"—that is, shall begin to lay by twelve pounds as a competency on which she can desert him in order to make an independent living. He is not convinced, but in a later scene the audience thinks it catches the look in the new wife's eyes, and suspects that soon again he will be alone in his pride.

Possibly the best of Barrie's plays is "Dear Brutus" (1917), produced during the war but in no way concerned with it. The theme and the setting have more than a touch of the weirdness and other-worldliness which the playwright's fancy has tended to embrace with greater warmth each year. On Midsummer eve a party of ladies and gentlemen come as guests to the house of an indeterminate old fellow named Lob, who encourages them after dinner to stroll out into the night. Pair by pair they reach the door and are astonished to see a vast wood extending where before was open ground. But they proceed, are stricken with midsummer wisdom, and for a few hours at least live the lives which character and circumstances have thwarted them from living in the light of common day. Barrie is too sensible to let it be understood that a complete reformation has been worked in any case. Here, as often, he has suggested more than he has said; he has led his audience to the verge of an unjustified emotion, and then before it was too late—but only just before—has withheld them from the leap with light laughter shining through tears. He has not always done this, and when he has not done it he has failed to be worthy of respect.

Maugham
1874–

Comedy of manners in the traditional sense of that term has never been long absent from the English stage, and neither has it been absent during the period since 1890. Neither Wilde nor Shaw has provided examples of it as clear as those of Somerset Maugham and his followers. Maugham is perhaps as important for his plays as for his novels and short stories.[1] Of the thirty which he wrote between "A Man of Honour" in 1903 and "Sheppy" in 1933 he hopes that all but twelve will be forgotten, and he insists that he has never written dialogue for any other purpose than entertainment. But he has been really entertaining, and therefore some of his plays will survive, though not perhaps as many as twelve. The two best known are "The Circle" (1921) and "Our Betters" (1923). The first of these shows how history repeats itself in society. Lord Porteous and Lady Kitty once ran away from Lady Kitty's husband Clive, and they still live together. Now in another generation they come to visit Lady Kitty's daughter-in-law Elizabeth, who is on the point of deserting her husband for a lover. The older couple with their triviality, their false teeth, and their sense of having done nothing noble would seem to be evidence that Elizabeth had better reconsider, and indeed Lady Kitty urges her to do so. But she does not, and the play ends with her going off in spite of what she has learned from her elders—if she can be said to have learned it. It is a comedy of manners in that it is not a comedy of

[1] For his fiction, see pages 226–231.

morals; or rather, if it deals in morals at all, it deals in a kind that cannot be distinguished from manners. Certainly Maugham passes no judgment, as indeed he never does; for he is most interested in observing what happens to people who know what they want. So in "Our Betters," although the expatriated American lady who is its central character is so immoral as to shock her young relatives fresh from the United States, and although the audience and even Maugham may share this shock, the fact is that Pearl seems not to incur the contempt of the guests whom she has offended, and the play ends with her being embraced by a duchess. The shock is registered because it is true; but Maugham finds other things as true, and the detachment with which he presents these other things is what makes him capable of the comedy of manners. His later plays were more tragic in their undertones, and barely concealed their author's bias. "The Breadwinner" (1930) exposes the spoiled arrogance of the young a generation following the war; "For Services Rendered" (1932) shows a family crushed by the war fifteen years after it ended; and "Sheppy" sardonically tells of a man who has an authentic religious experience only to incur the suspicion of insanity on the part of a people who cannot, Maugham seems to say, observe the difference. Certain of Maugham's earlier plays were in their fashion serious also. "Smith" (1909), for instance, commented clearly enough on the modern English woman when it showed its hero, returning from South Africa to look for a wife, finding the necessary qualifications only in his sister's servant. And most of Maugham's work for the stage has had in it somewhere a vein of satirical or critical venom. But he is best when he provokes laughter, which he knows perfectly how to do—as when, in the otherwise undistinguished "Home and Beauty" (1919), he writes a scene in which the two husbands of a woman (one of them having returned from the war after being announced as dead) draw lots to see who shall keep her, and each tries to cheat the other into winning. That is heartless. Yet the woman is a fool, and comedy of manners is always a little heartless.

Coward 1899– Among several younger playwrights who have learned much from Maugham about the art of comedy, the most successful and delightful is Noel Coward. Coward's many plays are not all comedies. "The Vortex" (1923), his first stage triumph, was something of a melodrama, though it contained elements which were to be reworked for comic purposes later on. Like several of its successors, it had for its heroine a beautiful, vain woman, a little past her prime and incapable of resisting the temptation to make young men fall in love with her; and like those same successors it gives this woman a sensible friend who tells her the truth. But it also gives her a son, Nicky Lancaster, who takes her conduct tragically and seeks forgetfulness of it in drugs. The last scene, in which Nicky and his mother cling to each other and promise to reform, is effective on the stage, but it lacks the weight of tragedy—as does "Cavalcade," which traces the fortunes of the Marryots from 1899 to 1930 in the effort to write a history of that English spirit during that period. "Cavalcade" is serious, but it does not escape the twin rocks of unexamined patriotism and over-emphasized sentiment. "Post Mortem" is Coward's contribution to literature against war, and it reaches a terrifying irony when it shows John Cavan, returning from his French grave after thirteen years, unable to convince anybody except his mother that the war had been unspeakably a mistake. But it tends on the whole to be hysterical, as "Bitter Sweet," a musical play in which the past of the Marchioness of Shayne is relived so that young Dolly Chamberlain may be convinced that she should marry the man she loves though she is engaged to another, tends to be mawkish. The lyrics scattered so profusely through it are, when read on the printed page, preposterously flat.

"The Vortex" has its comic counterpart in "Hay Fever," one of the funniest of modern plays. Coward has escaped in it from any necessity to be otherwise than what he is, namely an exquisite provider of ludicrous situations and an ineffable mimic of affected conversation. The scene is the Bliss household, all four members of which are as charming as they are idiotic—eccentric, histrionic, extravagant, rude, and childlike at the same time that they express in a curious way the farthest refinements of civilization. Among themselves they seem to be mannerless monsters, yet they like one another vastly better than they do the rest of the world, which comes to their house for a weekend in the persons of four friends each one of whom has supposed he was the only one invited. The upshot of many ridiculous confusions and farcical heartbreaks is that in the last scene the family sit peacefully down to breakfast while the four guests slip away for such peace as they can find elsewhere. Judith, the mother, is Florence Lancaster made over in the style of high farce. She is one of the most foolish women in dramatic literature, and one of the most captivating. Her dialogue, like that of the others in "Hay Fever," is Coward's dialogue at its best—brief, allusive, sophisticated, and simple quite beyond analysis. "Private Lives" extracts no less laughter from the spectacle of Amanda and Elyot, divorced because they cannot stop quarrelling yet ready to fall in love with each other again as soon as they meet—when they start quarrelling again, as they will undoubtedly continue to do throughout the rest of their lives. They are brilliant in the way that Beatrice and Benedick are brilliant, or Mirabell and Millamant; and Coward has provided foils for them in the well-meaning Victor and Sybil who have married them after their divorce but who are forgotten as soon as they set eyes on each other. "Design for Living" follows three bohemians, Gilda, Otto, and Leo, through many amusing adventures together and apart in Paris, London, and New York; ending up with their reunion when they realize that no one of them can live away from the other irresponsible pair. Coward has that rare thing in English or any other comedy, a truly light touch. The froth of laughter forms on his best subjects when he is free to handle them. He has contributed much gaiety to the life of his time.

**Hardy
1840–1928** Thomas Hardy [1] stands entirely outside of the contemporary dramatic design with his lone masterpiece, "The Dynasts" (1904–1908). This play is remarkable in the century first because it is poetry. In the greatest periods of its literary history the drama has been both poetic and popular. Poetry of no sort is popular to-day in the important sense that prose fiction is popular, and verse plays especially lack that kind of force which compels universal attention. Hardy is almost unique, then, in the form which he has given to his language. But he is even more extraordinary in the form which he has given to his material, and in the scope which his ambitions have led him to conceive. In mere size "The Dynasts" permits nothing to be compared with it except Shaw's "Back to Methuselah"; and incidentally a great deal could be said for the opinion that those two dramas have been the giants of their generation. But whereas Shaw's perspective has been scientific and philosophical, Hardy's, at least on the surface, has been historical. "The Dynasts" is a history of the ten years in Europe between 1805 and 1815, and the central figure is, of course, Napoleon. Here another comparison suggests itself—a comparison with Tolstoy's great novel in three volumes, "War and Peace," covering the

[1] For his poems, see pages 170–175.

same ground in point of time and place. But the concern of the famous Russian was different from Hardy's, as that of any one else must necessarily have been.

The nature of "The Dynasts" may partially be deduced from the sub-title: "An Epic-Drama of the War with Napoleon, in Three Parts, Nineteen Acts, and One Hundred and Thirty Scenes." Hardy has presented a panorama of mighty sweep—a sweep quite beyond the limits of stage artifice, a sweep which makes the poem fit only for "mental performance." On a certain occasion a few speeches were selected from the mammoth text and recited on a London stage; but the effect of the whole is one that can be wrought only upon the mind's eye. The mind's eye must travel in an instant from England to France, from France to Italy, from Italy to Germany, from Germany to Russia, from Russia back to an English village; and indeed there are moments when the continent of Europe becomes visible as an entity, as in the following stage-direction: "The nether sky opens, and Europe is disclosed as a prone and emaciated figure, the Alps shaping like a backbone, and the branching mountain-chains like ribs, the peninsular plateau of Spain forming a head. Broad and lengthy lowlands stretch from the north of France across Russia like a grey-green garment hemmed by the Ural mountains and the glistening Arctic Ocean. The point of view then sinks downwards through space, and draws near to the surface of the perturbed countries, where the peoples, distressed by events which they did not cause, are seen writhing, crawling, heaving, and vibrating in their various cities and nationalities." When the first terrestrial scene is presented at close hand, therefore, and a stage-coach appears upon an English highway along the sea, the voices of the people within, "after the foregoing, sound small and commonplace, as from another medium."

It is this alternation between the near and the far view

which gives to the action of the piece its uncanny significance. For Hardy has endeavored to see the Napoleonic years as a tragic unit, an episode in the life of man susceptible to special treatment as revealing all that is pitiful for Hardy in that life. Hardy conceives the war to have been an unrelieved calamity for which no single nation and no single man—not even Napoleon—was responsible. The spectacle which presents itself is rather a vast network of error growing more complex and inescapable each year only because fate persists in her attitude of indifference or even contempt toward the human race. To give voice to this view Hardy has invented a group of Phantom Intelligences—the Ancient Spirit of the Years, the Chorus of the Years, the Spirit of the Pities, the Chorus of the Pities, Spirits Sinister and Ironic, the Choruses of Sinister and Ironic Spirits, the Spirit of Rumor, the Chorus of Rumors, the Shade of the Earth, Spirit-Messengers, and Recording Angels—who from regions far above the earth look down and comment from time to time upon the conduct of the persons involved. The comment of these spirits is the comment of Hardy himself, and in every respect it is consistent with the philosophy which he expressed in his fiction and his poetry. It is comment of the most grandly poetical sort, and it contains some of the greatest writing of the twentieth century —writing comparable with that of Æschylus in Greece and with that of Milton in an older England. Yet it in no way suggests that Æschylus and Milton have been imitated. Æschylus, like Homer, peopled his sky with gods; Milton filled the universe with falling devils and soaring angels; Hardy, in another age, has had to be content with intellectual abstractions to which he could give no other human attribute than voice. For the gods no longer have shapes like men; they are remote, dwelling in the realm of pure, disembodied ideas.

The largeness of Hardy's perspective lends more than a

philosophical significance to the action as a whole. It lends an unexampled reality to the various parts. When the mists finally clear away, each scene, each army, each individual, becomes terribly clear by virtue of the fact that a gaze so comprehensive and so earnest has been momentarily concentrated thereupon. An incident becomes actual because its meaning, or perhaps its lack of meaning, has been so indelibly impressed upon the reader. No one character fully realizes the importance of what he does; the reader, in the capacity of divine spectator, realizes everything, as God would if he looked at men. There are literally hundreds of speakers, and if the armies be taken into account, literally hundreds of thousands of human beings. But there is no confusion in the mind of the audience, however much there may be upon the physical stage. After the play is over the reader remembers with ease, as if he had been actually upon the ground, dozens of scenes—Pitt in the picture-gallery, receiving the news of Austerlitz; Pitt on his death-bed; the peasants along the English coast guarding with their beacons against a rumored invasion by Napoleon himself, and comically solemn in the consciousness of their responsibility; the courts of Russia and Germany, splendid with gold and silk and humming with intrigue; Napoleon with Josephine, and later with Marie Louise; the ghastly winter at Moscow, with Frenchmen lying frozen around the remains of camp-fires; the ball-room at Brussels, just before the order comes to arm for Waterloo; Waterloo itself, with Napoleon reduced to despair and the armies charging in their respective sectors; the Peninsular Campaign, with fields full of struggling men and barns inhabited by sleeping or drunken soldiers; Nelson mortally wounded at Trafalgar; the death of George III; the English Prince Regent revoltingly indifferent to the news of George's death; the final defeat of Napoleon; and his escape from Waterloo through lonely woods.

Not the least interesting thing about "The Dynasts" is the story of its growth in the poet's mind. Hardy himself has told how as a boy, living on that portion of the English coast where tradition long persisted that Napoleon came in person one dark night and reconnoitered, he was seized with an insatiable curiosity concerning all things connected either with Napoleon or with the wars that he waged. When he grew up and became a writer he treated one aspect or another of the subject in short stories, in poems, and in a novel—"The Trumpet Major." But still the subject eluded him because it was so big. At last, when he had closed his career as a novelist, he settled down to researches of a comprehensive sort and in eleven years completed one of the most ambitious and at the same time one of the most successful literary ventures ever undertaken by an ancient or a modern man. Thus two great English dramas of the twentieth century, "The Dynasts" and "Back to Methuselah," are seen to be what great dramas have almost always been, works of a long and gradual growth, the growth indeed of a lifetime.

CHAPTER IV

ESSAYISTS

STRICTLY speaking, there is no body of English prose to-day which conforms to the traditional rules of the essay. There is a great wealth of miscellaneous writing by philosophers, historians, critics, economists, and humorists; yet the profession of essayist as such can hardly be said to exist. A writer who sits down at his desk with something specific to say in the twentieth century is more likely to call his product an article than he is to claim for it the artistic distinction of being an essay, thus implying that his subject is of more significance than his personality. Of the six authors considered in the present chapter, one is a caricaturist and satirist first of all, three have consistent theories about society which they wish to expound, one is a naturalist, and one is a biographer.

Beerbohm **1872–** Max Beerbohm is the only surviving writer who carries over to present times the full flavor of the eighteen-nineties. He was one of the cleverest members of that extremely clever and sophisticated group which contained Oscar Wilde and the illustrator Aubrey Beardsley, and it might have been supposed that with the new century he would wither as most of the fine flowers of his decade did. But he was saved by the fact that he was a wit; he never had taken his generation too seriously. Indeed, in a manner quite his own, he had been its satirist. He had been in the nineties, but not irretrievably of them. He had loved dandyism—the metropolitan elegance of irresponsible gentleman and wits—but he had known how to take it off in caricature. Himself a fastidious artist in everything, he yet had seen the ludicrous side of the esthetic movement, and had made gentle fun of it. When, at the not very advanced age of twenty-four, he collected the best of the essays which he had been contributing to periodicals characteristic of the time, he already foresaw the end of his generation, and affected to believe that his end also had come. He called his first book "The Works of Max Beerbohm" (1896), and closed it with a facetious, inimitable sketch in which he bade farewell. "Already I feel myself to be a trifle outmoded. I belong to the Beardsley period. . . . Indeed, I stand aside with no regret. For to be outmoded is to be a classic, if one has written well." This sketch, entitled "Diminuendo," is famous, as are several other pieces in the "Works." "The Pervasion of Rouge" he had written at Oxford, under the title "A Defence of Cosmetics"; it is a half-serious, half-comic plea for artifice in civilization. "Dandies and Dandies" glorifies Beau Brummel, the supreme dandy of all times, and "1880" is a history, with all the apparatus of formal history, of the esthetic movement. "1880" is unsparing of its subject, and is altogether a delicious piece of raillery; yet it would be difficult to determine just where the author's sympathy gives way to his satire. This is true of all his work; it is never obviously one thing rather than another, but is compounded of many elements furnished by his delicately imaginative temperament.

The next year Beerbohm published "a Fairy Tale for Tired Man" which he called "The Happy Hypocrite." This is beautiful in its own light, mocking way, but it is essentially a parody of the fantastic, pseudo-moral tales which Oscar Wilde and others had written during the eighties and nineties. Sir George Hell is a very bad man with a very evil face who is saved by his love for Jenny Mere, in whose company he wears a mask of goodness and goes by the name of Sir George Heaven, until one day when his mask is torn off he discovers that his real face has become angelic. Beerbohm followed this by "More," the reference in the title being to the original "Works." The temper of this volume is still that of the earlier book, but there is already a discernible tendency toward a greater range of subject and a greater simplicity of style. The satirist retains all his gift for insinuating that certain things are absurd, but he condescends to treat of popular things, such as bicycles and fire departments.

Ten years passed before he published another volume of essays. In the meantime he was busy drawing caricatures of the most famous of his contemporaries in letters and public life; and for a while he served as dramatic critic. When therefore he came out with a third volume of his collected works under the title "Yet Again" (1909), a new generation offered itself for his satire, and the nineties were dead. Beerbohm, with the agility of genius, landed on his feet; this third volume was better than either of the former two. It played over the surfaces of twentieth-century life with all the old subtlety and all the old power. This is yet truer of the fourth volume, "And Even Now" (1920), which is the funniest of its author's miscellaneous books. The best and most characteristic sketch is "A Clergyman." A study of this would reveal as well as it can be revealed the method of Beerbohm's humor. In the beginning there is nothing more to go on than a short passage from Boswell's life of Johnson in which an unnamed clergyman, venturing to make a remark in Johnson's company, is squelched by a dogmatic retort and never speaks again. Beerbohm plays upon this hint, building up a more and more elaborate structure of hypothesis concerning the nature and career of the clergyman, until he stands entirely revealed, or rather created, for the amusement and the not too serious sympathy of the reader. Such is Beerbohm's technic—to blow upon a trifling fact or idea until it swells into the dimensions of a swaying, iridescent soap-bubble and finally breaks silently in refined laughter.

This indeed is the secret of the many brilliant caricatures which Beerbohm has drawn of his contemporaries, and which are as well known as his writings to those who value wit for its own sake. The superiority of these caricatures in the last analysis resides in the fact that their artist has imagination enough to seize upon the essential trait in the person to be satirized; then he exaggerates that trait just enough to make his point and to deepen his criticism. It would naturally follow that Beerbohm was gifted as a parodist in literature, and he has proved this by a volume of parodies on contemporary prose writers called "A Christmas Garland." The essential qualities of men like Kipling, Wells, Chesterton, Hardy (in "The Dynasts"), Bennett, Galsworthy, Conrad, Shaw, and George Moore are singled out and enlarged until not only laughter is aroused but materials for criticism of these authors is furnished in abundance. "A Christmas Garland" is perhaps the most brilliant book of its kind in English. The same procedure on a greater scale explains the success of Beerbohm's one novel, "Zuleika Dobson" (1911), a burlesque of Oxford life which many readers call his masterpiece, and which, like the rest of his work, mingles affection for the subject with a clear perception of its occasional absurdity. A rival for the honor of being Beerbohm's masterpiece is "Seven Men" (1919), a collection of portrait-stories. Only six men are listed in the table of contents; the seventh, presumably, is Beerbohm himself. In his account of at least four of them he returns to the nineties, painting in Enoch Soames, Hilary Maltby, Stephen Braxton, and "Savonarola" Brown the plight of the minor author who flourished then. Soames, eager for fame, and willing to sell his soul for a glimpse of what posterity will think of him, is conducted by the Devil to the library of the British Museum a hundred years hence, only to find that the only reference to him in the catalogue is in a book by Max Beerbohm called "Seven Men." Maltby and Braxton, each the author of one popular book, are furious rivals; Brown spends ten years writing a pitiful play in verse upon Savonarola, and four acts of it are "quoted" by Beerbohm, who of course invented it along with its imaginary author.

Beerbohm has no message to the world other than that of his fastidious common sense. "I am a Tory Anarchist," he says. "I should like every one to go about doing just as he pleased—short of altering any of the things to which I have grown accustomed." His prose is as precise and pure as any in the language, and his wit belongs with the rarest —with that of Shakspere, Congreve, Sterne, and Oscar Wilde.

Shaw 1856– George Bernard Shaw was beginning to be known in London as a wit at about the same time with Beerbohm. But it did not take the public long to find out that he was what Beerbohm as a dandy could not possibly be, a serious man. The dandiacal humorist never deals with important things; he assumes them, and talks rather about clothes, cosmetics, walking-sticks, operas, or parties. Shaw has lighted the crackling fire of his wit under every significant question of his day in economics, politics, ethics, and art. He has been a painstaking student of formidable issues; he has dug for facts where other men had only opinions; he has been stern, direct, consistent. His ideas have been discussed in another chapter,[1] in connection with his most important work in literature, his dramas; so that it is necessary here only to indicate where his miscellaneous prose may be found, and what its singular quality is.

It divides itself naturally into three parts: the economic

[1] For his plays, see pages 249–264.

and political pamphlets, the criticism, and the prefaces to the plays. Under the first come the "Fabian Essays" and the "Fabian Tracts" which Shaw wrote as a socialist under the influence of the Fabian Society. These essays, with others which followed in various years on such questions as imperialism, finance, the eight-hour day, and municipal trading, are shrewd and carefully documented expositions of the socialist point of view. In some cases the research was made by other men and Shaw was used only to give the facts a brilliant expression; in all cases, however, the spectacle presents itself of a great and happy genius laboring with the most unpromising material in order to make truth and sanity prevail. Of more general interest, and perhaps of greater importance, have been the pamphlets written during the World War. "Common Sense about the War" (1914), issued soon after the conflict began, shocked a considerable portion of the public merely by virtue of the fact that it was common sense, and indeed for a few years it alienated Shaw's audience from him. The pamphlet was nothing more or less than an attempt to hush up the current talk about the high motives of the Allied statesmen, and to call attention to the real motives behind every policy. The real motive of any nation in any war, said Shaw, is self-preservation, and so it was in this case; Great Britain was fighting for her prestige, and ultimately for her life. One might think that a good or a bad motive—personally, Shaw wanted Great Britain to survive and prevail—but there was certainly every reason for recognizing it, and every reason against glozing it over with sentimental words about Belgium, a scrap of paper, and the war-lords of Europe. Five years later, when the Peace Conference was about to meet at Versailles, Shaw found no different opinion possible, and wrote a pamphlet which he called "Peace Conference Hints," urging the convened statesmen to be honest and frank in the hope that justice would be best served thus.

Shaw's various pamphlets in the department of economics and politics are by no means the least important of his works; they are a guarantee of his sincerity, and they possess not a little of the quality of the fugitive prose written by the greatest pamphleteer in English—Swift, with whom Shaw is often compared. The same quality is to be found throughout the large volume in which he finally brought together all of his ideas about society. "The Intelligent Woman's Guide to Socialism and Capitalism" (1928) is more serious than its title might suggest to one who has less respect for women than Shaw has. And it is of the first excellence in that literary kind—the outline of knowledge—which is perhaps better known through the compilations of H. G. Wells. If it is better than Wells, the reason is that it maintains a more steadily personal tone; and that Shaw is, first and last, a better writer than Wells— or, perhaps, than anyone else in his time.

Shaw's criticism was devoted first to art, then to music, and finally to the drama. In each field he found a more or less neglected master to champion, and he championed him with all the ardor at his command at the same time that he heaped scorn upon weaker artists or upon critical opponents. In painting his hero was Whistler, only then coming into recognition; in music it was Wagner; in the drama it was Ibsen. Shaw is in considerable measure responsible for the fame of these three men in modern England. Wagner he interpreted as a sociologist, a revolutionary whose chief hero, Siegfried, expressed his own passionate views regarding society. Such an interpretation is of course wholly personal with Shaw, and it is extravagant; but in the course of making it, in "The Perfect Wagnerite," he delivered himself brilliantly of many sound pronouncements upon both music and socialism, as indeed he did in all of the articles which have subsequently been reprinted under the title "London Music." Ibsen he treated in one of his earliest books, "The Quintessence of Ibsenism," as the destroyer for the nineteenth and twentieth centuries of cheap conventions, and as the enemy of all that false idealism which discourages the mind from facing or accepting facts. Shaw continued to talk of Ibsen in articles later collected in two volumes as "Dramatic Opinions and Essays" (1907). No more comprehensive or suggestive dramatic criticism has been published in recent years, for Shaw naturally discusses bad plays as well as good, and so sweeps the whole range of dramatic theory and practice. Incidentally he is unflaggingly witty; and he has much to say about the art of acting which deserves to become classic.

His most important work in the essay, however, and probably his most permanent, is found in the prefaces before the plays. They have been so interesting and so varied that the purchaser of a new play by Shaw is likely to look with as much eagerness to the disquisition at the beginning as to the dialogue which follows. They are generally long, running sometimes to a hundred pages; but they have seldom been called tiresome. They are long not because Shaw does not know how to say things quickly, but because he has so much to say. His restless mind turns up so many ideas by the way that he may seem slow in reaching the point. The fact is that he is making points all along. The subject is always the subject of the play— marriage, the superman, biology, linguistics, Christianity, martyrdom, or whatever is considered by the characters who speak the dialogue. The intellectual discipline behind the writing is great; it moves with great speed and clarity against the errors of the mind which Shaw most despises —fear, hypocrisy, sensuality, stupidity. Yet the result is never merely sober or heavily dogmatic. Shaw is in his highest spirits here. His irony and his contempt cut right and left. His style is sharp and final, with brilliant antith-

eses and with examples drawn suddenly in from a wide
world of reading and acquaintance. He does not scruple
to call names; people are fools, knaves, ignoramuses without qualification. There is no verbiage concealing real motives; there is anger in abundance, and fun, and eloquence;
and there is extravagance of statement whenever Shaw is
sure that the wisest of his readers will appreciate the extravagance. All in all, these prefaces make up a body of
prose which is as pungent and important as any so far in
the twentieth century.

**Wells
1866–**
Just as H. G. Wells began his career in fiction [1] with short stories more or less in the conventional form, so in the other department of his
prose he began with essays, and only later developed a
style and form of exposition which was perfectly suited
to his large purposes. One of his earliest essays, called
"Thoughts on Cheapness and Aunt Charlotte," seems in
the light of later books to be entirely characteristic of
Wells at all periods of his intellectual life. It is a protest
against the notion that furniture must be so durable and
good that it will last forever and serve posterity as an-
tiques. Wells confesses to a partiality for cheap, ephemeral
things which can be used carelessly now and thrown away
to-morrow when something different is desired. He looks
with favor on the Japanese custom of making a great many
articles out of paper; Europe, he says, could well cultivate
so free and rational an attitude toward possessions and institutions. Here speaks the philosopher who was to devote
the remainder of a busy career to swift intellectual experiment, who was to scheme year after year for a constantly
changing society.

In the intervals between the novels which he wrote during the first decade of the twentieth century, Wells poured
out six volumes of speculation upon social problems, and

[1] For his prose fiction, see pages 206–212.

it is here, perhaps, that his most interesting prose outside of the fiction may be found. The temper of this writing is very different from that of Shaw upon the same general subject. Whereas Shaw is terse, impatient, and dogmatic, Wells is tentative, skeptical, and smooth. He is as much of a socialist as Shaw, but he is a more comprehensive philosopher. He has never rested content with a single point of view or a single set of prejudices; in successive volumes he has elaborated, qualified, and enlarged his doctrine until certain of his readers have been bewildered. But he has really been consistent, as a swiftly growing plant is consistent. Chesterton once said of Wells, "One can lie awake at night and hear him grow." He has grown in the direction of freedom and common sense; his desire has always been to construct a social philosophy which should take into account every significant impulse of man. "First and Last Things" (1907) is the most cogent of these books, and the one in which Wells's mind can most profitably be studied. It begins with a metaphysical examination of the limits of knowledge and the limits of belief. Wells decides that present classifications of facts and ideas are not binding upon any individual who wishes to think for himself. His will to believe what he likes in the world is supreme. Philosophy is essentially a personal thing, an individual guess as to the composition and purpose of the universe. So while Wells refrains from insisting that other people believe with him, he proceeds to outline his own faith, hoping that many will find that they agree. He feels within himself a powerful sense of society, and therefore calls that sense fundamental in man. The social good is the highest good. Socialism must be an expression not of condescension or of revolution, but of love. One who knows that love is the greatest of all intellectual passions must try to increase the amount of it in the world; his duty is "to talk, teach, explain, write, lecture, read, and listen." He must endeavor to civilize his species by encouraging men to understand both themselves and one another. There will be no coercion in Wells's ideal state. There will be freedom under order, justice and yet individuality. The new earth will be roomy, a place where salvation will be achieved through social service, and where happiness will consist in the realization of beauty, knowledge, and power. Each person will want the best thing for himself, and nothing will stand in the way of his getting it. Least of all will any force run wild among men; war, which has some technical and disciplinary value, will not be a dangerous plaything in the hands of a child, but will be an instrument for peace and order in the hands of adult philosophers.

Wells eventually wished to make a historical approach to his social philosophy. From having urged men's thoughts forward toward a utopian future, he came to a point where he thought it necessary to survey for them the steps in the past through which the race according to his interpretation had advanced in the direction of unity and brotherhood. Once that tendency was clear, the future was safe. So he labored for a long time upon "The Outline of History" (1920), which proved to be of great popular influence and educational value. He rightly maintained that history at present lacks comprehensiveness. This or that period has been exhaustively studied; that or that nation knows itself completely. But what has each contributed to the whole story? It was the whole story which Wells set out to tell, from the point of view of one who was chiefly concerned for the harmony of human elements. He began with the earliest known facts about the earth, millions of years before man appeared. He introduced the first men, living in their caves or on their lakes; and as tribes and nations formed themselves out of savagery, he traced their developments through war, work, religion, politics, and art down to the present day. He treated

with contempt most heroes of history who were merely egotists—Alexander and Napoleon for instance—and dwelt
longer upon intellectual and moral leaders such as Buddha,
Socrates, and Christ. It was no superficial essay that he
wrote; he made real researches, and he wove a comprehensive plot out of innumerable data. "The Outline of History" is one of the most ambitious and serviceable of all
books ever written with a definite ethical purpose. Historians in one field and another object to its proportions;
all readers join in paying tribute to its purpose. The student of Wells may rightly consider it the grandest mani-
festation of its author's wide-ranging, liberal imagination.

Its range is certainly not exceeded by that of "The
Work, Wealth, and Happiness of Mankind" (1931), an
outline of economics and sociology, or by that of "The
Science of Life" (1931), an outline of biology compiled
with the help of Julian Huxley and G. P. Wells. Both of
these later works are full and valuable, but neither of them
has had anything like the success of their predecessor
among Wells's ambitious popularizations. They tend to
repeat that performance so far as their method is concerned, as indeed all of Wells's later non-fiction follows
familiar paths. "The Open Conspiracy" (1928) offers
"blue-prints for a world revolution." "The Way the World
is Going" (1929) and "After Democracy" (1932) are
more pessimistic about the future of civilization than Wells
has ever been before, yet both of them represent his
journalism in its old rather slapdash form. "The New
America" (1935) is one more book on a favorite subject;
and "World Brain" (1938) finds Wells still eagerly recommending international effort toward an understanding of
things as they are. "Experiment in Autobiography" (1934)
promised much, but after a good beginning it turned into
a tract on the thing of greatest interest to its author at the
moment—the world brain itself. Wells has never ceased

to be the restless man he began by being. That restlessness has been his strength, just as it has been his weakness.

G. K. Chesterton was a novelist and poet of **Chesterton 1874–1936** rank, but he is still most widely known as an essayist. A journalist by profession, turning out weekly articles for newspapers and magazines, he at one time or another touched upon nearly every subject under the sun, and his manner was primarily that of a busy journalist—rapid, nervous, and clever. But his cleverness is more than ordinary cleverness, though it is often dismissed as that by those who do not like his notions. It amounts to a genius for surprising juxtapositions of interesting ideas, a genius for paradox. Chesterton revels in antitheses, distinctions, identities, and absurdities. He argues usually by analogies and examples, though there is likely to be a real idea behind his display of fireworks, and often he is talking the plainest kind of sense. He has a gift for illustration worthy of a great poet; the world is constantly alive for him, and images occur to him naturally from the furthest ends of it. He writes with a perpetual relish for facts; he knows the habits of men and women as a reporter knows them, and he does not forget whatever has once engaged his eyes and ears. He is positive, dogmatic, and sudden in his statements, and seems to find a great deal of fun in speaking extravagantly to an age which has been trained to accept only qualified judgments, to be skeptical about everything. His gospel is the joy of life, and his duty as he sees it is to keep his audience reminded of the possibilities of that joy.

An ardent democrat and a despiser of useless aristocracy, Chesterton was yet the farthest thing from a socialist that could be imagined. Many of his essays ridicule the utopianism of Wells and the scientific socialism of the Fabians. Those philosophies spring, he implies, from a pessimistic view of human nature—a view of it as something which is sick, and needs heroic treatment. Human nature is not sick, roars Chesterton; it is healthy and "terribly solid." Sociologists do not understand it because they do not approach it in a sufficiently hearty spirit. They make a survey of society and find many maladjustments; but then they propose "altering the human soul to fit its conditions, instead of altering human conditions to fit the human soul." They are not aware, that is to say, of the primary desires of man— to be free, to be healthy, to be amused, to work at what is congenial, and to own a little property. They forget that society was made for man, and begin to think that man was made for society. Most of all they err in forgetting the infinite variety of human traits. In an essay on William Morris, the socialist-poet of the nineteenth century, Chesterton finds fault with Morris because "he seemed really to believe that men could enjoy a perfectly flat felicity." For Chesterton felicity is an extended landscape with mountains and rivers and valleys, and he has set out with boundless gusto to explore that landscape.

In the course of his exploration he finds many healthy and harmless habits among men which he wishes to defend against the rigid moralists who would reduce the race to a narrow form of behavior. He is moved to indignation against prohibitionists, particularly when they attack beer, which he often, more or less humorously, has championed as the bulwark of English civilization So with beef, which vegetarians like Shaw refuse to eat. And so with an infinite number of things for which human beings since the dawn of history have had affection. One of Chesterton's books is characteristically entitled "The Defendant." It is a collection of brief essays pointing out the salutary qualities of cheap fiction, pompous public statues, nonsense in literature, useless information in newspapers, heraldry, and so on. He makes these things out to be at least good for something, and insists that critics not make the mistake of judging them by standards not meant for them. Shilling novels are written to amuse or thrill; amusement and romance are legitimate appetites of the human animal; "Hamlet," therefore, has no business being brought in for comparison. In the introduction to "The Defendant" Chesterton inveighs against the "weird and horrible humility" of people who inveterately call good things bad. He will be the prophet of the earth as it is; he will be an optimist. Prophets have always been optimists in the sense that they have been "indignant, not about the badness of existence, but about the slowness of men in realizing its goodness." The only definitely evil thing in the world, he says elsewhere, is the institution of land-holding whereby a few rich men are permitted to gather God's acres into their lonely estates and so deprive most of the people of the natural air and sod.

In "What's Wrong with the World" Chesterton attempted to say the foregoing in a long and coherent volume; but he gradually reverted to the form of the occasional essay, and indeed it seems obvious that he is better at essays than at books. The titles of the numerous collections into which he put his best journalistic sketches are in themselves illuminating: "Heretics" (1905), "Orthodoxy," "Tremendous Trifles," "A Miscellany of Men," "All Things Considered," "Alarms and Discursions," "The Uses of Diversity," and "Fancies Versus Fads." The exuberance of these titles is reflected in the exuberance of the contents. There are essays on the advantages of having one leg, on cheese, on pokers, on running after one's hat, on rhyming, and on a thousand good things of life which as Chesterton examines them come to have an immense significance. He is also an ingenious and entertaining critic of individual men. Tolstoy he condemns, because he over-simplified the human problem; Scott he glorifies for his deathless and opulent romance. As a literary critic

Chesterton stands high among his contemporaries for the flashes of his intuition and the vigor of his judgments. He has lavished his genius for comment on Dickens and Shaw. Dickens he defends against the condescending slurs of modern criticism, maintaining that the great Victorian novelist excelled in the variety and richness of his portraiture, and deifying him for his healthy sentiment. Shaw he accuses of puritanism and a too rigid insistence upon the consistency of things, but he praises him for his wit, his intellectual strength, and his very great sincerity. In "The Victorian Age in Literature" (1913) Chesterton passes in review the outstanding writers of the nineteenth century, enlivening his pages on Carlyle, Arnold, Cobbett, Mill, and the rest with epigram, epithet, and paradox, and making distinctions which will be of permanent validity in English criticism.

Within the dozen years preceding his death he added to his list of critical studies five important new titles: "William Cobbett," "Robert Louis Stevenson," "Chaucer," "St. Francis of Assisi," and "St. Thomas Aquinas." He reflected his conversion to Catholicism—a conversion for which he had always been prepared—in "The Resurrection of Rome," "Avowals and Denials," and "The Well and the Shadows." And just as he died he finished one of the best of all his books, the "Autobiography" (1936) which, in addition to explaining his conversion, analyzed his own personality—his preference for definiteness, for clearness, for "smallness"—as nobody else could ever have done it. In addition it provided a feast of anecdote and epigram. For at no time did Chesterton ever fail to be witty, and at no time did he forget to be the good-natured man he was evidently born to be.

Hudson
1840 (?)–
1922

Naturalists in Great Britain who have also been good writers are comparatively few. The reason seems to be that in most cases the energy required for travel and observation is too great for much to be left over for art. When the combination is fortunate, however, the result is likely to be remarkable; for observation is two-thirds of literature. W. H. Hudson was an observer of the first rank—indeed, of a rank quite his own; and he wrote a peculiarly strong and limpid prose not exactly paralleled by that of any English author, and matched by that of very few. His observations of men and nature had been made in two hemispheres. Born in South America of American parents, he made public few details of his life. His biography was in his books, he said; the only important things which had happened to him had happened to his mind. "Far Away and Long Ago" (1918), a book which many readers call his masterpiece, is a kind of autobiography. This is a record of all the early impressions which his native pampas had made upon his imagination, and reconstructs the process, as accurately as he could remember it in old age, by which nature had wooed, won, and finally disciplined him into manhood. It is a particularly rich book, being crowded with memories of trees, flowers, weeds, thistles, and forests, of eagles, ostriches, owls, ducks, doves, and smaller birds, of snakes, armadillos, dogs, horses, cattle, and men. Over and above all these details, described as they are by the hand of a master in words, there runs a current of philosophy; Hudson explains the first ecstasy which he felt in the presence of living nature, and the ensuing resolve which he made to devote his life to understanding her, not altogether as a scientist, though he should be that, but as a poet and lover as well.

Circumstances removed him at about thirty to England, where he remained the rest of his long life. He did no successful writing for another ten years or so. Then began the series of books, based at first upon his memories of South America but later turning to the English scene for their subjects, which gradually earned him fame. His first book, "The Purple Land that England Lost," was a long romance of the Argentine, packed with fascinating details about the life of the gaucho, or South American cowboy, and taking the reader through many desperate adventures over the plains. Hudson was to try his hand at fiction on several occasions, but he was not often successful, and he approached "The Purple Land" only twice, in "Green Mansions" and "Tales of the Pampas." "Green Mansions" created against the southern background which always enchanted his imagination the figure of an ideal creature, half bird and half girl, who was all that a human being can be and more. In its ideal nature the book resembles a less effectual book by Hudson, "A Crystal Age," in which the reader is conducted forward in history thousands of years to look upon a society freed from the muddier elements of superstition, fear, ignorance, and jealous love. "Tales of the Pampas" contains a number of faultless short stories in a form which Hudson found best suited to his temperament, the form of reminiscential episode.

The fact that Hudson occasionally turned aside in fiction to paint an ideal existence suggests the possibility that he was dissatisfied with this one. That is only partially true. He never had any quarrel with those things which he believed to be natural, and nature herself he always loved with an austere love. But most men, and particularly men living in cities, he despised because of the narrowness, coldness, and pettiness of their dispositions. He was not a genial man when it came to men, and he never minced matters. Prehistoric man interested him a great deal and had his respect; for he imagined that the race in dim days long forgotten was a natural race—a collection of human beings who knew the wind and the rain at first hand, and possessed senses as keen and comprehending as those possessed by the finer animals now. Hudson often felt himself to be a lone survivor of this older race, a remnant of this vanished people. "The blue sky," he wrote in "Hampshire Days," "the brown soil beneath, the grass, the trees, the animals, the wind, the rain, and sun, and stars are never strange to me; for I am in and of and am one of them; and my flesh and the soil are one, and the heat in my blood and in the sunshine are one, and the winds and tempests and my passions are one. I feel the 'strangeness' only with regard to my fellow-men, especially in towns, where they exist in conditions unnatural to me, but congenial to them; where they are seen in numbers and in crowds, in streets and houses, and in all places where they gather together; when I look at them, their pale civilized faces, their clothes, and hear them eagerly talking about things that do not concern me. They are out of my world—the real world. All that they value, and seek and strain after all their lives long, are the merest baubles and childish things; and their ideals are all false, and nothing but by-products, or growths, of the artificial life—little funguses cultivated in heated cellars." He went on to express this hatred in even a more vivid and bitter form. He identified himself with the spirits of those prehistoric men who were buried under a mound on which he sat one day in Hampshire, and who now might be supposed to be looking with contempt toward the neighboring village where modern men lived their "artificial indoor lives." "It is not strange that they fear and hate. I look at them—their dark, pale, furious faces—and think that if they could be visible thus in the daylight, all who came to that spot or passed near it would turn and fly with a terrifying image in their mind which would last to the end of life. But they do not resent my presence, and would not resent it were I permitted to come at last to dwell with them forever. Perhaps they know me for one of their tribe—know that what they feel I feel, would hate what they hate."

Such was the uncompromising attitude of Hudson to-

ward his contemporaries. But most of the time in his books
he put this out of mind and attended to the nature which it
was his business to report. His most characteristic books
are collections of essays describing walks or other excur-
sions in South America and England. The South American
books are built up from notes and from long memory, the
consequence of this being that they glow with a far-away
beauty. "The Naturalist in La Plata," "Idle Days in Pata-
gonia," and "South American Sketches" contain inimitable
pictures of the fauna and flora of the pampas, pictures
which alternate with narratives of adventure in the pursuit
of difficult truth. The English books in this class are more
numerous, and many of them are soberer and more subdued, though they are written with even greater excellence.
At least six of them are wholly concerned with birds, which
of all animals most kept the devotion of Hudson. "Birds
in a Village," "British Birds," "Birds in London," "Birds
and Man," "Adventures among Birds," and "Birds in
Town and Village" establish Hudson in a position supreme
among all men who have observed the feathered world. He
liked his birds alive, and hated those collectors who stuffed
their specimens in order to write dry monographs about
them full of dull Latin words. Hudson knew all this side
of ornithology, but he knew in addition the warm, living
habits of birds; his mind dwelt among them, in their nests
and on the wing.

The rest of his English books dealt with landscapes,
quadrupeds, villages, and men, and with birds also upon
occasion. For years before his death this tall, silent man
with the powerful eyes had walked assiduously through
the southern counties of England, avoiding villages when
he could, but now and then entering towns and studying the
people, the houses, or the churches there with the care with
which he studied the wilder things on moor and down.
"Nature in Downland," "Hampshire Days," "The Land's

End," "Afoot in England," "A Shepherd's Life," "The Book of a Naturalist," "A Hind in Richmond Park," and "A Traveller in Little Things" contain a great wealth of observation and anecdote concerning not only adders, hawks, badgers, and voles, but shepherds and village wives and children as well. Hudson was a keen judge of men, perhaps because of the very fact that he felt so distant from them; and in spite of his sense of superiority he managed to converse with them most profitably. "A Shepherd's Life," one of his finest books, is largely a series of reports on conversations with an old Wiltshire shepherd, Caleb Bawcombe, concerning his dogs, his wife, and his infinitely long life on the downs. "Hampshire Days" is full of significant judgments upon various southern villages and their inhabitants, whom Hudson had classified much as he would have classified a community of foxes or swallows.

The style of Hudson is the despair of all who attempt either to study or to imitate it. It is perfectly simple to all appearances, yet it accomplishes wonders of illusion on every page. It is rapid, and it is as clear as water. There are few superlatives anywhere in it, but there is always a note of suppressed passion; and when that passion breaks out directly the effect is immeasurable. There are no obvious tricks by which "atmosphere" is built up, yet the atmosphere is there, and always appropriate to the subject. In particular is Hudson an adept at narrative. His best books are strewn with anecdotes. They begin naturally, almost without the reader's realizing that they have begun, and they continue for pages while the reader is absorbed in the action being unfolded. No naturalist has ever described the movements of animals to better effect. Hudson knows how to set the scene without any unnecessary stage-properties; then when the animal appears and begins to feed or look about him it is as if the reader were on the spot himself,

standing as motionless as Hudson always stood, and looking with a quiet intentness that could last three or four
days if necessary.

The art of the biographical essay, an art
practised at various times in England by skilful
hands, was revived shortly after the World War
by Lytton Strachey's "Eminent Victorians." The delight of
the readers of this volume was partly over the almost malicious ingenuity with which Strachey exposed the somewhat hypocritical temper of the Victorian mind; but it was
even more over the technic of the author as a biographer. It
had been virtually forgotten that the art of writing lives
could be as entertaining as fiction, and full of as many
sharp subtleties. "The art of biography," said Strachey,
"seems to have fallen on evil times in England. We have
had, it is true, a few masterpieces, but we have never had,
like the French, a great biographical tradition. . . . With
us, the most delicate and humane of all the branches of the
art of writing has been relegated to the journeymen of letters; we do not reflect that it is perhaps as difficult to write
a good life as to live one. . . . To preserve, for instance, a
becoming brevity—a brevity which excludes everything
which is redundant and nothing that is significant—that,
surely, is the first duty of the biographer. The second, no
less surely, is to maintain his own freedom of spirit. It is
not his business to be complimentary; it is his business to
lay bare the facts of the case, as he understands them."
Strachey, true to his profession, took pains to understand
himself as well as the people whose lives he studied. With a
condensed and glittering style, and with irony flickering
over every page, he analyzed the careers of a famous Roman
Catholic bishop, a famous humanitarian and woman, a famous fighter in the wilds of Africa, and a famous school-
master. In each case he implied, though he did not state, that
a point of view might be taken of the subject less com-

Strachey
1880–1932

plimentary than that usually taken; he arranged his facts, dug out of heaps upon heaps of original materials, in such a way that the inferences he wished to be made could not be avoided.

Strachey followed "Eminent Victorians" with a volume devoted wholly to Queen Victoria, who now received the same kind of treatment that had been given to her subjects. But the scale was larger. Not only was the queen set forth in all her rather appealing absurdity, but the long procession of notable men and women with whom she had to do filed by the reader in the clear, unforgettable outlines of life. A third book, "Books and Characters," was more miscellaneous, gathering up the best of Strachey's past performances in periodicals. But it contained brilliant sketches of certain French personages of the eighteenth century who were particularly suited to the author's temper. Still later, an early book on "The Landmarks of French Literature" was reprinted; and it became obvious just whence emanated the spirit behind Strachey's incomparable work; for he was essentially Gallic in his gifts, as so many novelists, dramatists, and poets have been in modern England.

Before his death he was to publish another collection of critical essays, "Portraits in Miniature" (1931), and in the year following his death appeared "Characters and Commentaries." The first of these volumes is especially characteristic of his method, offering as it does the opportunity to see it applied in minimal space. But he had applied it at length in one further biographical work. "Elizabeth and Essex, A Tragic History" (1928) is chiefly concerned with the dramatic and sometimes grotesque relation which existed between Elizabeth and the favorite whose head she was finally obliged to have cut off. Strachey has his own interpretation of the famous love affair, if it was a love affair. He builds it upon the foundation of his theory about Elizabeth, namely that her central trait was procrastination. His development of this theory is one of his ablest achievements. It is in the same class with his portrait of Victoria, and with his portraits of her most astounding subjects. Since his death he has been somewhat drastically discounted, and his exaggerations have become easier to detect. But he is sure of an interesting seat in the hall of English biographers.

Nicolson 1886–

Another biographer who rose to prominence during the twenties because of a gift he had for the definition of personality was Harold Nicolson. Nicolson began with a series of literary biographies each one of which was notable for the clarity with which it brought the author's figure out. Verlaine, Tennyson, Byron, and Swinburne had all been written about many times before, but it was as if they now had determined to exist again. Nicolson remained behind them better than Strachey remained behind his subjects; his art was quieter, and often it was subtler. Eventually he turned to the subject which interested him most. He had been born to a diplomatic career, being the son of Sir Arthur Nicolson, whose life he wrote in 1930; and he had served adventurously under Lord Curzon, the end of whose life he took for the subject of a book in 1934. But he made other capital out of his experience, for in "Some People" (1927) he extracted its essence in a series of brief, imaginary biographies of types he had met in his travels. This has been his most successful book, and its mingling of the methods of biography and fiction, taken together with its cool, ironic, aristocratic style, is certainly the reason. Miss Plimsoll, J. D. Marstock, Lambert Orme, the Marquis de Chaumont, Jeanne de Hénaut, Titty, Professor Malone, Arketall (Lord Curzon's valet), and Miriam Codd are all in their various ways foolish, affected, obsessed, wrong, or by some other standard remarkable. But Nicolson's point of view toward them, while consistently superior, is neatly and impeccably humane. They are specimens, yet a liking for them makes itself felt between the apparently heartless lines. The art of their portraiture, in other words, is complex. No other book of its sort exists in English, and it is likely to outlive many another book of its time assumed to possess a greater importance.

T. E. Lawrence 1888–1935 The importance of Colonel T. E. Lawrence's "Seven Pillars of Wisdom" is more than assumed; it is proved, at any rate if proof consists in such a case of universal agreement to admire a clearly unique book. Published privately in 1926, abridged as "Revolt in the Desert" in 1927, and given to the public in its original form only in the year of its author's death, it has furnished the great literary legend of its time. This is partly because of the peculiar interest inhering in the life and character of Lawrence. A young archaeologist stationed in the Near East when the World War broke out, he became devoted to the cause of Arab independence from Turkey and, after failing to secure permission from his government for an Arab campaign, disappeared into the desert to lead one without permission. The difficulties and dangers were enormous, but so were his talents; or rather his genius, for he has been declared one of the military geniuses of all time. His military triumph, however, was also a personal one, for his initial task was to secure the confidence of the Arabs both in himself and in a government in whose name he made promises. When the promises were not fulfilled he became a changed man; he returned to England and wrote his book, but once that duty to the truth was discharged he endeavored to disappear from the world. His fame was a handicap, but he took extraordinary measures to submerge himself, altering his name, enlisting as a private soldier, and encouraging the rumor that Lawrence had died or effectively disappeared. His death in 1935 was probably welcome to him, for he had never forgiven himself for what he chivalrously called his betrayal of the Arabs. He will live, of course, in "Seven Pillars," which might seem to have no place in the present chapter but which cannot be ignored in any account of contemporary literature. It is long, difficult, and often painful to read, because it tells everything about two hot, perilous, romantic, and dirty years spent by an Englishman at the limit of his endurance among fanatical tribesmen. It offers to the reader, in fact, the same arduous kind of experience that is offered by another classic of Arabian adventure, Charles M. Doughty's "Arabia Deserta," a nineteenth-century work which of course Lawrence knew, and his introduction to an edition of which is filled with noble praise. Arabia would seem to be a place from which no sensitive traveller emerges unchanged. It is a place he feels compelled to talk about at length, and yet he is sure that he cannot communicate the secret of its dreadful fascination. He tries hard, and that is the reason for the difficulty of such books. But he does not wholly succeed. And that is the reason, in part at least, for Lawrence's final "strangeness." "Seven Pillars of Wisdom" is both real and strange. It is, in other words, a great book.

PART THREE

IRISH LITERATURE

IRISH LITERATURE

THE late nineteenth and early twentieth centuries have seen the creation of an important body of Irish literature which has its roots in the soil of genuine Irish culture and is an expression of the Irish genius. That this literature is written in the English language rather than in the ancient language of Ireland, Gaelic, does not make it any the less national. Gaelic as a medium for literature has been dead for a considerable period, and still is dead in spite of an attempt in the generation just passing to revive it. Even as a medium for speech it is dying, and there is little likelihood that any distinguished use will be made of it in the future. The new literature has employed English to express for a wider world than would otherwise have been reached the ideals and temper of an exceedingly self-conscious race.

Until the nineteenth century was well under way, Irishmen who wrote in English were scarcely distinguishable from Englishmen. The literary capital for Swift, Goldsmith, and Sheridan was London, just as in recent years it has been for Oscar Wilde, Bernard Shaw, and George Moore. These great writers have contributed preëminently to English literature, and have dealt with universal European themes. The more specifically Irish literature, by evoking the ancient spirit of Ireland, has made her speak for herself before the world, presenting the natural and permanent claims for her culture. The deeds and heroes of that ancient time were best made available for literary purposes by Standish O'Grady, whose "History of Ireland" (1878–1880) has thrilled the latest generation of poets and dramatists by its color and its impetuosity, and may now be looked back upon as the source of all that is most energetic and beautiful in the new literature. O'Grady explored the voluminous poetical literature of the remote Gaelic past, with its many epics and lays, and recreated for modern readers the brilliant figures of Cuchulain, Conchobar, Queen Maeve, Deirdre, and others, causing them once more to be a possession of the living Irish mind. Cuchulain particularly, the supreme hero, the champion of the knights of the Red Branch of Ulster, the mainstay of King Conchobar and the arch-enemy of Queen Maeve of Connaught, was rendered in glorious terms so that he still is a fruitful subject in Ireland for poems, novels, and plays. Here also was told the great story of Deirdre, the "girl of the sorrows," who, chosen by Conchobar to be his future bride and kept apart from other men in the wilds of the forest, one day met Nasi, one of the three young sons of Usnach, and escaped with him and his brothers to Scotland. The four lived happily abroad for seven years, until Conchobar, sending them word by his innocent old counselor Fergus that they would be pardoned if they returned, slew the three boys upon their return and lost Deirdre through her suicide. These two stories, together with those of the heroes Finn and Oisin, of Diarmuid and Grania, and of Etain, have since become familiar classics, and have furnished the material upon which many poets have based their researches into the Irish genius.

Other materials for a future literature, no less fertile in suggestion and inspiration than those of O'Grady, were furnished by two poets and scholars, George Sigerson and Douglas Hyde, who labored at the close of the nineteenth century to make available the vast body of old bardic songs and folk-tales of their race. Their translations of these precious pieces were valuable particularly because they preserved the true Gaelic speech-accent, and revealed the possibilities for poetic and dramatic use of an entirely indigenous idiom. Douglas Hyde, in his "Love Songs of Connacht" and his "Religious Songs of Connacht," has been the inspiration of a multitude of later writers who without his aid would never have been able to give a completely national turn to their phrases, to enrich their books with an authentic local flavor. With the subject-matter of Irish epic and folk-lore close at hand, and with a speech already invented, the new generation was able to proceed rapidly and intelligently with a literature which should be profoundly national, whether it took the form of poetry, drama, prose fiction, or essay.

POETRY

Yeats 1865-1939 One of the contributors to "Poems and Ballads of Young Ireland," a volume which in 1888 announced the entry of a new generation of poets upon the Irish scene, was William Butler Yeats, who with four poems struck a fresh note, not only of artistic perfection but of national personality. Yeats was at that time a young man, but discerning readers at once saw promise in him, and such readers were impressed by his evident absorption in native legendry or fairy lore. The first volume of his own verse, called "The Wanderings of Oisin and Other Poems," established him in a leading position among contemporary poets. The title-poem went back for its inspiration to the days of Ireland before the dawn of Christianity, the pagan days which Yeats always loved for their shadowy beauty; and incidentally it touched upon the whole material of heroic life which he was later to treat in many a poem or many a play. His second volume, "The Countess Cathleen and Various Legends and Lyrics," increased his reputation. He consolidated his supremacy with "The Wind among the

Reeds" (1899), in which may now be found many of his very famous poems. "The Wind among the Reeds" was marked by a certain touch of philosophical mysticism which rendered some of the pieces difficult to understand, and in subsequent volumes this tendency toward a misty obscurity increased. Eventually, however, he developed an austere simplicity, and continued to write verse of the first quality.

Yeats is now recognized everywhere in the English-speaking world as the chief poetic spokesman of modern Ireland. He was also a playwright and essayist of great importance, but he remains supreme only in the field he first entered. For years, until the appearance in the drama of J. M. Synge, Yeats was easily the leader in his nation's literature, and the principal support of the claim of Ireland that she was artistically independent of England. He has had many imitators both in Ireland and in England; his brooding temperament, by the casual reader rather superficially identified with the Celtic temperament in general, has been influential upon a host of less inspired writers. There is perhaps a touch of artificiality and affectation about even his own work—parodists have not been lacking to point out these weak places—though on the whole he was a great artist, and probably the best of all the poets who have to be considered in the present book. His limitations—his dreamy, vague languor and his cool, impalpable thought—have been described for all time by his contemporary George William Russell in a critical essay. "For a generation the Irish bards have endeavored to live in a palace of art, in chambers hung with the embroidered cloths and made dim with pale lights and Druid twilights, and the melodies they most sought for were half sound-less. The art of an earlier age began softly, to end its songs with a rhetorical blare of sound. The melodies of the new school began close to the ear and died away in distances of the soul. Even as the prophet of old was warned to take off his shoes because the place he stood on was holy ground, so it seemed for a while in Ireland as if no poet would be accepted unless he left outside the demesnes of poetry that very useful animal, the body, and lost all concern about its habits. He could not enter unless he moved with the light and dreamy footfall of spirit. Mr. Yeats was the chief of this eclectic school, and his poetry at its best is the most beautiful in Irish literature. But there crowded after him a whole horde of verse-writers, who seized the most obvious symbols he used and standardized them, and in their writings one wandered about, gasping for fresh air and sunlight, for the Celtic soul seemed bound for ever by the pale lights of fairyland on the north and by the darkness of forbidden passion on the south, and on the east by the shadowiness of all things human, and on the west by everything that was infinite, without form, and void."

The rarest beauty in the poetry of Yeats consisted in the limpid and languorous ease of his lines. Few poets in English have so completely mastered the art of being natural and at the same time precious. The phrases of Yeats flow in delicate, cool curves that suggest the draperies upon the slender bodies of fairy queens. It had been his endeavor, following after the researches of Sigerson and Hyde into the genius of Irish speech, to fabricate an idiom which should be essentially Irish even though it used English words. In this endeavor he may be said substantially to have succeeded. There is not a trace of English practicality or English energy in his verse; all is moody and slow, and the prevailing accent is one of unspoiled speech—the speech of a melancholy man who has brooded long upon the ancient beauties of his land. Perhaps the best specimen is his famous poem, "The Lake Isle of Inisfree":

I will arise and go now, and go to Inisfree,
And a small cabin build there, of clay and wattles made;
Nine bean rows will I have there, a hive for the honey bee,
And live alone in the bee-loud glade.

And I shall have some peace there, for peace comes dropping slow,
Dropping from the veils of the morning to where the cricket sings;
There midnight's all a glimmer, and noon a purple glow,
And evening full of the linnet's wings.

I will arise and go now, for always night and day
I hear lake water lapping with low sounds by the shore;
While I stand on the roadway, or on the pavements gray,
I hear it in the deep heart's core.

The tone of Yeat's devotion, whether in love of woman or in love of country, is quiet and pure. He is not always explicit regarding the object of this devotion. Sometimes it seems to be nothing more tangible than the spirit of perfection which he worships under the mystical title of the Rose.

All things uncomely and broken, all things worn out and old,
The cry of a child by the roadway, the creak of a lumbering cart,
The heavy steps of the ploughman, splashing the wintry mould,
Are wronging your image that blossoms a rose in the deeps of my
     heart.

The wrong of unshapely things is a wrong too great to be told;
I hunger to build them anew and sit on a green knoll apart,
With the earth and the sky and the water, remade, like a casket
     of gold,
For my dreams of your image that blossoms a rose in the deeps
     of my heart.

The best instance of the tentative, unlilting quality in Yeats's verse is to be found in a brief poem called "He Wishes for the Cloths of Heaven," in which there is subtle and intricate music yet no positive song.

> Had I the heavens' embroidered cloths,
> Enwrought with golden and silver light,
> The blue and the dim and the dark cloths
> Of night and light and the half light,
> I would spread the cloths under your feet:
> But I, being poor, have only my dreams;
> I have spread my dreams under your feet;
> Tread softly because you tread on my dreams.

The separate lines here have a sound of prose; the whole, however, is poetry of a high order, and poetry of a kind which in recent years has been often attempted by other writers in Ireland, England, and America.

Around his fiftieth year, in other words, Yeats began to modify his style. He kept the grace which had always been his distinction, and indeed he never was to lose it; but his verse took on a new definiteness and solidity. It was as if he had changed his allegiance from the moon to the sun. Angles appeared in the contours of his verse; the language approached nearer to that of men's speech; and an intellectual content gave fresh weight to his rhythms. All this was not because growing older had weakened him. It had in fact strengthened him, as it strengthens great poets; and if he became within two decades the greatest poet writing in the English language, as there seems to be little doubt he did, the reason was merely that he had grown at last to full stature. The change was noticeable in "Responsibilities" (1914) and "The Wild Swans at Coole" (1919), though not everywhere in those volumes. The fine poem in the first of them, "To a Friend whose Work has come to Nothing," was for one thing written in a short, crisp line like that which we associate with the poetry of Jonathan Swift; and for another thing it said things quickly, sharply, and even harshly.

> Be secret and exult,
> Because of all things known
> That is most difficult.

Yeats had emerged from his Celtic twilight to say things which are true everywhere, and to say them, it would seem, in the fewest possible words, and in the clearest. His poem in honor of those who lost the rebellion of Easter, 1916, and were executed by the English, ended with a line whose power came partly at least from its brevity:

A terrible beauty is born.

But the later poetry of Yeats, the poetry which will be the basis for his future fame, is by no means limited to the short, bare line. In two volumes of the first importance to contemporary poetry in any part of the English-speaking world, "The Tower" (1928) and "The Winding Stair" (1933), he regained all of his old fluidity without a return to the vagueness and relaxed tunefulness which were the weaker side of his original talent. The first poem in "The Tower," "Sailing to Byzantium," has become one of the most famous of modern poems. It expresses his final intention and his final wisdom. He will put off the aging body, the "dying animal" to which his soul is fastened, and sail to Byzantium where art has always occupied itself with truth rather than nature, intellectual patterns rather than patterns of water, sunlight, growth, desire, and mortality. The lines of nature are curved; only the intellect can draw straight lines, and that is what he will do henceforth. This was his way of saying that the callow mysticism of his youth had given place to a sterner one. He remained a mystic, but the content of his vision was now richer, more abstract, more difficult. All of his later work shows him adding to this content and so ballasting his poetry with thought. This would not matter were the result something other than poetry, as it would be in most cases. In his case, since his natural endowment was never decreased, and since he had solved the problem of how as an

artist to absorb the matter of his thought into forms which
gain rather than lose by the experience, the result is something very rich and profound.

Æ
1867–1935
By general consent George William Russell,
who wrote always under the pseudonym Æ,
ranks next to Yeats among modern Irish poets,
some of his admirers indeed preferring him to the better-
known "poet of the shadows." Æ was an important leader
of the new literary movement as editor, essayist, publisher,
and philosopher. A man of singular integrity and beauty
of character, he encouraged the profession of letters in
Dublin in many unselfish ways; never, however, in the
rôle of narrow nationalist. He early assisted in the forma-
tion of a philosophical group in the Irish capital which
considered the foundations of a future national literature,
and which gave body to the general literary movement.
The members of this group were mystics, devoted to the-
osophic studies and drawn closer each year to the religious
speculations of the East. The poems of Æ are prevailingly
mystical in tone, being concerned with the "Universal
Being" who has nourished their author's mind and imagination through many years. Being an honest and humble
mystic, Æ clung to a single vision; and being less interested
in literary effect than Yeats, he did not trouble to search
his fancy for fresh symbols by which to express himself.
As a consequence his poetry tends toward monotony both
of structure and of theme; this monotony irks those readers who do not sympathize with the author's mood, but
for others it is a guarantee of sincerity. Few poets have
been more sincere than Æ; few have been more profoundly
respected. There is a monotony even about his landscapes,
the settings of his visions. He confines himself to those
hours of the day when time seems merging into eternity—
dawn and twilight—and the colors of his skies are the

delicately tinted colors of changing moments. The two following poems are typical, both in their spirit and in the fine modulation of their language.

Still as the holy of holies breathes the vast,
Within its crystal depths the stars grow dim;
Fire on the altar of the hills at last
    Burns on the shadowy rim.

Moment that holds all moments; white upon
The verge it trembles; then like mists of flowers
Break from the fairy fountain of the dawn
    The hues of many hours.

Thrown downward from that high companionship
Of dreaming inmost heart with inmost heart,
Into the common daily ways I slip
    My fire from theirs apart.

Twilight, a timid fawn, went glimmering by,
    And Night, the dark-blue hunter, followed fast,
Ceaseless pursuit and flight were in the sky,
    But the long chase had ceased for us at last.

We watched together while the driven fawn
    Hid in the golden thicket of the day.
We, from whose hearts pursuit and flight were gone,
    Knew on the hunter's breast her refuge lay.

O'Sullivan
1879–
Among the many younger poets whom Æ had encouraged as friend and editor, Seumas O'Sullivan stands forth as one gifted with extraordinary facility and sweetness of style. Like Æ he is partial to twilight hours, and sensitive to the evanescent beauty that passes with the dying day. Like Æ also he lacks any great variety. But he is a more perfect master of form than Æ; he comes close, in fact, to Yeats in the matter of verbal felicity. "The Starling Lake" will recall the older poet in its limpid cadences:

My sorrow that I am not by the little dún
By the lake of the starlings at Rosses under the hill,
And the larks there, singing over the fields of dew,
Or evening there and the sedges still.
For plain I see now the length of the yellow sand,
And Lissadell far off and its leafy ways,
And the holy mountain whose mighty heart
Gathers into it all the colored days.
My sorrow that I am not by the little dún
By the lake of the starlings at evening when all is still,
And still in whispering sedges the herons stand.
'Tis there I would nestle at rest till the quivering moon
Uprose in the golden quiet over the hill.

Colum
1881–

Another protégé of Æ in the early years of the twentieth century was Padraic Colum, a man of remarkable force and originality who in one view has earned a greater reputation as a playwright than as a poet. Yet his poetry ranks high among his contemporaries by virtue of its sterling honesty and its purity of observation. Colum, at present a resident of the United States, was once in close contact with the Irish soil, and drew his strength directly from that. His pictures of peasants at their work, of old women by firesides, of young girls spinning, are notably free from sentimentality; they are almost bare in their truthfulness, and they are wholly independent of any inspiration save personal experience. "A Drover" brings to life a man following his beasts over the hills.

> To Meath of the pastures,
> From wet hills by the sea,
> Through Leitrim and Longford,
> Go my cattle and me.
>
> I hear in the darkness
> Their slipping and breathing—
> I name them the bye-ways
> They're to pass without heeding.

"What the Shuiler Said as She Lay by the Fire in the Farmer's House" realistically enumerates the comforts which an old pauper-woman dreams of having as she nods in the chimney-corner; while several spinning songs with rollicking refrains speak for girls at their daily labor. An even greater vigor shows in "River Mates," which deals with the king of river animals.

> I'll be an otter, and I'll let you swim
> A mate beside me; we will venture down
> A deep, full river when the sky above
> Is shut of the sun; spoilers are we:—
> Thick-coated; no dog's tooth can bite at our veins,
> With ears and eyes of poachers: deep-earthed ones
> Turned hunters; let him strike past,—
> The little vole; my teeth are on an edge
> For the King-Fish of the River!
>   I hold him up,
> The glittering salmon that smells of the sea:
> I hold him up and whistle!
>   Now we go
> Back to our earth: we will tear and eat
> Sea-smelling salmon; you will tell the cubs
> I am the Booty-bringer—I am the Lord
> Of the River—the deep, dark, full and flowing River.

The brilliant achievements of James Stephens in the novel have tended to overshadow his work as a poet, but he is a vivid and amusing poet, and it happens that his verses are marked by the same qualities for which his fiction is famous. "Insurrections" (1909), his first volume, with the others which followed it in fairly rapid succession, established him early in his career as an impish poet, humorous, grotesque, and occasionally profound, and by no means disposed to take too solemn a view of the materials which had already become conventional in Irish poetry. He wrote of cities and men rather than of hillsides and fairies, or if he wrote of fairies and heroes he treated them with a familiarity

Stephens
1882–

sometimes bordering on levity. At the same time that he is
a humorist in verse, however, Stephens is a devotee of the
rarer forms of beauty, and many passages in his poetry
are lovely beyond the power of many more serious writers.

"What Tomas an Buile Said in a Pub" quotes a drunk-
ard on the subject of God:

> I saw God. Do you doubt it?
>   Do you dare to doubt it?
> I saw the Almighty Man. His hand
> Was resting on a mountain, and
> He looked upon the World and all about it:
> I saw him plainer than you see me now,
>   You mustn't doubt it.
>
> He was not satisfied;
>   His look was all dissatisfied.
> His beard swung on a wind far out of sight
> Behind the world's curve, and there was light
> Most fearful from His forehead, and He sighed,
> "That star went always wrong, and from the start
>   I was dissatisfied."
>
> He lifted up His hand—
>   I say he heaved a dreadful hand
> Over the spinning Earth, then I said, "Stay,
> You must not strike it, God; I'm in the way;
> And I will never move from where I stand."
> He said, "Dear child, I feared that you were dead,"
>   And stayed His hand.

In his later books Stephens has widened his range, reaching, for instance, to the heights of this beautiful and profound lament for Deirdre, his favorite among the mythi-
cal personages of ancient Ireland:

> Do not let any woman read this verse;
> It is for men, and after them their sons
> And their sons' sons.

The time comes when our hearts sink utterly;
When we remember Deirdre and her tale,
And that her lips are dust.

Once she did tread the earth; men took her hand;
They looked into her eyes and said their say,
And she replied to them.

More than a thousand years it is since she
Was beautiful: she trod the living grass;
She saw the clouds.

A thousand years! The grass is still the same,
The clouds as lovely as they were that time
When Deirdre was alive.

But there has never been a woman born
Who was so beautiful, not one so beautiful
Of all the women born.

Let all men go apart and mourn together;
No man can ever love her; not a man
Can ever be her lover.

No man can bend before her; no man say—
What could one say to her? There are no words
That one could say to her!

Now she is but a story that is told
Beside the fire! No man can ever be
The friend of that poor queen.

Such a poem is effective in part because its author has not
stood too much upon his dignity. He has not been conventionally and vaguely worshipful before his legendary
queen, but has been simply, even painfully, impressed by
her human beauty; he has been a man with all of man's
complex and varying motives, and that is the secret of
Stephens's success in anything that he has written.

**Campbell
1881–**

"The Mountainy Singer," "Irishry," and other volumes by Joseph Campbell have contributed to contemporary Irish poetry a remarkably large number of ingenuous and affecting songs. Campbell first announced himself through the following stanzas:

> I am the mountainy singer—
> The voice of the peasant's dream,
> The cry of the wind on the wooded hill,
> The leap of the fish in the stream.
>
> Quiet and love I sing—
> The cairn on the mountain crest,
> The cailin in her lover's arms,
> The child at its mother's breast.
>
> Beauty and peace I sing—
> The fire on the open hearth,
> The cailleach spinning at her wheel,
> The plough in the broken earth.

He went on to say that he would sing of travail and pain, of sorrow and death, of the only life in fact that peasants lead. For he is the singer *par excellence* of peasant life. He has gone much about the hills and lanes of certain counties, observing the inhabitants in their infinitely varied attitudes and callings; and he has copied them with always a becoming fidelity. He has paid particular attention to Christian ritual and folk-belief, treating this with as much affection as he has treated the more pagan aspects of the popular imagination. Perhaps the best known of his poems is "The Old Woman," in which he has preserved the image of tranquil old age not only for Ireland but for all places and times:

> As a white candle
> In a holy place,
> So is the beauty
> Of an aged face.

As the spent radiance
  Of the winter sun,
So is a woman
  With her travail done,

Her brood gone from her,
  And her thoughts as still
As the waters
  Under a ruined mill.

DRAMA

The development of a national Irish drama proceeded
rapidly during the first quarter of the twentieth century,
and it is this department of the new national literature
which is best known abroad. One reason for the latter fact
is that the Irish playwrights have numbered several particularly brilliant persons among themselves; another reason is that the circumstances attending a new departure in
the drama draw wide-spread attention from critics and
critical periodicals. Chief among such circumstances in the
present case was the founding of special theaters in Dublin,
as in other capitals during the same period, in order to meet
the needs of a special and at first unpopular drama. Of the
two important theaters founded in Ireland for such a purpose, the first was the Irish Literary Theater, which com-
menced its career in 1899 with a play by Yeats. Yeats
had been the chief mover in the enterprise, but he had
been materially assisted by Edward Martyn, George
Moore, Æ, and others. Eventually he found the Literary
Theater unsuited to his personal dramatic program, which
provided for a predominance of folk and legendary plays,
and withdrew into another movement. Edward Martyn,
at first with the help of George Moore, but latterly alone,
has directed the Literary Theater in accordance with his
own program, which provides especially for intellectual
plays in the general European tradition of Ibsen. He him-

self has written and produced in Dublin half a dozen plays in the manner of Ibsen, and in addition has presented a number of worthy plays from writers of the Continent. The most interesting career of the Irish drama, however, has been run in connection with the theater to which Yeats withdrew. With him as president, the Irish National Theater Society was formed, and after two years a theater, now famous as the Abbey Theater, came into possession of the society. Since 1904 the Abbey Theater has been the home, properly speaking, of the Irish national drama; it is here that the most famous Irish plays have been first presented; it is here that the most significant reputations have been made.

**Yeats
1865-1939**
With the one exception of Synge, Yeats is the best-known Irish playwright. If he was greater as poet than as dramatist, if his gift was really for lyric and narrative utterance, he at least was one of the glories of the stage he labored to found, and his influence has been incalculable. His plays are somewhat lacking in structure, and they occasionally fail in dramatic effect; they are often vague and inconclusive; but all of them are beautifully written, and the best of them have stirred their audiences to a profound and poetic response. "The Countess Cathleen" tells the story of a wealthy noblewoman of old times who when her people were suffering from famine sold her soul to the devil in order that they might not be forced from necessity to sell theirs. As a play it hardly succeeds, but as poetry it ranks high among Yeats's works. "The Land of Heart's Desire" (1894) is also more a poem than a play. It deals with the fairy material which Yeats likes so much to resurrect from the Celtic past; it returns to the pagan world. Mary Bruin, the young daughter of peasants "at a remote time," hears the call of the Sidhe, or fairies, outside her father's door. At last Mary allows herself to dance with a strange

child who has entered the house, and at the close of the dance her spirit leaves her body to dwell in the world of spirits forever. "The Shadowy Waters" was at one time preferred by Yeats himself to all his other plays. But again it is preferable only on the ground of its poetry; no action, and therefore no drama, is possible in a piece which attempts to express the abstract longings of a soul for absolute, imperishable love. The scene is a ship in the shadowy waters of the western sea, and the hero is Forgael, who at first rejects the mortal love of Queen Dectora, bestowed upon him as the ship adventures through quiet waves, but who accepts that love when its owner is made to understand the nature of his quest, and unites with him in spirit.

"On Baile's Strand" was the first of Yeats's plays in verse to achieve a distinct dramatic success. It retells the story which he told in his poem "The Death of Cuchulain," and tells it with all the power of which the author is capable. Excellent material for drama of course is furnished by the episode of the coming of Cuchulain's unknown son to fight him, and by the determination of Cuchulain to die in battle with the waves after he has killed the young warrior. Much in the way of reality is contributed by a fool and a blind man who talk in idiomatic prose in the intervals of heroic verse. Equally dramatic, "Deirdre" is Yeats's contribution to a great body of literature which in recent years has collected around this epic figure. The story of Deirdre lends itself to poetic, narrative, or dramatic treatment in almost every one of its episodes, but particularly in the episode of Deirdre's return to Ireland with Nasi and his two brothers. Yeats has handled this scene, ending with the murder of the three brothers and the suicide of the heroine, with rare dramatic tact and with profound human feeling.

The most popular play by Yeats is in prose. "Cathleen ni Houlihan" (1902) relates with simplicity and effectiveness the tragic story of the appearance to Michael Gillane in 1798 of a Poor Old Woman who urges him off to the wars. Despite his plans to marry, and despite his duties at home, Michael follows this personification of patriotism out of the village. Not until the end of the play does any one on the stage become aware that the Poor Old Woman is the ancient queen of Ireland in disguise. Peter, Michael's father, asks Patrick, the younger son, if he had seen an old woman going down the path away from the house. "I did not," answers Patrick, "but I saw a young girl, and she had the walk of a queen." The accent of this last speech is what is fairly rare in Yeats's work, the peasant or folk accent. Faithfully as he labored for the peasant drama, he never succeeded in saturating himself for long, as certain later playwrights have, in the homely speech of common people. The Old Woman's speech before she leaves is an approximation to it, and it is beautiful: "It is a hard service they take that help me. Many that are red-cheeked now will be pale-cheeked; many that have been free to walk the hills and the bogs and the rushes will be sent to walk hard streets in far countries; many a good plan will be broken; many that have gathered money will not stay to spend it; many a child will be born, and there will be no father at its christening to give it a name. They that had red cheeks will have pale cheeks for my sake; and for all that, they will think they are well paid."

Yeats wrote a few other plays in prose, none of which is of the first rank, though two of them have been popular. "The Hour-Glass" is a morality play, and "The Pot of Broth" (written in collaboration with Lady Gregory) is a farce. "Where There Is Nothing," rewritten with Lady Gregory as "The Unicorn from the Stars," contains more social criticism than is usually to be found in Yeats's plays. Martin Hearn revolts against conventional industry, ethics, and religion in favor of an ideal world of which he has been dreaming, a world where "the battle goes on always, always." This world is to be apprehended only by one who has "put out the senses" as one puts out a candle; in short, Yeats approached his mystic's universe once more, this time through the medium of prose, and in the language of social criticism. In 1928 he published a prose translation of Sophocles's "King Oedipus" which was excellently suited to the modern theater, and in 1935 there appeared a volume, "Wheels and Butterflies," containing four plays in which Yeats returned to his favorite themes of magic, spiritualism, and myth. "The Words upon the Window-Pane," the first of these, is taken up with a séance in which Jonathan Swift speaks out of his two-century-old grave. And "The Resurrection" is interesting for the drama it extracts from the miracle of Christ's appearance out of the tomb. A skeptical Greek, placing his hand on the breast of what he considers an apparition dressed in winding-sheets, screams and declares: "The heart of a phantom is beating!" "The Herne's Egg and Other Plays" (1938) returns to verse, at any rate in part, offering two versions of the same theme in "A Full Moon in March" and "The King of the Great Clock Tower." The story in each case is of a queen who has a lover beheaded because he has insulted her and then, as he had predicted while he lived, dances with his head in her hands and kisses his lips. These last plays are of little significance, though they are interesting for their evidence that Yeats had never ceased to experiment either with ideas or with dramatic devices.

Synge 1871–1909 The peasant accent spoken of above found its most perfect employer in John Millington Synge, who without any doubt is the greatest Irish playwright to date, and indeed by general consent is one of the most powerful dramatic writers who have used the English language. As a young man he had left his university and wandered to Paris, where Yeats on a visit found him miserably existing in a vain hope to master French literature and become a critic of it. Yeats, immediately perceiving in him great creative powers, and encouraged in this faith by the fact of Synge's linguistic training, persuaded him to return to Ireland and go for a while among the peasants of the west coast, where primitive conditions still obtained and the original speech of the country had not lost its flavor. Synge was willing to try the experiment, and took up a residence in the Aran Islands, off the west coast. His stay here, though it was not a continuous one nor very long, was richly productive in literary results. He adjusted himself easily to the life of the peasants and fishermen among whom he lived; learned to talk their language; heard many old stories, some of which he later worked into plays; observed man and beast and sky and sea always with a poet's eye; and in general prepared himself for a series of dramatic pieces which should be charged with this atmosphere and in which the people should talk a kind of English like no other English ever heard—at once more beautiful and more real, and real with the reality of purely Irish life. Synge left a record of this sojourn in a volume called "The Aran Islands" (1907), which many of his readers enjoy equally with the plays; another volume of observations repeated the process for other parts of the Irish world—Wicklow, West Kerry, Galway, and Mayo.

The six plays of Synge are in the form of prose, but they are among the most highly poetical writings of modern times. The people in them are more than peasants; their eloquence, their singing passion as they speak of death or love or loneliness or pain, raises them to the rank of great tragic poets. There is no lack of comedy at the same time; but the comedy is that of irony, of sardonic commentary upon the elements of existence. The words have a deep, vibrant melody in them which strikes a similar melody, or seems to strike it, from the hills and glens which always rise in the background. The sense of place is very strong in the reader or spectator as the play proceeds; the atmosphere—often misty or murky—rolls close about him, and he all but participates himself in the tragedy or the comedy that is being lived. The stories tell themselves with apparently no effort; the characters are natural, even when they are possessed by extraordinary passions. Yet the art of these plays is an intricate art, and the significance of these actions tends always to be a universal significance.

Synge's first play contained in its one short act most of the qualities now associated with his name, and contained them in their full intensity. Synge seems never to have had to go through a period of dramatic preparation; he felt from the beginning exactly what effect he wished to achieve, and he achieved that effect by the best because the most natural means. "In the Shadow of the Glen" (1903) tells a story heard by Synge in the Aran Islands; but he has set the scene in "the last cottage at the head of a long glen in County Wicklow." A tramp appears one misty night at the cottage of Dan Burke, a farmer, and upon being welcomed with unexpected fervor by Nora Burke, the young wife, discovers that the man of the house is lying dead under a sheet at the back of the room. At first it seems that Nora wishes to have him there for company only, but soon she puts on her shawl and leaves to find a young farmer who will be somewhere in the neighborhood, to tell him of her misfortune. While she is gone the dead man rises and tells the tramp that he has merely feigned death in order to test his wife's fidelity. He is an old man, and Nora, he suspects, has fallen in love with young Michael Dara. Before Nora returns with Michael, Dan resumes his former appearance, and when the two come in out of the darkness he hears his wife tell Michael that she had been a fool ever to marry an old man, even though he had given her a

farm. At last Dan hears enough to satisfy him and con-
fronts the two conspirators with his living presence. He
orders Nora to leave forever, and when Michael hesitates
to go with her, she angrily accepts the tramp as her companion.

"Riders to the Sea" (1904) is perhaps the best known
of Synge's pieces for the stage, though it is not necessarily
the greatest. Like his first play it is based upon his observations in the Aran Islands, not only of the fact that death
comes often and suddenly to many island fishermen, but
of the more particular fact that the body of a drowned
islander was washed up during his residence there in much
the same way that Michael's body is washed up here. The
play is actually a lyric poem, a cry from the heart of a poor
people against the cruelty and waywardness of death. Like
all good poets Synge thought much about the ravages of
old age and death; his characters feel those two evils more
deeply than any other. Old Maurya here has lost five sons
in the sea, and presently she loses her sixth and last. Her
"keening," or sorrowing, provides a kind of continual
chorus which is poetic in every word: "They're all gone
now, and there isn't anything more the sea can do to me.
. . . I'll have no call now to be up crying and praying when
the wind breaks from the south, and you can hear the surf
is in the east, and the surf is in the west, making a great
stir with the two noises, and they hitting one on the other.
I'll have no call now to be going down and getting Holy
Water in the dark nights after Samhain, and I won't care
what way the sea is when the other women will be keening."

"The Tinker's Wedding" was Synge's first comedy, and
it was scarcely successful. The reckless fun of two tinkers
who for some strange reason desire the respectability of
marriage furnishes excellent material for farce, but Synge
has not justified the length of his piece; the amusement of
the spectator flags. It is interesting at the same time to note

this evidence that Synge had an unusual endowment in comedy, and important to remember that his high spirits expressed themselves on many occasions in other than sorrowful accents.

"The Well of the Saints" (1907) was Synge's first full-length play, and it is one of his best. Two old blind beggars, Martin Doul and his ugly wife Mary, have illusions not only about the beauty of each other but about the beauty of the whole world. Happening to cross the path of a saint who possesses the power of healing the afflicted, they permit him to cure them of their blindness, only to commence a career of disillusionment that ends with the gradual loss of their sight again. At the conclusion of the play they indulge in rhapsodies upon the beautiful dark ideal world which has been restored to them, rhapsodies in which Synge has expressed all of his own powerful idealism and all of his own poet's delight in the sounds and sights of the world.

I'll be getting my death now, I'm thinking, sitting alone in the cold air, hearing the night coming, and the blackbirds flying round in the briars crying to themselves, the time you'll hear one cart getting off a long way in the east, and another cart getting off a long way in the west, and a dog barking maybe, and a little wind turning the sticks. . . .

Ah, it's ourselves had finer sights than the like of them, I'm telling you, when we were sitting a while back hearing the birds and bees humming in every weed of the ditch, or when we'd be smelling the sweet, beautiful smell does be rising in the warm nights, when you do hear the swift flying things racing in the air, till we'd be looking up in our own minds into a grand sky, and seeing lakes, and big rivers, and fine hills for taking the plough. . . .

I'm thinking it's a good right ourselves have to be sitting blind, hearing a soft wind turning round the little leaves of the spring and feeling the sun, and we not tormenting our souls with the sight of the gray days, and the holy men, and the dirty feet is trampling the world.

"The Playboy of the Western World" (1907) made Synge quickly famous in Great Britain and America. The reason was not merely that the piece was so excellent as to inspire many to call it his masterpiece—fortunately this question can never be decided—but that the performance of it was attended by a scandal among those sections of the Irish who were jealous of their good name. These latter people, absurdly enough it now seems, were outraged by a story of an Irish boy who began to feel respect for his manhood only when he thought he had killed his father and who passed as a hero among strange people as long as they believed the tale of his deed to be true. Christy Mahon stumbles into a village on a wild coast of Mayo with the news that he has split his father's skull with a potato-digger. Pegeen Mike, the daughter of the local tavern-keeper, immediately falls in love with him and the towns-women throng about him—all to be disappointed, along with Christy himself, when the father turns up with only a wound in his head. The morals of the piece, which incidentally are natural enough, are entirely irrelevant to a discussion of its artistic qualities. Those qualities are of the highest. The talk is as rich and racy and beautiful as any in Synge; and the story is marvelously told. In a preface to the printed version Synge has explained that the source of his linguistic inspiration lay in the genius of the Irish people. "For in countries where the imagination of the people, and the language they use, is rich and living, it is possible for a writer to be rich and copious in his words, and at the same time to give the reality, which is the root of all poetry, in a comprehensive and natural form. . . . In a good play every speech should be as fully flavored as a nut or an apple, and such speeches cannot be written by anyone who works among people who have shut their lips on poetry." No better analysis has been made of the combination in Synge of poetry with realism.

Synge's last play represented a new departure for him; he returned to the world of Irish legend. His "Deirdre" tells once more the deathless story, and tells it with greater power and beauty than are to be found in any other modern version. This is due partly to his skill and insight in the matter of human motives, and partly to the fact that he retained the peasant language which he had perfected into so fine and natural a dramatic instrument. His Deirdre is a living woman, possessed of great power in love and death; and in the course of the play she expresses for the last time in Synge the poet's profound dread of death and old age. She, equally with him, is thinking of the time when she and Nasi will be no longer young and beautiful; in the light of such a possible future, death now at the hands of Concho-bar is in some measure a blessing. "Deirdre" was not per-formed until a year after Synge's death. Then it was a forcible reminder how great a writer has been lost to Ire-land and the world.

Colum 1881– Equal to Synge in originality and artistic in-tegrity, Padraic Colum has yet failed to make an equivalent impression outside of Ireland be-cause of the peculiarly local materials with which he has dealt. He is a realist, a writer essentially of prose plays, and a penetrating analyst of Irish social conditions. With the scrupulous technic and care of an Ibsen he has bent himself to the task of interpreting the conflicts which exist in the minds of representative Irish peasants. He is a peasant playwright in even a stricter sense than Synge; in so strict a sense, indeed, that he has paid the penalty of lesser fame. But he is an admirable craftsman; his plays are real in a more fundamental sense than is implied by mere fidelity to conditions; they are genuinely if soberly moving. Par-ticularly in their dialogue are his dramas excellent. His people, care-worn perhaps, or puzzled by problems which they scarcely have the information or the intellect to solve, move slowly across the simple stage, thinking as they speak, and speaking with an utter, appealing naturalness. To a

greater extent than a reader realizes at the time, he hears
their conversation and accepts it as he would accept the
actual talk of neighbors.

"The Land" deals with the agrarian problem in Ireland,
a problem which is more complicated than the corresponding problem in the United States because while here it is
merely a question of how people shall be induced to stay on
their farms, in Ireland the question is in addition how
people shall be induced to resist the call of America. Matt
Cosgar in "The Land" leaves for America just at the time
when his father has succeeded in gaining possession of the
farm on which the family has always lived. The inefficient
elders remain while the youth is drawn toward the industrial, indifferent New World. "Broken Soil," later entitled
"The Fiddler's House," shows a peasant being wooed from
his home and his work by the call of the road. An artist by
temperament, Conn Hourican abandons duty for vagabondage and so joins the company of Synge's poetic tramps.
Colum has created another such person in "Thomas Muskerry" (1910), probably his best play. Myles Gorman, a
blind piper, symbolizes for Muskerry, the old master of a
workhouse, the freedom which he has never known because of his long attention to duty and because of his long
sacrifices for his family. His last days, as seen in the play,
are relieved for a brief period by dreams of happy independence when he shall retire from office; but his tragedy
is to be hedged about by his grasping relatives until he dies
of neglect and depression. "Thomas Muskerry" is not only
an exceedingly pathetic spectacle; it is a subtle study of a
problem of great importance in Ireland, the problem of the
family.

Lady Gregory 1881-1932   Lady Augusta Gregory became one of the
stanchest supporters of the new literature in Ire-
land after the beginning of the twentieth century. Her finest contribution to that literature belongs to

the department of fiction, but she also contributed plays. No Irish playwright has produced more; nor for that matter has any Irish playwright of to-day been more widely popular. This is true in spite of the fact that Lady Gregory was not possessed of the highest talents. She was first of all an entertainer, and her forte was first of all the farce. Her "Seven Short Plays" (1909) contains the most famous of her farces; later compositions rather monotonously continued similar themes, though they attained an equal success in the Abbey Theater. "Spreading the News" is best known. The idea upon which it is based is slight but of genuine value for comedy. The scene is the outskirts of a fair, and the story tells of the absurd lengths to which a rumor grew in the space of a few minutes out of a remark that Bartley Fallon had been seen running after Jack Smith with a hay-fork. As a matter of fact, Bartley was merely attempting to overtake Jack and give him the fork which he had forgotten to take with him from an apple-stall where he had stopped to talk; but legend had it that he looked like murder, and soon the belief is general that the murder has been committed. The ensuing complications are resolved only when the two men stroll amicably back to the original scene. In "The Rising Moon" a fugitive from political justice prevails upon the police who are detailed to catch him, and escapes into a boat while they sentimentalize about their country. "The Workhouse Ward," one of the funniest of Lady Gregory's farces, is nothing but a conversation between two old men on their workhouse beds; their habitual bickering promises for a moment to separate them, but it soon becomes clear that it is by such quarrels of the tongue that they live, and one of them who is offered release refuses to go because he cannot leave his neighbor—whom immediately he begins to berate again as the curtain goes down.

Lady Gregory produced in addition to these farces sev-

eral folk-history plays, dealing with periods in the past of
Ireland both before and after the dawn of recorded history.
The best of them, "Grania," uses purely legendary material,
and introduces a heroine who strangely enough has been
neglected by most Irish poets and playwrights. Grania is
not unlike Deirdre. Brought to the court of Finn, an old
Irish king, to be Finn's bride, she elopes before the cere-
mony with young Diarmuid, whom formerly she had seen
and loved, and lives with him abroad for seven years until
Finn follows and kills him. Many circumstances render the
story different from that of Deirdre, but the appeal of it is
powerful, and Lady Gregory has treated it with a dignity
and beauty not often to be found in her pages. A writer of
unusual talent, she almost nowhere deserves the title of
genius, as Synge nearly always does.

**Dunsany
1878–**
Coming somewhat later to the Irish theater
than any of the playwrights so far discussed,
Lord Dunsany has made a swift and brilliant
reputation for himself without ever treating conventional
Irish themes. He writes of neither peasants nor heroes. His
scenes are romantic, far-off scenes, laid in countries to
which he has given strange names and which are inhabited
by people of a sort never met with in other books. "The
Glittering Gate" is a parable of agnosticism and faith. Two
tramps, Jim and Bill, attempt to scale the wall of their
Heaven after death, only to find that the great gate when
it is swung open reveals vast empty space: "Stars. Blooming great stars." Lord Dunsany has always been especially
interested in gods. "The Gods of the Mountain" is a terrifying story of seven beggars in an Eastern land who dress
like the seven stone gods of the mountain and palm themselves off on the people until the real gods—of green stone
—walk down and turn the beggars to the stone from which
they are pretending to have changed themselves. This is effective on the stage, as is another play on a similar theme,

"A Night at an Inn" (1917). Three Englishmen have stolen the great ruby from the forehead of the stone god of the East, Klesh. Three priests of Klesh who follow to recover the ruby are murdered without much trouble by the thieves, but eventually Klesh comes himself with heavy stony steps, screws the ruby back into its socket, and calls the three miscreants out of the room to a mysterious and horrible death. "The Queen's Enemies" relates the awful vengeance visited by an Egyptian queen upon the kings who are her enemies. She invites them to dinner in an underground chamber and at the proper moment gives the signal which lets in the Nile. It is perhaps clear from these summaries just where the strength of Lord Dunsany lies—in theatrical devices moving to terror and to ironic contemplation of human fate. Within this domain he is a startling and memorable dramatist; but it is a narrow domain, and scarcely the highest powers are demanded for success in it. The spectator becomes aware of devices rather than ideas, and is willing to credit the author with little more than ingenuity. The best Irish drama has never departed too far from purely Irish themes—peasants and folk-heroes.

O'Casey
1884–

After 1925 Yeats had a formidable rival for the honor of being the best modern Irish playwright save Synge. This was Sean O'Casey, whose "Juno and the Paycock" startled Dublin in that year and led its author to international fame. He had come out of the slums of Dublin an obscure man with nothing but a genius for the theater—nothing but that and an uncanny skill in dialogue. He put a phase of Irish drama forever behind him. He wrote what may be called peasant plays, but his peasants have moved into the city and have been degraded by their new life. They are drunken, unscrupulous, hopeless, cynical, and withal greatly comical; at least the men among them are, for the women are long-suffering and sometimes noble. O'Casey, who knew what he was talking about because he had lived it, opened the door on a hitherto uncelebrated area of Irish life. He showed people degraded and brutalized by unspeakable poverty; and furthermore, without taking sides himself, he showed them in crises when the terrors of war, chiefly civil, bore down upon them with a depressing and again a degrading weight. He proceeded to write other plays which established him as a tradition, and which proved beyond any doubt his power as a contriver of grim comedy. He is very funny, but at the same time he is terrifying; and always he is a master of the theatrical situation.

"Juno and the Paycock" takes place in the household of the Boyles during the civil warfare of 1922. "Captain" Jack Boyle, O'Casey's first old rogue in a series which has run throughout the plays, is the shiftless, irresponsible, and divinely eloquent peacock-husband of Juno Boyle (so named because she was born in June), who is driven to distraction not only by her spouse but by his drinking companion Joxer Daly. Joxer and the "Captain" keep their Irish lingo up while the plot, such as it is, goes on; it has to do with the daughter Mary's deception by a Mr. Bentham who brings false news of an inheritance for the family so that he can be free to seduce her, with the ridiculous behavior of the "Captain" in the expectation of riches, and with the panic of John Boyle, the son who has informed on a Die-Hard comrade and at the end is taken out by Irregulars to be shot like a dog in the streets. It is not the plot that matters so much as the atmosphere and the talk— the talk coming with a special richness from the "Captain's" mouth, but coming from every mouth as well, and not least from that of Mrs. Maisie Madigan, a neighbor woman. The formula is repeated with signal success in "The Plough and the Stars" (1926), where the "Captain" is succeeded by Fluther Good, Mrs. Madigan by Bessie Burgess, and—with a difference—Mrs. Boyle by Mrs. Jack Clitheroe. Jack

Clitheroe is a young commandant in the Irish Republican Army of 1916, and is in love with his wife but no less so with Ireland. She cannot stand up under the strain of waiting to know whether he has been killed, nor can he bear her nerves. The tension between them is created by O'Casey with relentless skill, as is the irony of their sacrifice of themselves for such worthless specimens as Fluther and his friends.

These are O'Casey's best known plays, and they are his best ones. "The Silver Tassie" (1928), which Yeats refused to produce at the Abbey Theater, departs from O'Casey's familiar subject matter; and though it has much merit it must be said to lose by the departure. It opens in a Dublin tenement from which the athlete Harry Heegan is leaving for the World War; but it ends with the scattered effect of several scenes which with wild, ironic song and dance tend to show expressionistically the consequences of war. Its tendency to hysteria is relieved only by the presence in it of two old rogues, theatrical descendants of "Captain" Boyle. Sylvester Heegan and Simon Norton have "the lingo" almost at its best in O'Casey. Yet they cannot save the play from dissipating its own energies in extravagant experiments. Admirers of O'Casey hoped he would return to his old materials in his next play. "Within the Gates" (1934), however, went farther in the direction of symbolism; using, like "The Silver Tassie," recitative and song to break up its effects and taking all of four scenes in a London Park to say one does not know exactly what about Life. It seems clear that O'Casey has a unique opportunity in the subject of Ireland as it is. And his admirers still hoped after "Within the Gates" that he would recognize the nature of his own best powers.

FICTION

Neither the novel nor the short story in Ireland has pursued anything like the consistent course which poetry and the drama have pursued. Irish fiction as a whole cannot be summed up in a phrase; there are no lines of development, no common themes. Most of its more brilliant representatives have been as little concerned with nationality as Yeats and Æ have been, or even as Synge was. In their realism, or their satire, or their principles of art, they have contributed not so much to the Irish stream of literature as to the general European stream.

Lady Gregory 1881–1932 Lady Gregory early published two volumes of adaptations or translations from the old Irish romances which promised at the time to inaugurate a line of modern fiction dealing with folk-heroes. But "Cuchulain of Muirthemne" and "Gods and Fighting Men" (1904) had few or no followers. They have been of immense influence in the field of poetry and the drama; they have been the source-book for all who wished to resurrect the shining folk of the past; they are still unique as fiction. They tell the whole story of Cuchulain, Conchobar, Queen Maeve, the battle of the bulls, Deirdre, Nasi, Finn, and Oisin with a vigor and a beauty not found in any similar work since Standish O'Grady's "History of Ireland." A typical tribute to her books is Yeats's in an appendix to the first collection of his plays: "If my present small Dublin audience for poetical drama grows and spreads beyond Dublin, I shall owe it to these two books, masterpieces of prose, which can but make the old stories as familiar to Irishmen everywhere as are the stories of Arthur and his knights to all readers of books. I cannot believe that it is from friendship that I weigh these books with Malory and feel no discontent at the tally, or that it is the wish to make the circumstantial origin of my own art familiar, that would make me give them before all other books to Irish boys and girls. I wrote for the most part before they were written, but all or all but all is there, Oisin wandering, Cuchulain killing his son and fighting the sea, Maeve and her children, Baile and Aillin, Angus and his fellow-immortals, all literally translated, though with much condensation and selection, from the old writings." One of the reasons for the charm of Lady Gregory's stories is that they are written in peasant speech, in the Kiltartan dialect which the author best knew; therefore they preserve a great deal of the original flavor of legends, and are a living force as literature to-day.

Moore
1852–1933
Attention has been given in another chapter,[1] the chapter on English fiction, to the novels and stories of George Moore that deal with Ireland or were written there. Moore was for all practical purposes an English author, since most of his life had been spent in London, and most of his books had been issued among English audiences. But he had an Irish period, and at last three of his books can be said to belong to Irish literature. "The Untilled Field" is a collection of short stories upon Irish subjects; "The Lake" (1905) is a novel of Irish religious life; and "Hail and Farewell," his autobiographical record in three volumes of his stay in Ireland, is in a sense a piece of Irish fiction—fiction, indeed, of a high if curious order.

Joyce
1882–
One of the strangest geniuses in the history of literature is James Joyce, a novelist who began his career in Ireland but who has since taken up his residence in Paris and has succeeded in reaching an international audience which may in time divest him of his more purely national characteristics. His first prose book, "Dubliners," was a collection of short stories more or less in the conventional forms, describing and satirizing Irish

[1] See pages 192–194.

types. His "Portrait of the Artist as a Young Man" (1916) attracted wide attention as promising a new form for fiction. Its hero was Stephen Dedalus, and the author's method was to give all of Stephen's thoughts as they passed pell-mell through his mind rather than to make him talk in the orderly fashion which is customary in the novel. The attitude of the author toward the Dublin through which Dedalus moved was savagely satiric; he reveled in disclosures of physical, intellectual, and moral filth; he painted the Irish capital as a hopelessly rotten city, corrupting to all sensitive and ambitious minds. But this was only a beginning for Joyce. Later there appeared from a private press in Paris an enormously long novel called "Ulysses" (1922)—one of the longest in existence—setting forth the actions, moods, reveries, thoughts, and words of a Dublin Jew named Bloom over a period of twenty-four hours. The savage cynicism of the "Portrait of the Artist as a Young Man" was magnified a hundredfold in "Ulysses"; the spectacle was presented of an author spreading his discontent and disillusionment over hundreds of pages of amazingly frank discourse. The book will never have a wide audience because of the difficulty experienced in reading it; much of it is obscure; many passages are subtle parodies on books which Joyce likes or dislikes; the style is radically elliptical. The aim is to show the entire contents of a man's mind during one day—the whole stream of thought—without reservation or shame. Competent critics predict that "Ulysses" will be permanently a masterpiece; if so, it will have such a life as Rabelais has had, or certain less-known marvels of literature.

The difficulties which "Ulysses" presented to its first readers have to some degree disappeared with the passage of years and with the coming into existence of commentaries explaining Joyce's method. It was not always clear in 1922, for instance, that passages in the novel were parodies of old or new styles; and it certainly was not clear that the title had significance. It is now well known that the book is a translation into modern terms of the great myth of Ulysses and his son Telemachus—the difference between Homer and Joyce residing in the latter's inability to make anything heroic out of the world he knows. Quite the contrary. "Ulysses" is an indictment of the twentieth century in that it shows how much or how little an old story can mean in the language of our life. But if "Ulysses" has become easier to read than it was, Joyce's next book bids fair to remain forever formidable. His so-called "Work in Progress"—subsequently known under the title "Finnegan's Wake"—takes him to the limit of his tendency toward word-play and the study of style for its own sake. This tendency was not observable in "Dubliners," and only barely so in the "Portrait." It seemed to have reached a climax in "Ulysses," but that was not the case. "Finnegan's Wake" is the exercise of a man intoxicated with the many meanings and the possible derivations of words. His passion for linguistics has obsessed him until he can write mere streams of vocables which echo each other and throw up puns as they flow. The culmination of Joyce's life work as a novelist is either tragic, or sublime, according as one demands human documents from an artist in the field or looks for nothing beyond verbal triumphs.

Dunsany 1878– Lord Dunsany began his career as an author with prose tales somewhat on the order of his plays. He has written several volumes of these, ingeniously treating psychological or philosophical themes in exotic settings and appealing as always to the instincts in the reader of wonder and terror. He has invented a special geography for his purpose, and a special mythology; the names of his people, his gods, and his places are sometimes haunting and sometimes merely grotesque, but they are always strange. It is a question whether these tales are of

permanent value, and it is almost certain that they are inferior to the plays; but a few of them are extraordinarily
memorable. In a volume called "Fifty-one Tales" (1915),
for instance, there is the story of Charon conveying the last
mortal across the waters of Hades; there is the story of
"The Guest," wherein a young man dines with Death at a
restaurant; there is "Taking Up Piccadilly," which shows
two workmen destroying London because it has not satisfied the gods—revealing, as they pick a hole in the pave-
ment, the Southern stars.

**Stephens
1882–**
James Stephens is the most popular Irish novelist of the twentieth century. He is also the best
of those younger novelists who are definitely
Irishmen. The same qualities which were discussed in connection with his poetry are to be found in his prose. It is
exceedingly lively prose, sparkling with wit, colored with
beauty borrowed from its creator's fanciful and often mystical nature, and running rapidly through many moods—
sarcasm, tenderness, satire, worship, and lyrical exaltation.
The nearest equivalent in English fiction is the prose of
Barrie, but there is no possibility of confusing the two
writers; Stephens is perhaps the safer from sentimentality
and the stronger in his likes and dislikes. In "The Char-
woman's Daughter," for instance, published in America as
"Mary, Mary," the scene is laid in mean streets; but, miser-
able as are the circumstances of the characters, there is a
charm about the faculty which they possess of flying to a
world of fantasy. The border between the two worlds is
constantly crossed, and the realism in both cases is remarkable; Stephens always has been equally at home in the actual
world and in the world of imagination. He can laugh at
both worlds, for he finds them both entertaining; also, he
can write tenderly on both sides of the mysterious boundary.

"The Crock of Gold" (1912) has as brilliant a beginning
as can be boasted by any British novel. There seems to be no

disagreement about that, though there are numerous persons who deny to the later portions of the book the same high rank. The scene is set "in the center of the pine wood called Coilla Doraca," and two philosophers are introduced whose wives, the Grey Woman of Dun Gortin and the Thin Woman of Inis Magrath, are the terror of their lives. Within a few pages the laughable habits of the philosophers and the not so laughable habits of the two wives are masterfully sketched. By the end of the second chapter one of the philosophers and his wife are dead; the field is then left clear for the Philosopher. His conversations with various neighbors who come through the pine wood to ask his advice about important matters are delicious satires on pedantry; his adventures through the world in search of the Irish god of love and life, Angus Og, are alternately beautiful and ludicrous. Pan comes into the story for a while, straying from the distant world where he is no longer welcome; but the great god of gods is Angus Og, who for Stephens represents the finest human qualities—spontaneous love, positive delight in life, and constant search for beauty in the world. Armies of fairies troop across the pages also, mingled with peasants and policemen; and the Thin Woman of Inis Magrath somewhat modifies her asperity as the action gets under way. The idealism of Stephens is expressed through the beautiful daughter of Meehawl MacMurrachu, Caitilin ni Murrachu. As she grows up she becomes conscious of aspirations within her that cannot be satisfied by mortal companionship; wandering off at first with Pan, whom she finds playing his thin pipes in the long grass, she eventually leaves him for Angus Og, with whom she inhabits a wonderful cave. "The Crock of Gold" is a medley of marvelous elements, but all of them are the product of an integral and superior imagination.

Stephens has also published short stories. Because of its variety and sprightliness, its wit and its understanding,

"Here Are Ladies" is the favorite with many of Stephens's readers. But "The Demi-Gods" (1914) is more important. In it Stephens returns to the borderland between this world and the other. Patsy McCann and his daughter Mary and their donkey, three beggars on the roads of Ireland, are visited one day by three celestial visitors who put away their wings and their gold to wander with their mortal friends. The conversations of the angels with Patsy and Mary, their attempts to understand the world into which they have dropped, and their comments upon it are handled with the deftness, the tact, and the almost sublime humor which must now be familiar in their author.

Having published four volumes of fiction in four years, Stephens rested for six years, meanwhile studying Gaelic, making researches into the legendary past, and concerning himself with Irish politics. The first fruit of his studies in the ancient myths was "Irish Fairy Tales," one of the finest volumes of fairy stories in modern times. Stephens here lavishes his mingled humor and imagination on Finn, Oisin, Bran, and other famous persons who were treated by Lady Gregory in her translations. His stories are rapid and fascinating, and they always take a turn which is entirely consonant with his genius. They have proved deservedly popular. The second fruit of his antiquarian studies was "Deirdre" (1923), a retelling of the inexhaustible story with which nearly every first-rate Irish author has undertaken to test himself. Although Stephens sticks closely enough to the original incidents, he of course applies his own fancy, his own humor, and his own philosophy. Incidentally he has never told a more interesting story; and he has never written more passionately or more devotedly of beautiful and mystical things—Deirdre, Nasi, and the spirit of the wood in which they met. "In the Land of Youth" goes still further with the heroic legends of Ireland.

The third decade of the century produced in
Liam O'Flaherty an Irish novelist who insisted
on a close view of recent history, and on an uncompromising report of its terrors. The political life of
Ireland between 1915 and 1925 was overshadowed by an
incessant struggle, first with England and then between
rival parties at home. Assassination was the order of the
day, and many men lived either in hiding or in disguise. It
was a bloody time, and O'Flaherty was one of the first to
make literature out of the fact. "The Informer" (1925) is
best known perhaps as the source of a great moving picture, but it is a powerful work in its own right, telling as it
does of Gypo Nolan who informed on his former comrade
in The Revolutionary Organization, Frankie McPhillip,
and finally paid with his own death for the death of Frankie.
Gypo is a memorable figure—hulking, well-meaning, ignorant, and pressed by poverty to do a thing which violates all
his instincts as a patriot. His degeneration into a wild
animal driven by panic to desperate or grotesque acts is
one of the finest achievements in contemporary fiction. A
sort of companion novel is "The Assassin" (1928), in
which Michael McDara, politician, poet, and madman,
gathers aid about him so that he can kill an official who in
his opinion is blocking the future of the Irish people. The
first faith of the revolutionists has evaporated by this time,
and only a fanatical young man like McDara, visited by hallucinations and ecstasies, could carry through such a program. He does carry it through, and escapes to England
with Kitty Mellett who has helped him. The psychology of
the political assassin has rarely been studied in more convincing detail. O'Flaherty's short stories, as for instance
in "The Mountain Tavern and Other Stories" (1929), have
not the importance of his novels, though the tale which gives
the title to this volume illustrates bitterly the hatred of
the Irish people for all soldiers finally, no matter what their

programs or their pretenses. "Return of the Brute" (1930) extends the scope of this hatred to include the World War. It describes the extermination, except for one man, of Corporal Williams's squad in March of 1917, amid the most hideous paraphernalia of mud, quagmire, shell-hole, insanity, and rotting death ever assembled in one book. It is effective and terrible, but O'Flaherty was still more so, and indeed quite uniquely so, in the record he left of death in Ireland during and after the war.

O'Faolain 1900– The fiction of Sean O'Faoláin is less sensational than that of O'Flaherty, being the work of a more reflective temperament; but it is as serious, and it is as much concerned with Ireland, though it reveals no obsession with the details of war. "A Nest of Simple Folk" (1934) is one of the most searching studies ever made of life all over Ireland. It is the record of a family through three generations, and by backward reference through five, first in the country near Limerick and later in Rathkeale and Cork. The unifying individual is Leo Donnell, husband of Julie Keene. His spoiled, wild youth leads to a maturity during which he takes part in three important revolutionary movements—Fenianism, the Irish Republican Brotherhood, and Sinn Fein. These matters have their great interest, but still more interesting is the rich picture we get of Irish life in its amusing and amazing variety. O'Faoláin's continuing concern with the larger theme is reflected in "A Purse of Coppers" (1937), a volume of short stories distinguished for their subtlety of observation and analysis. The time is post-revolutionary, and the temper is relaxed. Life in certain parts of Ireland is "lying broken and hardly breathing," for now that the English masters have gone the Irish servants do not want the privileges that are theirs. "The land was kept from them too long, and now they have lost the knack of it." All they can be is factory hands and soldiers. O'Faoláin is writing of a new country—one scarcely recognizable as yet in Synge, Yeats, O'Flaherty, or O'Casey—but one that has its interest too.

ESSAYISTS

Yeats 1865–1939 The miscellaneous prose of the Irish Renaissance has dealt chiefly with literary criticism or politics, or with the philosophy of the new and spiritualized Ireland. One of its ablest representatives is William Butler Yeats, who in the course of his busy career wrote many influential essays announcing new authors or suggesting dramatic and poetic programs. He began with stories or sketches based upon folk-lore, the two best volumes in this field being "The Celtic Twilight" (1893) and "The Secret Rose." They contain some of the most beautiful prose in Irish literature, and take a position near the front of Yeats's work. His essays on various literary, philosophical, and political subjects may most profitably be studied in two other volumes, "Ideas of Good and Evil" and "The Cutting of an Agate." In these books Yeats has given as complete an expression as possible of his rather difficult and impalpable thought; the style is limpid and pure, while the metaphysical basis of the new literature is searched with characteristic sobriety.

The importance of his "Autobiography" and of his strange work called "A Vision" (1925, 1937) is that in them we learn much that we needed to know about the deepening of his mind, and therefore of his poetry,[1] after his fiftieth year. "I put 'The Tower' and 'The Winding Stair' in evidence to show that my poetry has gained in self-possession and power," he writes in "A Vision." "I owe this change to an incredible experience." There follows a record of his adventures with automatic writing, talking in his

[1] For his poetry, see pages 311–317.

sleep, the hearing of voices, the mystical interpretation of odors, the exploration of new philosophies, and finally the geometry of a vision so elaborate that a large book must be devoted to its explication. It is a weird book which to some readers makes only nonsense. Taking it at its face value, however, one will find it an indication of the new paths into which Yeats's mind had turned after a lifelong search for ways of escape from the narrow rationalism and scientific orthodoxy of the nineteenth century. His name will continue to be connected with this escape, as well as with his great poetry and with the plays with which for a generation he pleased and instructed the people of Dublin.

Æ
1867–1935

Æ's noble spirit and his gentle style show best in three volumes of prose, two of which "Imaginations and Reveries" (1915) and "The Candle of Vision," are collections of miscellaneous critical or philosophical essays, and the other of which, "Interpreters," is an attempt at a statement of the eternal issue in Irish politics. Among the first may be found sensitive descriptions of the poetry of Yeats, Seumas O'Sullivan, and James Stephens; there are also numerous musing disquisitions on his own mystical view of the universe—analyses of his dreams, and declarations as to the paramount importance of the imagination in human life. "Interpreters," though it is political in subject-matter, is entirely free from nationalism; rather it is a treatise on "the politics of eternity"—an inquiry into the questions which always and everywhere arise in connection with man's desire for freedom.

SUGGESTIONS FOR STUDY

AMERICAN LITERATURE

A useful bibliographical guide, containing lists of books by various modern authors and critical references concerning them, is "Contemporary American Literature: Bibliographies and Study Outlines," by John Matthews Manly and Edith Rickert (New York: Harcourt, Brace and Company, 1929). "A History of American Letters," by Walter F. Taylor (Boston: The American Book Company, 1936), also contains extensive bibliographies, by Harry Hartwick.

A critical discussion of some of the authors considered in this section may be found in "New American Literature, 1890-1930," by Fred Lewis Pattee (New York: D. Appleton-Century Company, 1930); and in "I Hear America: Literature in the United States Since 1900," by Vernon Loggins (New York: Thomas Y. Crowell Company, 1937).

CHAPTER I: POETRY

ANTHOLOGIES:

There are numerous anthologies of contemporary American verse, but the two most convenient are "The New Poetry: An Anthology of Twentieth-Century Verse in English," edited by Harriet Monroe and Alice Corbin Henderson (New York: The Macmillan Company, 1932), and "Modern American Poetry," edited by Louis Untermeyer (New York: Harcourt, Brace and Company, 1936). The first includes both American and British poems; the second is the more comprehensive as regards time, covering the period since Whitman. In the lists of recommended poems below (*) will indicate that a poem may be found in "The New Poetry" and (**) that it may be found in "Modern American Poetry." Poems quoted in full in the text above are not listed below.

There are three critical discussions in which the subject of this chapter may be studied in greater detail: "Tendencies in Modern American Poetry," by Amy Lowell (Boston: Houghton Mifflin

Company, 1917), "American Poetry Since 1900," by Louis Unter-meyer (New York: Henry Holt and Company, 1923), and "This Modern Poetry," by Babette Deutsch (New York: W. W. Norton and Company, 1935).

JAMES WHITCOMB RILEY:
  Complete Works (Indianapolis: Bobbs-Merrill Company, 6 vols.).
  Biography: "The Life of James Whitcomb Riley," by Marcus Dickey (Indianapolis: Bobbs-Merrill Company, 1919–1922, 2 vols.).
  Recommended: "The Old Swimmin'-Hole."
                ** "When the Frost Is on the Punkin."
                  "Little Orphant Annie."
                  "The Old Man and Jim."

GEORGE SANTAYANA:
  Poems (New York: Charles Scribner's Sons).
  Recommended: Sonnets IV, VII, XIII, XV, XXV, XXIX, XLIV, XLIX.

EMILY DICKINSON:
  Complete Poems (Boston: Little, Brown and Company).
  Biography: "This Was a Poet: A Critical Biography of Emily Dickinson," by George Frisbie Whicher (New York: Charles Scribner's Sons, 1938).
  Recommended: ** "I Taste a Liquor Never Brewed."
               ** "I Like to See It Lap the Miles."
               ** "I Dreaded That First Robin So."
               ** "A Bird Came down the Walk."
                  "A Narrow Fellow in the Grass."
                  "The Mountain Sat upon the Plain."
               ** "Elysium Is as Far as to."
                  "If You Were Coming in the Fall."
               ** "I Never Saw a Moor."
                  "Because I Could Not Stop for Death."
                  "I Have Not Told My Garden Yet."
               ** "The Soul Selects."
               ** "After Great Pain a Formal Feeling Comes."

RICHARD HOVEY:
  Poems and dramas published by Small, Maynard & Company (Boston) and Duffield and Company (New York). "Along the Trail" (New York: Duffield and Company).

Recommended: ** "At the Crossroads."
                ** "Unmanifest Destiny."
                ** "Love in the Winds."
                ** "A Stein Song."
                "Spring" ("Along the Trail").

WILLIAM VAUGHN MOODY:
Poems and Plays (Boston: Houghton Mifflin Company, 2 vols.).
Recommended: ** "Gloucester Moors."
                "An Ode in Time of Hesitation."
                "The Quarry."
                "The Menagerie."

EDWIN ARLINGTON ROBINSON:
Collected Poems (New York: The Macmillan Company).
Criticism: "Edwin Arlington Robinson," by Mark Van Doren
(New York: The Literary Guild, 1927).
Recommended: * "The Master." **
                * "Richard Cory." **
                * "Miniver Cheevy." **
                * "Mr. Flood's Party." **
                ** "The Gift of God."
                ** "Ben Jonson Entertains a Man from Strat-
                   ford."
                "The Poor Relation."
                "Uncle Ananias."
                ** "Luke Havergal."
                ** "The Sheaves."
                ** "New England."
                "Old King Cole."
                "The Man Against the Sky."

ROBERT FROST:
Collected Poems (New York: Henry Holt and Company).
Criticism: "Recognition of Robert Frost," edited by Richard
Thornton (New York: Henry Holt and Company, 1937).
Recommended: * "Mending Wall." **
                * "After Apple-Picking." **
                ** "The Tuft of Flowers."
                * "Mowing."
                * "An Old Man's Winter Night." **
                ** "The Death of the Hired Man."
                ** "The Runaway."

** "Birches."
** "Good-bye and Keep Cold."
"The Wood-Pile."
** "The Road Not Taken."
* "Fire and Ice." **
* "Once by the Pacific." **
* "Stopping by Woods on a Snowy Evening." **
** "To Earthward."

VACHEL LINDSAY:
Collected Poems (New York: The Macmillan Company).
Recommended: * "General William Booth Enters into Heaven." **
* "The Eagle That Is Forgotten." **
* "The Congo." **
* "The Chinese Nightingale." **
* "Abraham Lincoln Walks at Midnight." **
** "A Negro Sermon:—Simon Legree."

EDGAR LEE MASTERS:
Selected Poems (New York: The Macmillan Company).
Recommended: * "Fiddler Jones."
* "Archibald Higbie."
* "Father Malloy."
* "Lucinda Matlock." **
* "William H. Herndon."
* "Rutherford McDowell."
* "Aaron Hatfield."
"Cassius Hueffer."
"Blind Jack."
"Elliott Hawkins."
"Magrady Graham."
"Lydia Humphrey."

CARL SANDBURG:
Selected Poems (New York: Harcourt, Brace and Company).
Recommended: * "Chicago."
* "The Harbor."
* "Lost."
* "The Poor."
* "Killers."
* "Nocturne in a Deserted Brickyard." **

* "Old Timers."
* "Prayers of Steel."
* "Cool Tombs." **
** "Fog."
"The Hangman at Home" ("Smoke and Steel").
* "Grass." **
** "Wing Song."
** "Broken-Face Gargoyles."
** "Precious Moments."

AMY LOWELL:
Selected Poems (Boston: Houghton Mifflin Company).
Biography: "Amy Lowell, A Chronicle," by S. Foster Damon (Boston: Houghton Mifflin Company, 1935).
Recommended: * "Patterns." **
* "Venus Transiens."
* "A Lady." **
* "Chinoiseries."
* "Red Slippers."
* "Meeting-House Hill." **
* "Four Sides to a House."

"H.D.":
Collected Poems (New York: Liveright Publishing Company).
Recommended: * "Oread." **
* "Hermes of the Ways."
* "Orchard."
* "The Pool."
* "At Baia."
** "Heat."
** "Lais."
** "The Islands."
** "Helen."
"Sea Gods."
"Adonis."
"Evadne."
"Centaur Song."

EDNA ST. VINCENT MILLAY:
Works published by Harper & Brothers (New York).
Recommended: ** "Renascence."
* "Recuerdo."

      * "Sonnets."
      * "Spring." **
      * "The Buck in the Snow."
      * "Prayer to Persephone."
      * "Dirge Without Music."
    ** "Wild Swans."
    ** "Justice Denied in Massachusetts."
    ** "Oh, Sleep Forever in the Latmian Cave."
        "The Ballad of the Harp-Weaver."
        "Portrait by a Neighbor."
        "Sonnets from an Ungrafted Tree."
        "Keen."
        "The Singing Woman from the Wood's
          Edge."
        "She Is Overheard Singing."

ELINOR WYLIE:
  Collected Poems (New York: Alfred A. Knopf).
  Recommended: * "The Eagle and the Mole." **
              * Sonnets from "One Person." **
           ** "Escape."
           ** "Puritan Sonnet."
           ** "Let No Charitable Hope."
           ** "Confession of Faith."
           ** "Epitaph."
              "True Vine."
              "Address to My Soul."

THOMAS STEARNS ELIOT:
  Collected Poems (New York: Harcourt, Brace and Company).
  Criticism: "The Achievement of T. S. Eliot" by F. O. Matthies-
  sen (Boston: Houghton Mifflin Company, 1935).
  Recommended: * "The Love Song of J. Alfred Prufrock." **
              * "Portrait of a Lady." **
              * "Sweeney Among the Nightingales." **
              * "Marina."
              "Morning at the Window."
           ** "Rhapsody on a Windy Night."
           ** "The Hollow Men."
              "The Hippopotamus."
              "The Waste Land."
              "Ash Wednesday."

EZRA POUND:
  "Personae: Collected Poems" (New York: Horace Liveright,
    1926).
  Recommended: * "The Garret."
                  * "The Garden."
                  * "The River-Merchant's Wife: A Letter."
                  * "The Return." **
                 ** "An Immortality."
                 ** "A Virginal."
                 ** "Greek Epigram."
                 ** "A Girl."
                 ** "Portrait d'une Femme."
                 ** "Canto I."
                  * "Canto XIII." **
                    "The Tree."
                    "Les Millwin."
                    "The Age Demanded an Image."

WALLACE STEVENS:
  "Harmonium" (New York: Alfred A. Knopf, 1923, 1931).
  Recommended: * "Peter Parasol."
                  * "Peter Quince at the Clavier." **
                  * "Sunday Morning." **
                 ** "Sea Surface Full of Clouds."
                    "Stars at Tallapoosa."
                    "Bantams in Pine-Woods."
                    "Anecdote of the Jar."

JOHN CROWE RANSOM:
  Poems by Alfred A. Knopf (New York): "Chills and Fever,"
    1924; "Two Gentlemen in Bonds," 1927.
  Recommended: * "Bells for John Whitesides' Daughter." **
                  * "Blue Girls." **
                  * "Parting, Without a Sequel."
                 ** "Here Lies a Lady."
                 ** "Antique Harvesters."
                 ** "Piazza Piece."
                 ** "Captain Carpenter."
                    "Miller's Daughter."
                    "Two in August."

ALLEN TATE:
Selected Poems (New York: Charles Scribner's Sons).
Recommended: * "Ode to the Confederate Dead." **
     ** "Mr. Pope."
     ** "Death of Little Boys."
     ** "Mother and Son."
     ** "The Cross."
     ** "The Mediterranean."
     "The Last Days of Alice."
     "The Wolves."
     "Emblems."

HART CRANE:
Collected Poems (New York: Horace Liveright).
Biography: "Hart Crane: The Life of an American Poet"
(New York: W. W. Norton Company, 1937).
Recommended: * "Repose of Rivers."
     ** "Praise for an Urn."
     * "The Bridge" (selections). **
     "Legend."
     "Paraphrase."
     "Recitative."
     "At Melville's Tomb."
     "To Shakespeare."
     "To Emily Dickinson."

ARCHIBALD MACLEISH:
"Poems, 1924–1933" (Boston: Houghton Mifflin Company,
1934).
Recommended: * "Ars Poetica." **
     * "Immortal Autumn." **
     * "You, Andrew Marvell." **
     ** "In My Thirtieth Year."
     ** "Memorial Rain."
     "Conquistador."
     "Panic."

ROBINSON JEFFERS:
"The Selected Poetry of Robinson Jeffers" (New York: Ran-
dom House, 1938).
Recommended: * "Night." **
     * "Hurt Hawks." **
     ** "Age in Prospect."

** "Noon."
** "To the Stone-Cutters."
** "Apology for Bad Dreams."
** "Credo."
"Birds."
"Continent's End."
"Bixby's Landing."
"The Tower Beyond Tragedy."

STEPHEN VINCENT BENÉT:
"Ballads and Poems" (New York: Farrar and Rinehart, 1931).
Recommended: ** "The Ballad of William Sycamore."
"John Brown's Body."

CHAPTER II: PROSE FICTION

The subject of this chapter may be studied in greater detail in "The American Novel," by Carl Van Doren (New York: The Macmillan Company, 1939).

STEPHEN CRANE:
Collected Works (New York: Alfred A. Knopf, 10 vols.).
Biography: "Stephen Crane," by Thomas Beer (New York: Alfred A. Knopf, 1923).
Recommended: "The Red Badge of Courage" (New York: D. Appleton-Century Company).

FRANK NORRIS:
Collected Works (New York: Doubleday, Doran and Company, 7 vols.).
Recommended: "The Octopus."

JACK LONDON:
Collected Works (New York: The Macmillan Company).
Biography: "The Book of Jack London" by Charmian London (New York: D. Appleton-Century Company, 1921, 2 vols.).
Recommended: "The Call of the Wild."

O. HENRY:
Collected Works (New York: Doubleday, Doran and Company, 14 vols.).
Biography: "O. Henry Biography," by C. Alphonso Smith (New York: Doubleday, Doran and Company, 1916).
Recommended: "The Four Million."

HAMLIN GARLAND:
Collected Works (New York: Harper & Brothers).
Recommended: "Main-Travelled Roads."

THEODORE DREISER:
Works published chiefly by Simon and Schuster (New York).
Criticism: "Theodore Dreiser," by Burton Rascoe (New York: Robert M. McBride Company, 1925).
Recommended: "Sister Carrie."

BOOTH TARKINGTON:
Works published chiefly by Doubleday, Doran and Company (New York) and Harper & Brothers (New York).
Recommended: "Seventeen."

GEORGE ADE:
Works published chiefly by Duffield and Company (New York), Doubleday, Doran and Company (New York), and Harper & Brothers (New York).
Recommended: "Ade's Fables" (New York: Doubleday, Doran and Company).

EDITH WHARTON:
Works published chiefly by Charles Scribner's Sons (New York) and D. Appleton-Century Company (New York).
Criticism: "Edith Wharton," by Robert Morss Lovett (New York: Robert M. McBride and Company, 1925).
Recommended: "Ethan Frome" (New York: Charles Scribner's Sons).

WILLA CATHER:
Works published by Houghton Mifflin Company (Boston) and Alfred A. Knopf (New York).
Criticism: "Willa Cather," by Rene Rapin (New York: Robert M. McBride Company, 1930).
Recommended: "My Ántonia" (Boston: Houghton Mifflin Company).

JAMES BRANCH CABELL:
Works published by Robert M. McBride and Company (New York).
Criticism: "James Branch Cabell," by Carl Van Doren (New York: Robert M. McBride and Company, 1925).
Recommended: "Domnei."

Upton Sinclair:
Works published by Upton Sinclair (Pasadena).
Recommended: "The Jungle."

Sinclair Lewis:
Works published by Harcourt, Brace and Company (New York) and Doubleday, Doran and Company (New York).
Criticism: "Sinclair Lewis," by Carl Van Doren, with a bibliography by Harvey Taylor (New York: Doubleday, Doran and Company, 1933).
Recommended: "Main Street."
"Arrowsmith."

Sherwood Anderson:
Works published by The Viking Press (New York) and Charles Scribner's Sons (New York).
Recommended: "A Story Teller's Story."

Ring W. Lardner:
Works published by Charles Scribner's Sons (New York).
"Round-Up" (New York: Charles Scribner's Sons).
Recommended: "Alibi Ike."
"Champion."
"A Day with Conrad Green."
"Haircut."
"Some Like Them Cold."
"I Can't Breathe."

Thomas C. Wolfe:
Works published by Charles Scribner's Sons (New York).
Recommended: "Look Homeward, Angel."

William Faulkner:
Works published by Random House (New York).
Recommended: "As I Lay Dying."

Erskine Caldwell:
Works published chiefly by The Viking Press (New York).
Recommended: "God's Little Acre."

Elizabeth Madox Roberts:
Works published by The Viking Press (New York).
Recommended: "The Time of Man."

ERNEST HEMINGWAY:
  Works published by Charles Scribner's Sons (New York).
  Recommended: "A Farewell to Arms."
              "Men Without Women."

JAMES T. FARRELL:
  Works published by The Vanguard Press (New York).
  Recommended: "The Studs Lonigan Trilogy."

PEARL S. BUCK:
  Works published by The John Day Company (New York) and
    Reynal and Hitchcock (New York).
  Recommended: "The Good Earth."

CHAPTER III: THE DRAMA

Useful information may be found in "Playwrights of the New American Theatre," by Thomas H. Dickinson (New York: The Macmillan Company, 1925). For criticism, particularly of the later dramatists, see "American Drama Since 1916," by Joseph Wood Krutch (New York: Random House, 1939) and "American Playwrights, 1919–1938)," by Eleanor Flexner (New York: Simon and Schuster, 1938).

Recommended plays appearing in "Chief Contemporary Dramatists," edited by Thomas H. Dickinson (Boston: Houghton Mifflin Company) will be marked (*).

CLYDE FITCH:
  Collected Plays (Boston: Little, Brown and Company, 4 vols.).
  Recommended: * "The Truth."

AUGUSTUS THOMAS:
  Recommended: * "The Witching Hour."

WILLIAM VAUGHN MOODY:
  Collected Poems and Plays (Boston: Houghton Mifflin Company, 2 vols.).
  Recommended: * "The Great Divide."

SUSAN GLASPELL:
  Plays (Boston: Small, Maynard and Company).
  Recommended: "Trifles."
              "Bernice."

EUGENE O'NEILL:
Collected Plays (New York: Random House).
Criticism: "Eugene O'Neill." By Richard Dana Skinner (New
York: Longmans, Green and Company).
Recommended: "Beyond the Horizon."
* "The Emperor Jones" ("Chief Contempo-
rary Dramatists, Third Series.")
"The Hairy Ape."
"Strange Interlude."
"Mourning Becomes Electra."

SIDNEY HOWARD:
Works published chiefly by Charles Scribner's Sons (New
York) and Doubleday, Doran and Company (New York).
Recommended: "They Knew What They Wanted."

MAXWELL ANDERSON:
Works published chiefly by Dodd, Mead and Company (New
York).
Recommended: "Winterset."

GEORGE S. KAUFMAN:
Recommended: "Beggar on Horseback" (New York: Boni and
Liveright, 1924).

S. N. BEHRMAN:
Works published chiefly by Farrar and Rinehart (New York)
and Random House (New York).
Recommended: "Biography" (New York: Farrar and Rinehart).

CLIFFORD ODETS:
Works published by Random House (New York).
Recommended: "Waiting for Lefty."

CHAPTER IV: ESSAYISTS

JOHN MUIR:
Collected Works (Boston: Houghton Mifflin Company, 8 vols.).
Biography: "The Life and Letters of John Muir," by William
Frederic Badé (Boston: Houghton Mifflin Company, 1924,
2 vols.).
Recommended: "The Mountains of California."

EDGAR WATSON HOWE:
  Works published by Alfred A. Knopf (New York) and Harper
    & Brothers (New York).
  Recommended: "Ventures in Common Sense" (New York: Al-
          fred A. Knopf).

HENRY ADAMS:
  Works published by Houghton Mifflin Company (Boston) and
    The Macmillan Company (New York).
  Recommended: "The Education of Henry Adams" (Boston:
          Houghton Mifflin Company).

GEORGE SANTAYANA:
  Works published by Charles Scribner's Sons (New York).
  Recommended: "Soliloquies in England."

RANDOLPH BOURNE:
  Works published by Houghton Mifflin Company (Boston) and
    The Viking Press (New York).
  Recommended: "Youth and Life" (Boston: Houghton Mifflin
          Company).

VAN WYCK BROOKS:
  Works published chiefly by E. P. Dutton and Company (New
    York).
  Recommended: "The Flowering of New England."

HENRY LOUIS MENCKEN:
  Works published by Alfred A. Knopf (New York).
  Recommended: "Prejudices: Third Series."
          "The American Language."

JOSEPH WOOD KRUTCH:
  Recommended: "The Modern Temper" (New York: Harcourt,
          Brace and Company).

DONALD CULROSS PEATTIE:
  Works published by G. P. Putnam's Sons (New York) and
    Simon and Schuster (New York).
  Recommended: "An Almanac for Moderns."

THOMAS STEARNS ELIOT:
  Works published by Alfred A. Knopf (New York) and Har-
    court, Brace and Company (New York).
  Recommended: "Selected Essays."

ENGLISH LITERATURE

A useful bibliographical guide, containing lists of books by various modern authors and critical references concerning them, is "Contemporary British Literature: Bibliographies and Study Outlines," by John Matthews Manly and Edith Rickert (New York: Harcourt, Brace and Company, 1935).

A critical discussion of most of the authors considered in the present volume may be found in "Modern English Writers: Being a Study of Imaginative Literature, 1890–1914," by Harold Williams (New York: Alfred A. Knopf, 1919).

CHAPTER I: POETRY

ANTHOLOGIES:

There are numerous anthologies of contemporary British verse, but the two most convenient are "The New Poetry: An Anthology of Twentieth-Century Verse in English," edited by Harriet Monroe and Alice Corbin Henderson (New York: The Macmillan Company, 1932), and "Modern British Poetry," edited by Louis Untermeyer (New York: Harcourt, Brace and Company, 1936). The first includes both British and American poems; the second is the more comprehensive as regards time, covering the period since 1860. In the lists of recommended poems below (*) will indicate that a poem may be found in "The New Poetry" and (**) that it may be found in "Modern British Poetry."

OSCAR WILDE:

Collected Works (New York: William H. Wise and Company).
Biography: "Oscar Wilde: His Life and Confessions," by Frank Harris (New York: The Author, 1918, 2 vols.).
Recommended: ** "Requiescat."
       ** "Impression du Matin."
       ** "The Ballad of Reading Gaol."
       ** "Hélas."

ERNEST DOWSON:
Poems and Prose (New York: Boni and Liveright).
Recommended: ** "You Would Have Understood Me."
** "To One in Bedlam."
** "Cynara."

FRANCIS THOMPSON:
Collected Poems (New York: Charles Scribner's Sons, 2 vols.).
Recommended: ** "Daisy."
** "To Olivia."
** "An Arab Love-Song."
** "The Hound of Heaven."
** "The Poppy."

ALICE MEYNELL:
Collected Poems (New York: Charles Scribner's Sons).
Recommended: ** "A Thrush before Dawn."
** "Renouncement."
** "The Shepherdess."
"The Poet and His Book."
"A Poet of One Mood."
* "Chimes."

RUDYARD KIPLING:
Collected Poems (New York: Doubleday, Doran and Company).
Criticism: "Rudyard Kipling," by John Palmer (New York: Henry Holt and Company, 1915).
Recommended: ** "Gunga Din."
** "The Return."
** "The Conundrum of the Workshops."
** "An Astrologer's Song."
** "Boots."
** "Danny Deever."
** "The Ladies."
** "Mandalay."
** "Recessional."
"The Ballad of East and West."
"The Overland Mail."
"The Vampire."
"The White Man's Burden."

A. E. HOUSMAN:
  "A Shropshire Lad"; "Last Poems" (New York: Henry Holt
  and Company). "More Poems" (New York: Alfred A. Knopf,
  1936).
  Recommended: ** "Reveillé."
                 ** "When I Was One-and-Twenty."
                 ** "With Rue My Heart Is Laden."
                 ** "To an Athlete Dying Young."
                 ** "Loveliest of Trees."
                    "Farewell to Barn and Stack and Tree."
                    "If It Chance Your Eye Offend You."
                    "Think No More, Lad."
                    "Could Man Be Drunk Forever."
                 ** "I 'listed at Home for a Lancer."
                 ** "Oh, When I was in Love with You."
                 ** "Bredon Hill."
                 ** "Eight O'Clock."
                 ** "Epilogue."

THOMAS HARDY:
  Collected Poems (New York: The Macmillan Company).
  Criticism: "The Art of Thomas Hardy," by Lionel Johnson
    (New York: Dodd, Mead and Company, 1923); "Thomas
    Hardy, A Critical Study," by Lascelles Abercrombie (New
    York: The Viking Press, 1927); "Thomas Hardy, Poet and
    Novelist," by Samuel C. Chew (New York: Longmans, Green
    and Co., 1923).
  Recommended: * "She Hears the Storm."
                 * "The Voice."
                 * "In the Moonlight."
                 * "The Man He Killed." **
                 * "The Two Houses."
                 * "In Time of 'The Breaking of Nations.' " **
                ** "Going and Staying."
                ** "The Roman Road."
                   "Let Me Enjoy."
                   "On an Invitation to the United States."
                   "Drummer Hodge."
                   "God-Forgotten."
                   "The Pine Planters."
                   "The Face at the Casement."

"Old Furniture."
"The Fallow Deer at the Lonely House."
"An Ancient to Ancients."

ROBERT BRIDGES:
  Collected Poems (New York: Oxford University Press, 1912).
  Recommended: ** "Winter Nightfall."
               ** "Nightingales."
               ** "London Snow."
                  "The Testament of Beauty."

GERARD MANLEY HOPKINS:
  "Poems" (New York: Oxford University Press).
  Biography: "Gerard Manley Hopkins," by G. F. Lahey (New
    York: Oxford University Press, 1930).
  Recommended: ** "Pied Beauty."
               ** "The Habit of Perfection."
               ** "God's Grandeur."
               ** "The Starlight Night."
               ** "Spring."
               ** "Hurrahing in Harvest."
               ** "Felix Randal."
                  "Thou Art Indeed Just, Lord."

JOHN MASEFIELD:
  Collected Poems (New York: The Macmillan Company).
  Criticism: "John Masefield," by Gilbert Thomas (London: But-
    terworth, 1932).
  Recommended: * "Ships."
                * "Cargoes." **
                * "Watching by a Sick Bed."
                * "What Am I, Life?"
                * "The Passing Strange." **
                * "The Frontier."
               ** "A Consecration."
               ** "Sea Fever."
               ** "The Choice."
               ** "The West Wind."
                  "Spanish Waters."
                  "Biography."
                  "The Everlasting Mercy."
                  "Reynard the Fox."

W. H. DAVIES:
"Collected Poems: First Series" (New York: Alfred A. Knopf); "Second Series" (New York: Harper & Brothers).
Recommended: ** "Days Too Short."
     ** "The Moon."
     ** "The Villain."
     ** "The Example."
     "Sweet Stay-at-Home."
     "Truly Great."
     "Child Lovers."
     "Strong Moments."
     "A Child's Pet."
     "The Song of Life."

WALTER DE LA MARE:
Collected Poems (New York: Henry Holt and Company).
Recommended: * "The Listeners." **
     * "An Epitaph." **
     * "When the Rose Is Faded."
     * "The Little Salamander."
     * "The Linnet."
     * "All That's Past."
     ** "Tired Tim."
     ** "Old Susan."
     ** "Nod."

RUPERT BROOKE:
Collected Poems (New York: Dodd, Mead and Company).
Recommended: * "Retrospect."
     * "Nineteen-Fourteen." **
     ** "The Fish."
     ** "The Great Lover."
     ** "Grantchester."

WILFRID OWEN:
"Poems" (New York: The Viking Press).
Recommended: * "Anthem for Doomed Youth." **
     * "Strange Meeting." **
     ** "Dulce et Decorum Est."
     ** "The Unreturning."

ROBERT GRAVES:
Collected Poems (Random House).

Recommended: ** "Neglectful Edward."
      ** "Escape."
      ** "In the Wilderness."
      ** "A Forced Music."
      ** "Lost Music."
      " 'The General Elliott.' "
      "Pure Death."
      "The Cool Web."

W. H. AUDEN:
  Works published by Random House (New York).
  Recommended: ** "Chorus from a Play."
      ** "Ode: To My Pupils."
      ** "The Strings' Excitement."
      ** "Ballad."

STEPHEN SPENDER:
  Works published by Random House (New York).
  Recommended: ** "Farewell in a Dream."
      ** "What I Expected."
      ** "The Prisoners."
      ** "The Landscape Near an Aerodrome."
      "Pylons."
      "New Year."
      "I Think Continually of Those Who were Truly Great."

CHAPTER II: PROSE FICTION

GEORGE MOORE:
  Collected Works (New York: Boni and Liveright).
  Criticism: "A Portrait of George Moore in a Study of His Works," by John Freeman (New York: Dodd, Mead and Company, 1922).
  Recommended: "Esther Waters."

SIR JAMES MATTHEW BARRIE:
  Collected Works (New York: Charles Scribner's Sons).
  Recommended: "Sentimental Tommy."

RUDYARD KIPLING:
  Collected Works (New York: Doubleday, Doran and Company).
  Criticism: See Suggestions for Study under Chapter I.

Recommended: "The Man Who Would Be King."
"The Phantom 'Rickshaw."
"The Man Who Was."
"Without Benefit of Clergy."
"Rikki-Tikki-Tavi."
"The Brushwood Boy."
" 'They.' "

All these short stories may be found in "Selected Stories from Rudyard Kipling" (New York: Doubleday, Doran and Company).

JOSEPH CONRAD:
Collected Works (New York: Doubleday, Doran and Company).
Criticism: "Joseph Conrad," by Hugh Walpole (New York: Henry Holt and Company, 1916).
Recommended: "Youth"; "Heart of Darkness"; "The End of the Tether" (1 vol.).

H. G. WELLS:
Collected Works (New York: Charles Scribner's Sons).
Criticism: "The World of H. G. Wells," by Van Wyck Brooks (New York: Mitchell Kennerley, 1915).
Recommended: "Tales of Space and Time."
"Tono-Bungay."

ARNOLD BENNETT:
Works published by Doubleday, Doran and Company (New York).
Criticism: "Arnold Bennett," by F. J. V. Darton (New York: Henry Holt and Company, 1915).
Recommended: "The Old Wives' Tale."

JOHN GALSWORTHY:
Collected Works (New York: Charles Scribner's Sons).
Criticism: "John Galsworthy," by Sheila Kaye-Smith (New York: Henry Holt and Company, 1916); "John Galsworthy," by Hermon Ould (London: Chapman, 1934).
Recommended: "The Forsyte Saga."

W. SOMERSET MAUGHAM:
Works published by Doubleday, Doran and Company (New York).

Criticism: "W. Somerset Maugham," by Richard A. Cordell (New York: Thomas Nelson and Sons, 1937).
Recommended: "Of Human Bondage."

D. H. LAWRENCE:
Works published by Alfred A. Knopf (New York).
Biography: "The Savage Pilgrimage: A Narrative of D. H. Lawrence," by Catherine Carswell (New York: Harcourt, Brace and Company, 1932).
Recommended: "Sons and Lovers."
"England, My England."

ALDOUS HUXLEY:
Works published by Doubleday, Doran and Company (New York).
Recommended: "Point Counterpoint."

KATHERINE MANSFIELD:
"The Short Stories of Katherine Mansfield" (New York: Alfred A. Knopf, 1937).
Recommended: "Prelude."
"Bliss."
"The Daughters of the Late Colonel."
"Mr. and Mrs. Dove."
"The Garden-Party."

VIRGINIA WOOLF:
Works published by Harcourt, Brace and Company (New York).
Criticism: "Virginia Woolf," by Winifred Holtby (London: Wishart and Company, 1932).
Recommended: "Mrs. Dalloway."

CHAPTER III: THE DRAMA

A convenient collection of modern British plays will be found in "Chief Contemporary Dramatists," edited by Thomas H. Dickinson (Boston: Houghton Mifflin Company). Plays recommended below will be marked (*) if they are to be found in this collection.

SIR ARTHUR WING PINERO:
"The Social Plays of Arthur Wing Pinero" (New York: E. P. Dutton and Company, 4 vols.).
Recommended: * "The Second Mrs. Tanqueray."

HENRY ARTHUR JONES:
Collected Plays (Boston: Little, Brown and Company, 4 vols.).
Recommended: * "Michael and His Lost Angel."

OSCAR WILDE:
See Suggestions for Study under Chapter I.
Recommended: * "Lady Windermere's Fan."
"The Importance of Being Earnest"

GEORGE BERNARD SHAW:
Works published by Dodd, Mead and Company (New York).
Biography and Criticism: "George Bernard Shaw," by Archibald Henderson (New York: Boni and Liveright 1916);
"George Bernard Shaw" by G. K. Chesterton (New York: Dodd, Mead and Company, 1909).
Recommended: "The Devil's Disciple."
"Man and Superman."
"Saint Joan."

JOHN GALSWORTHY:
See Suggestions for Study under Chapter II.
Recommended: * "Strife."
"Justice."

SIR JAMES MATTHEW BARRIE:
See Suggestions for Study under Chapter II.
Recommended: "Dear Brutus."

W. SOMERSET MAUGHAM:
See Suggestions for Study under Chapter II.
"Six Comedies" (New York: Doubleday, Doran and Company, 1937).
Recommended: * "The Circle" ("Chief Contemporary Dramatists, Second Series").

NOEL COWARD:
"Play Parade" (New York: Doubleday, Doran and Company, 1934).
Recommended: "Hay Fever."

THOMAS HARDY:
See Suggestions for Study under Chapter I.
Recommended: "The Dynasts" (New York: The Macmillan Company).

CHAPTER IV: ESSAYISTS

MAX BEERBOHM:
Collected Works (New York: E. P. Dutton and Company, 12 vols.).
Recommended: "Seven Men" (New York: Alfred A. Knopf).

GEORGE BERNARD SHAW:
See Suggestions for Study under Chapter III.
Recommended: The prefaces to the plays read for Chapter III.
"Selected Passages from the Works of Bernard Shaw," chosen by Charlotte F. Shaw (London: A. C. Fifield, 1915).

H. G. WELLS:
See Suggestions for Study under Chapter II.
Recommended: "A Modern Utopia."
            "An Experiment in Autobiography."

G. K. CHESTERTON:
Works published by Dodd, Mead and Company (New York).
Criticism: "G. K. Chesterton," by Julius West (New York: Dodd, Mead and Company, 1916).
Recommended: "George Bernard Shaw."
            "Varied Types."
            "Autobiography."

W. H. HUDSON:
Collected Works (New York: E. P. Dutton Company, 24 vols.).
Biography: "W. H. Hudson," by Morley Roberts (New York: E. P. Dutton and Company).
Recommended: "Far Away and Long Ago."
            "A Shepherd's Life."

LYTTON STRACHEY:
Works published by G. P. Putnam's Sons (New York) and Harcourt, Brace and Company (New York).
Recommended: "Eminent Victorians."

HAROLD NICOLSON:
Works published chiefly by Houghton Mifflin Company (Boston).
Recommended: "Some People."

T. E. LAWRENCE:
Works published by Doubleday, Doran and Company (New York).

Criticism and Biography: "Colonel Lawrence: The Man Behind the Legend," by Liddell Hart (New York: Dodd, Mead and Company, 1934); "Lawrence and the Arabian Adventure," by Robert Graves (New York: Doubleday, Doran and Company, 1928).

Recommended: "Seven Pillars of Wisdom."

IRISH LITERATURE

An historical and critical account of modern Irish literature will be found in "Ireland's Literary Renaissance," by Ernest Boyd (New York: Alfred A. Knopf, 1922).

In addition to the two anthologies referred to in the Suggestions for Study in connection with American and English Literature, reference will be made below to the "Anthology of Irish Verse," edited by Padraic Colum (New York: Boni and Liveright, 1922). Poems appearing in "The New Poetry" will be marked (*) ; poems appearing in "Modern British Poetry" will be marked (**) ; poems appearing in the "Anthology of Irish Verse" will be marked (***).

STANDISH O'GRADY:
  Recommended: "Selected Essays and Passages from Standish O'Grady," edited by Ernest Boyd (London: Fisher Unwin, 1918).

POETRY

WILLIAM BUTLER YEATS:
  Collected Works (New York: The Macmillan Company, 6 vols.). Collected Poems (New York: The Macmillan Company, 1933).
  Criticism: "William Butler Yeats," by Forrest Reid (New York: Dodd, Mead and Company, 1915).
  Recommended: "To an Isle in the Water."
                ** "The Lake Isle of Innisfree."
                ** "The Song of the Old Mother."
                ** "The Cap and Bells."
                ** "An Old Song Resung."
                 * "The Cold Heaven."
                 * "That the Night Come."
                 * "No Second Troy."
                 * "The Collarbone of a Hare."
                 * "The Dawn." **
                 * "The Magi."
                 * "The Fisherman."

        * "The Wild Swans at Coole." **
     *** "Pity of Love."
     *** "The Folly of Being Comforted."
       "The Hosting of the Sidhe."
       "The Death of Cuchulain."
       * "To One Whose Work has Come to Noth-
          ing."
       * "The Leaders of the Crowd."
       ** "Sailing to Byzantium."

Æ:
  Collected Poems (New York: The Macmillan Company).
  Criticism: "Æ," by Darrell Figgis (New York: Dodd, Mead
    and Company, 1916).
  Recommended: ** "The Great Breath."
              ** "The Unknown God."
              *** "Immortality."
              *** "A Farewell."

SEUMAS O'SULLIVAN:
  Recommended: * "My Sorrow."
              * "Splendid and Terrible."
              * "The Others." ***
              ** "Praise."
              *** "The Starling Lake."
              *** "The Sedges."
              *** "The Half Door."

PADRAIC COLUM:
  "Poems" (New York: The Macmillan Company, 1932).
  Recommended: * "Polonius and the Ballad Singers."
              * "The Sea Bird to the Wave."
              "Old Men Complaining."
              * "A Drover." ** ***
              * "An Old Woman of the Roads." **
              * "The Wild Ass." **
              ** "The Plougher."
            *** "River-Mates."
              ** "Interior."

JAMES STEPHENS:
  Collected Poems (New York: The Macmillan Company).
  Recommended: * "What Tomas an Buile Said in a Pub." **

> * "Bessie Bobtail."
> * "Hate." **
> ** "The Red-Haired Man's Wife."
> ** "Blue Blood."
> *** "Righteous Anger." **
> * "The Waste Places." **
> * "Hawks."
> * "Dark Wings."
> ** "The Shell."
> *** "The Daisies."
> *** "The Goat Path."

JOSEPH CAMPBELL:
  Recommended: * "At Harvest."
                 * "On Waking." ***
                 * "The Old Woman." **
                ** "I Am the Mountainy Singer."
               *** "The Blind Man at the Fair."

DRAMA

Recommended plays appearing in "Chief Contemporary Dramatists," edited by Thomas H. Dickinson (Boston: Houghton Mifflin Company) will be marked (*).

WILLIAM BUTLER YEATS:
  See Suggestions for Study under Poetry, above.
  Recommended: "The Land of Heart's Desire."
                "Cathleen Ni Houlihan."
            * "The Hour-Glass."

JOHN MILLINGTON SYNGE:
  Complete Works (New York: Random House).
  Recommended: * "Riders to the Sea."
              "The Playboy of the Western World."

PADRAIC COLUM:
  "Three Plays" (New York: The Macmillan Company).
  Recommended: "Thomas Muskerry."

LADY GREGORY:
  "Seven Short Plays" (New York: G. P. Putnam's Sons).
  Recommended: * "The Rising of the Moon."

LORD DUNSANY:
"Plays of Gods and Men" (New York: G. P. Putnam's Sons).
Criticism: "Dunsany the Dramatist," by Edward Hale Bierstadt
(Boston: Little, Brown and Company, 1919).
Recommended: "The Queen's Enemies."

SEAN O'CASEY:
Works published by The Macmillan Company (New York).
Recommended: * "Juno and the Paycock" ("Chief Contempo-
rary Dramatists, Third Series").

FICTION

LADY GREGORY:
Recommended: "Gods and Fighting Men" (London: John
Murray).

JAMES JOYCE:
Works published by Random House (New York).
Criticism: "James Joyce" by Herbert S. Gorman (New York:
The Viking Press, 1924); "James Joyce's Ulysses, A Study,"
by Stuart Gilbert (New York: Alfred A. Knopf, 1931).
Recommended: "Dubliners."
"A Portrait of the Artist as a Young Man."

LORD DUNSANY:
Recommended: "Fifty-One Tales" (Boston: Little, Brown and
Company).

JAMES STEPHENS:
Works published by The Macmillan Company (New York).
Recommended: "The Crock of Gold."

LIAM O'FLAHERTY:
Works published by Harcourt, Brace and Company (New
York).
Recommended: "The Informer."
"The Assassin."

SEAN O'FAOLÁIN:
Works published by The Viking Press (New York).
Recommended: "A Nest of Simple Folk."

ESSAYISTS

WILLIAM BUTLER YEATS:
  See Suggestions for Study under Poetry.
  Recommended: "Ideas of Good and Evil."
          "Autobiography."

Æ:
  Recommended: "Imaginations and Reveries" (Dublin: Maunsel).

INDEX